MW00891605

ENLIGHTENED MEDICINE YOUR POWER TO GET WELL NOW

AN INTEGRATIVE APPROACH TO HEALING THE SEVEN DEADLY LIFESTYLE DISEASES

MICHELLE S. FONDIN

Also by Michelle S. Fondin

The Wheel of Healing with Ayurveda: An Easy Guide to a Healthy Lifestyle

The Wheel of Healing with Ayurveda Companion Workbook

Help! I Think My Loved One Is an Alcoholic: A Survival Guide for Lovers, Family, and Friends

How to Run a Successful Yoga Business and Not Go Broke: Lessons from a Yoga Teacher, Entrepreneur, & Modern Hippie

Chakra Healing for Vibrant Energy: Exploring Your Seven Energy Centers with Mindfulness, Yoga, and Ayurveda

Copyright © 2018 by Michelle S. Fondin.

All rights reserved. No part of this publication may be reproduced, distributed or transmitted in any form or by any means, including photocopying, recording, or other electronic or mechanical methods, without the prior written permission of the publisher, except in the case of brief quotations embodied in critical reviews and certain other noncommercial uses permitted by copyright law. For permission requests, write to the publisher, addressed "Attention: Permissions Coordinator," at the email address below.

Michelle S. Fondin
michellefondinauthor@gmail.com
www.michellefondinauthor.com

Ordering Information:
Quantity sales. Special discounts are available on quantity purchases by corporations, associations, and others. For details, contact the "Special Sales Department" at the address above.

Enlightened Medicine Your Power to Get Well Now/ Michelle S. Fondin. —1st ed.
ISBN 978-1545587676

This book is dedicated to my Dad, Ramzi M. Dalloo, who despite all the medical procedures of Western medicine, has managed to keep on ticking like the Energizer bunny. Your ability to bounce back and keep on going shows me that there is something greater to healing that no one can bottle up and sell on a shelf. Love you Dad! Shelly

Dear Dad,
Wishing you
health, happiness, and
love always!
Love,
Michelle

Acknowledgments

I want to give special thanks to Jay Fondin for all of your support during my writing process. I couldn't have done it without you. I also want to thank Dr. Mitch Prywes, Dr. Melissa Delgado, and Dr. Julie Seely for giving me great insight into the medical world.

Contents

Health is a state of complete physical, mental, and social well-being and not merely the absence of a disease or infirmity.

-*World Health Organization*

PREFACE

MY MOTHER'S BELIEFS AND MY EXPERIENCE WITH WESTERN MEDICINE

THE PSYCHOLOGY OF ILLNESS is a funny thing. Our beliefs form who we are and how we react to sickness. I remember being sick often as a child, but I don't know if I was actually sick a lot or if I'm recalling my mother's stories of how I was always sick. The undeniable fact was that in my family, I was always the one with the flu, cold, strep throat, or gastrointestinal virus. At the first cough or stomach pain, my mother would whisk me off to the doctor's office. So all the way through age eighteen, I remember sitting for hours in the waiting room at the doctor's office. My childhood doctor's office catered to low-income families, and served more as a walk-in clinic than a traditional office. More often than not we would wait for three to four hours to be seen by the doctor. Everyone would be sitting shoulder to shoulder, kids crawling on the floor and playing in groups, sick people all stuffed into a narrow room, coughing, sneezing, and waiting to somehow get better.

My mom trusted the doctor like a god. She wanted the antibiotics, the cough syrup, the cold remedy, the throat spray, or anything else to make her daughter better. So I was poked, prodded, medicated, bedridden, and stuffed into a crowded waiting room time and again for years. And yet going to the doctors' office never seemed to help. My immune system was constantly compromised. I would miss days and weeks of school. Never did I hear my mother say, "Trust your body, it knows how to get well." Instead, all I heard was worry in her voice when she told me "You must finish your medicine." "Michelle," she would say, "you are always the one who gets sick." To say the least, I was not very empowered in my health.

To make matters worse, I was extremely sensitive to medications and allergic to several antibiotics. I had an intense gag reflex that to this day makes it difficult for me to take pills. It felt like my body had an innate intelligence to reject the strong medications that my mother and the doctors were stuffing down my throat. Somehow my body knew there must be a better way.

Even though my body wanted to heal naturally, my mind seemed to have other plans. When I say illness is a funny thing, I mean the dynamics of illness are strange. Experiencing ill health is a negative thing, but sometimes people use it consciously or unconsciously for positive rewards. As a small child I feel I unconsciously used illness to get more attention in a dysfunctional household.

My parents divorced when I was five years old. It was a traumatic experience for me. The divorce immediately plunged my family into poverty, because my mom had to go back to school and work as a waitress. My sister was nearly two at the time. Even though my mom wanted the divorce, she was sad and bitter about my dad's lack of commitment and how the relationship ended. She held onto that sadness and bitterness for a long time. As a result, I had to grow up a lot faster than most kids my age: at age five, I had to console my mom and help raise my little sister.

After the divorce, I didn't get a lot of attention. In retrospect, I think on a subconscious level, I chose to get sick often because it made my mom pay attention to me. She was the one who took me to the doctor's office. She was the one who cooked me chicken noodle soup and served it to me in bed. And she was the one who cared for me, but only when I was sick.

On the flip side, I hated being sick. I loved everything about school and longed to be there.

I hated those awful doctors' offices, the long waits, the smelly rooms, and the medications that felt like poisons to my body. I loathed not feeling normal, since most kids were much healthier than I was. I felt embarrassed when I got stacks of homework and Get Well cards from my classmates, like an invalid. But somehow, the reward of my mother's attention outweighed the pain of being constantly sick. And what's even more ironic is that it's only through my experience with illness that I can write about wellness.

Throughout my childhood, my mother taught me to completely mistrust my body. By the time I was eighteen, I learned to hate doctors' offices so much that I never wanted to step foot into one ever again. To me, it equaled pain – lots of pain. I was never taught preventative medicine. My mom, terrified of "the world out there" and determined that germs would somehow always get me, never taught me how to build up my immune system so I would be strong and healthy.

When I was eighteen, a man came into my life and changed my perspective.

Chris was vegetarian, drank tons of water, and practiced yoga. I was completely enamored with him, and my affection for him made me want to adopt his lifestyle. He taught me to respect and love my body. In 1988, he took me to food co-ops to search out organic food. He introduced me to a vegetarian diet and taught me mindfulness.

For the first time in my life, I learned that I could do something to help my weak immune system.

Thanks to this epiphany, I made some major changes. For one, I stopped eating red meat completely and opted for some occasional chicken or fish. Secondly, I began to drink water (what a concept, right?). Up until then, no one had ever encouraged me to drink water. Throughout my childhood, I remember being crippled by severe stomach cramps from constipation and headaches. Once I started drinking water, all of those symptoms stopped. I had been severely dehydrated and had no idea. I also started running, doing yoga, and aerobics.

The other thing that motivated me was an enormous fear of my family's genes. My maternal grandmother suffered from deep depression. My uncle was manic-depressive. My father suffered his first heart attack at age forty-nine. To make a long family medical history short, I did not want to turn out like any of my relatives.

But my relationship with Chris came early enough in life that it turned my belief about health completely upside down – and for the better. Still, sometimes I saw Chris taking his healthy living to extremes. In the few years we were together, I saw him go from a vegetarian diet to a vegan diet, and for months at a time, even a macrobiotic diet.[1] He was already fairly thin, but when I saw him eating only brown rice for weeks at a time and losing even more weight, I thought surely there must be a happy medium to getting healthy.

Then about eight years later, I was hit with thyroid cancer. I had gotten lazy about my strict and healthy diet, I wasn't exercising regularly, and I had forgotten yoga altogether. Furthermore, I was the mother of two small children, and I was unhappy with my marriage. As I wrote in my first book, *The Wheel of Healing with Ayurveda: An Easy Guide to a Healthy Lifestyle*, I was able to get rid of the cancer with Western medicine, but was able to truly heal with Ayurvedic medicine.

After my cancer diagnosis, everything I had learned from my relationship with Chris came back to me. It was a major wake up call. I knew it was time to take complete responsibility for my health and wellbeing. And if I didn't, I knew I might suffer from other devastating illnesses in the future.

The biggest source of frustration with the medical community, at the time of my diagnosis and treatment, was the mechanical way in which I was "processed". From the OB/GYN who diagnosed a potential problem, to the endocrinologist who did my fine needle biopsy, and then on to more doctors, nurses, and pathologists, I felt less like a human being with concerns and fears and more like a product on a conveyor belt. I do, however, remember one tender moment: a German surgeon who, seeing how nervous I was, lovingly tickled my toes before I went under. I'll never forget that gesture of affection. It was his way of saying, "Trust me, you're going to be okay in my care." And I did trust him, because he made me feel human.

Until I found integrative medical expert Dr. Leonard Wisneski, I didn't feel that a single doctor actually listened to me. It wasn't that I was a bad patient, either; I wasn't loud, boisterous, or overly chatty. After all, I grew up in doctors' offices with a mother who took doctors' word as gospel. As a result, I was obedient most of the time. But contracting cancer at age twenty-eight leaves some questions. The cancer – compounded with the array of negative symptoms I experienced once I had my thyroid removed – left me really suffering. And every single doctor dismissed my symptoms and discomfort because my blood tests showed my thyroid levels were fine.

Maybe you have a story like mine. Perhaps you've been diagnosed with a disease like cancer, hypertension, heart disease, hypothyroidism, diabetes, or an autoimmune disease. Since you're reading this book, maybe you haven't had the answers you seek on getting well. It's possible that you're just as frustrated as I was, not only from needing answers, but also from lack of compassionate care by your health care provider. The good news is physicians can learn better bedside manner with better awareness and practice The more physicians are able to practice medicine in a way that aligns with their moral values, the more they can then take the time to show attention and love to each patient. It's my belief that Western medicine must arrive at this point: the medical system must create trusting relationships between patients and providers, and not treat them like just another name on a sheet. We must turn the medical system upside down.

The bigger picture is that Western medicine is extremely limited in the solutions it can bring to solve your illness. The doctors treating my illness were not bad people, they simply had their hands tied. They were doing what they were trained to do. They took my thyroid levels. Those levels were fine according to blood tests, so in conclusion, I was supposedly fine and healthy.

Unfortunately, within the model of Western medicine, there was nothing more they could do for me. In fact, one endocrinologist even sent me to a psychiatrist because he said all the symptoms were in my head. And since doctors prescribe medications, the psychiatrist prescribed an anti-anxiety medication (this, by the way, was not the solution to the problem I was experiencing).

Imagine if you gave a few construction workers one hammer each – no other tools – and a whole pile of wood, and instruct them to build a house. If they are versed in the art of construction, they could probably figure out a way to build a house. They might find things in nature to create nails, and identify a way to cut the wood. They *could* build a house – probably not a very elaborate one – but it's possible. But those construction workers could build a much better house if they had an entire toolbox on hand. And if they each had electric saws, drills, and machines to hoist up beams, they could build an even more solid one.

It took a doctor versed in integrative medicine to diagnose, treat, and help me solve the problem. Why did this work? The answer is simple: he had more tools at his disposal. The first tool he had was love over fear. He loved his patients enough to listen to them. He loved me enough to find solutions that were unconventional according to Western medicine, and was determined to go against conventional practice if it meant getting me healthy. He believed in giving his patients bear hugs, like a loving parent, for those who needed consoling upon hearing an upsetting diagnosis. He had knowledge in herbal medicine, vitamins, and minerals. He taught me to not let my family medical history cloud my perception of my own health. He sent me to his nurse practitioner to do guided meditation. He even had in-house massage therapists.

Doctors in the Western model are much like the construction workers with one hammer. They can help you get healthy, but your health is not going to look as stellar as it would if they had other tools to help you build a mansion of health. And I don't know about you, but I'd rather have the mansion than the makeshift house built with only hammers.

INTRODUCTION

WHY SHOULD WE EVEN CARE?

We in the United States are in the midst of an epidemic of which most people aren't even cognizant. This national epidemic doesn't involve terrorism, economic crisis, or unemployment. Rather, this – the most rapidly growing epidemic to which we are all subject – is chronic disease, also known as lifestyle disease, exacerbated by the impermanent fix that Western medicine offers.

The state of health in the United States is bad. As of 2014, about half of all U.S. adults – a total of 133 million people – had one or more chronic health conditions. A fourth of US adults had two or more.[2] According to ImprovingChronicCare.org, that number is increasing by more than one percent per year. By the year 2030, they project that more than 171 million Americans will require chronic disease management.[3] But more recent statistics from the RAND Corporation, a research organization, shows that in 2017 the statistic from 2014 of 133 million had already risen to 150 million Americans with one chronic illness and 100 million with at least two.[4] If we take into account the Centers for Disease Control and Prevention (CDC) statistic in 2014, in a three-year span the number of Americans with chronic illness has not gone up one percent per year but rather more than three percent per year.

1

Lifestyle diseases not only create dependency on Western medicine, but also produce a global financial burden. Furthermore, they have a direct impact on our environment and society as a whole. The direct social impact is multilayered from increased work absenteeism or inability to work to heightened family responsibilities as when younger working adults must take care of their still young parents due to multiple chronic lifestyle diseases. In addition, increased use of prescription drugs has a direct impact on our environment, as we'll discuss in chapter five. Even in the light of these truths, apathy or lack of social awareness will not cause a global change. In other words, the common citizen must feel compelled in a big way to make monumental changes.

Let's take diabetes as an example since it constitutes a huge part of our chronic illness epidemic. Between the years 1980 and 2015 the number of patients with diagnosed diabetes quadrupled.[5] In 2015 the CDC estimated that 30.3 million Americans had diabetes.[6] Out of those 30.3 million only 5% had type 1 diabetes. From that 2015 statistic, 132,000 diagnosed were children under the age of eighteen. Furthermore, of those who had diabetes in 2015 87.5% of adults were overweight or obese, 73.6% had high blood pressure, and 58.2% had high cholesterol. Children of parents with type 2 diabetes are at a much higher risk of developing type 2 diabetes in childhood. One of the reasons is that children of overweight and obese parents are likely to adopt similar lifestyle habits. According to a study by the Harvard School of Public Health, in the past three decades, obesity in U.S. children between the ages of two and nineteen has tripled.[7] In 1970, five percent of U.S. children were obese compared to 17 seventeen percent in 2008. Unfortunately, a child has a one in seven chance of being diagnosed with type 2 diabetes if their parent was diagnosed before the age of 50.[8] So you can see that a chronic lifestyle disease like diabetes can have a ripple effect in families.

The previous example highlights how people with diagnosed *and* undiagnosed diabetes also have other health problems (high blood pressure, high cholesterol, heart disease), which magnify the global problem. Diabetics are hospitalized more for hyperglycemic crises (low blood sugar), have heart disease and stroke rates that are 1.7 times higher than the general population, and suffer from eye problems, blindness, and kidney disease, Furthermore, diabetics suffer from neuropathy which can lead to amputation.

The disease of diabetes has become so common that it's easy to overlook the more serious side of this disease. Hopefully you can now better understand the gravity of the problem.

CHRONIC DISEASE DOES NOT HAPPEN OVERNIGHT

Regardless of what you might be inclined to believe, the eruption of chronic disease does not happen overnight. Chronic diseases, differentiated from acute infectious or communicable diseases, take years – and often decades – for symptoms to become apparent. They are the culmination of choices we make over a long period of time. While definitions of chronic illness may slightly vary, the RAND corporation defines chronic illness as any physical or mental health condition that lasts more than a year and either limits ability or requires ongoing treatment.[9]

- Chronic diseases include, but are not limited to:
- Cardiovascular disease
- Hypertension
- Stroke
- Certain types of cancer
- Chronic respiratory diseases
- Arthritis
- Diabetes

- Certain mental and neurological disorders (anxiety, depression, Alzheimer's)
- Alcohol and drug addiction[10]

According to The CDC, 70% of all deaths in the U.S. are due to chronic diseases.[11] Treating people with chronic diseases accounts for 86% of all American health care costs.[12] The top modifiable causes for chronic disease are unhealthy diet and excessive energy intake (too many calories), physical inactivity, tobacco use, and excessive alcohol use and abuse.[13]

My focus in this book is to help you prevent and reverse the risk of what I call the seven deadly chronic lifestyle diseases: type 2 diabetes, certain types of cancer, heart disease, stroke, obesity, respiratory illness, and addiction. Other chronic diseases certainly exist but many of the top seven encompass other chronic conditions. For example, under the umbrella of heart disease falls hypertension (high blood pressure) and high cholesterol. Chronic mental health disorders, such as anxiety and depression, are not in my top seven even though they can be just as crippling. Be that as it may, our main focus in this work is on chronic physiological diseases. Then again when you begin to transform your physical health, you'll often find that your mental health improves too. All things considered, in recognition of the fact that millions of people suffer from mental illness or emotional distress, I've also included a chapter on emotional health.

It's Costing Us More to Stay Sick Than to Be Well

In the aforementioned 2017 CDC report, diabetes alone costs U.S. citizens an estimated $245 billion and the average medical expenditures for people with diagnosed diabetes were about $13,700 per year.[14] A recent Milken Institute analysis determined that treatment of the seven most common chronic diseases, coupled with the resulting work absenteeism and loss of productivity, costs the U.S. more than $1 trillion annually.[15]

What the Milken Institute study suggests – and what I'm proposing in this book – is that we take a serious look at prevention and early intervention. In our current health care model, we spend a small fraction of our national budget on the promotion of healthier behavior. Allocating so few resources to prevention and early intervention continues to cost us dearly in human lives, quality of life, and prosperity.

What's worse, those numbers don't even take into account the percentage of money that is coming out of your pocket. Forty years ago, we could actually afford to be sick. Medical costs were lower and more reasonable. Insurance companies covered more illnesses, and prescription medication costs weren't astronomical. Pre-existing condition clauses weren't a part of health insurance contracts, and family doctors could afford to stay in practice.

Unfortunately, the U.S. healthcare system has changed a lot since then. In the litigious American society, a physician must always carry medical malpractice insurance, and in most cases even if he or she is unemployed. While the cost varies state by state, the median cost of medical malpractice insurance premiums are around $20,000 per year. In some regions in New York in 2011, some malpractice insurance premiums for OB/GYNs reached $206,913.[16] At the same time, with one-third of the country insured by Medicare, reimbursement to physicians for the cost of care continues to drop.[17] Add to this the overwhelming average debt of medical school at around $100,000 and you have a recipe for physicians going out of business or leaving the profession altogether.

In addition, pharmaceutical companies lure us in through enticing ads, exceeding $6 billion in 2016 on direct-to-consumer ad campaigns,[18] and ensnare your physician with promises of financial rewards. Not to mention that even though the Affordable Care Act allowed millions of Americans to afford health insurance, the annual rise in premiums and reduction in benefits has made access to quality care a distant dream. In 2018 the situation is even bleaker. Our current politicians are debating another health care reform that will inevitably cause millions of Americans to lose health care coverage once again.

So: with Americans getting sicker and health care benefits declining, what are we to do?

It is tempting to believe in the American dream. You might even be proud that the United States has some of the greatest medical technology and the best research on how to cure disease. But with no affordable access, what is the use of such advancements? What is the use if you have to put yourself $100,000 in debt for a chance at curing your cancer? The stress of the medical debt alone is likely to hinder your recovery.

The truth is we cannot rely on our current medical system to take care of us. Instead, you now must rely on taking preventive healthcare measures into your own hands by way of researching lifestyle changes that will work to your benefit. Furthermore, you'll need to open your mind to investing in yourself and your health. It may cost a little more but will pay off in the long run.

Your Children Have a Shorter Lifespan Than You

We've become so disconnected with our bodies and our state of well-being that many of us have a hard time trusting that wellness is a normal state. People constantly search for an outside fix, whether in the form of a pill, a medical procedure, a miracle food, or a vitamin. Many also seek that fix in alcohol and drugs. In the senior community, there is a recent surge in treatment with medical marijuana. While marijuana may help alleviate symptoms in certain cases, just like all other temporary methods, those symptoms return shortly after the effects of the drug wear off.

Statistics for disease in American adults are tragic. But the pending tragedy lies in future generations – starting with children today. If we, as adults, have no idea how to bring our bodies back to health naturally, how can we expect our children to trust their bodies? Children model what they see, hear, think, and feel. We have already seen the beginning of a problem with childhood obesity and diabetes on the rise in the twenty-first century. In 2005, The New England Journal of Medicine reported that for the first time in two centuries, the current generation of children in America might have shorter life expectancies than their parents due to obesity.[19] Even I have seen small children – ages eight to ten years old – with high blood pressure and elevated blood cholesterol levels. This should never happen.

WE HAVE BECOME A SOCIETY OF TOO MUCH ACCEPTANCE

Our need to become politically correct has caused us to overlook the crisis of the last three decades. We've hailed phrases like "big is beautiful" and have embraced plus-sized models. With an extreme modern need to embrace acceptance, we're hesitant to even address our family and friends and tell them, for their health and wellbeing, that they really need to lose weight.

One of my favorite comedians, Gabriel Iglesias – also known as "Fluffy" – used to comment about his weight early in his career. In his late twenties, he used to tell the audience that he was completely comfortable with his weight. He stated that he loved to eat and live life to the fullest, in the most literal sense. While I loved his comedy act, I cringed when I heard those words, because I knew his mentality was going to have to change or he would never live to see his 30th birthday. Sure enough, in his more recent stand-up shows, he comments on how he lost close to 100 pounds because he had to. He was diagnosed with type 2 diabetes, high cholesterol, and high blood pressure. He was given two to three years to live. Mr. Fluffy also talks about how he was frightened into making these changes because he was certain he was going to die. It's not cute to be fat. It's unhealthy.

The more we ignore this life of excess in every way, the more we're killing ourselves. To demonstrate, the philosophy of the younger generation to accept everyone without question about lifestyle choices further proves my point. One day, I was talking with one of my older children about potential clients. I explained that they were optimal candidates for lifestyle coaching because, while they were extremely successful in business, they were obese. They looked like they had been ignoring their bodies for a long time. My child retorted, "Don't judge them. Maybe they're comfortable with the way they are." Wow, I thought. They might be comfortable. But pretty soon, they're going to be pretty dead if they continue along the same route. In fact, I believe it's our search for comfort that has driven us to where we are.

If we're to transform into a society of people focused on preventive versus curative health, we need to realize that not all behavior is okay. It's not okay to overeat, over sleep, live a sedentary life, drink too much alcohol, take too many pills, and succumb to addictions. We need to stop lying to ourselves and to our friends and family. It's simply not okay. It's not that we don't accept you, it's that we want you alive and healthy.

OUR HEALTH IS NOT THAT COMPLICATED

Repeat that title phrase to anyone who has gone through medical school and you will receive a very different response. I'm not denying the fact that the biology and anatomy of the human body is extremely complex. Pathology is often perplexing. Rather, what I'm asserting is that given all factors, seeking and maintaining health is relatively simple.

Given everything we're presented with in the way of toxins, microorganisms, processed and artificial foods, and environmental and socioeconomic factors, most of us manage to stay relatively healthy.

Our bodies can take a lot of abuse and still keep us alive and running. Take a moment and marvel in the wonder of that fact.

Now, if you consider yourself relatively healthy, think about how much healthier you would feel and be if you were able to tweak a few things. Let's suppose you had the discipline, know-how, and resources to:

- Eat organic, local fruits and vegetables
- Consume organic grass-fed dairy
- Eat organic grains and only grass-fed meat
- Abstain from any processed or artificial foods and drinks
- Drink filtered or distilled water
- Exercise for at least an hour daily
- Learn and implement stress management techniques
- Practice some form of meditation twice daily
- Abstain from alcohol or any type of drug
- Learn effective methods of communication to have more fulfilled relationships

These are just a few examples of what you could do to exponentially improve your health – and none of them are difficult. Many of them require self-discipline, but they are not hard to do.

You might read over that list and say to yourself, "I know I'm supposed to be doing these things, or at least some of them, but..." That big "but" is the main reason for the health epidemic today. Rather than coming up with the normal list of excuses, you might want to explore reasons why you would rather take many prescriptions or go to your doctor frequently rather than find the power within to make the necessary changes to improve your health.

Here is the absolute and stark truth: the medicine you need or choose to take will not cure the root cause of the problem. With the first regular prescription pill, you enter into the world of dependency on Western medicine.

Why Has Illness Become the New Normal?

Humans have dealt with sickness and ailments from the dawn of humanity. However, disease was not the norm. If it *were* normal, how have human beings survived thousands of years or at least long enough to procreate and raise their young?

As you'll learn in these pages, modern medicine, as we know it today, is relatively new. In fact, it's a little more than 200 years old. Compared to 200,000 years of modern human existence, 200 years is a drop in the bucket. Yet in the midst of these 200 years, we've managed to normalize disease like never before. It's true that our life expectancy has risen in the span of that time, but not by much considering the major advances in medical science and technology we have at our disposal.

The main reason life expectancy was lower, prior to the advent of good hygiene, vaccinations, and antibiotics, was due to high infant and child mortality. In the 1800s, if a child made it to their tenth birthday, they had a good chance of living until age 60. The same child born in 2016 in the U.S. could expect to live to age 76, maybe. But health and wellness statistics are changing rapidly – and not for the better. Despite being one of the wealthiest countries, and especially as the country that spends the most on health care, the United States ranks a sad number 43 in world life expectancy.[20]

A 2016 report from the National Center for Health Statistics stated that in 2015, U.S. life expectancy fell for the first time since 1993.[21] While the decline is not big, falling one-tenth of a year – from 78.9 in 2014 to 78.8 in 2015 – it's highly unusual.[22] While the top ten causes of death rose across the board, the two biggest jumps came from Alzheimer's disease and unintentional or accidental death due to overdoses from drugs, alcohol, and other chemicals, as well as motor vehicle crashes. While the correlation might not be clear now, you'll soon see how death due to chronic lifestyle diseases tie into the increases in death overall.

Changing the Collective Mindset

In order to change the collective mindset about health and wellness, we need to reach critical mass. Enough people have to take constant action either towards a common goal, or away from destructive behavioral patterns.

In 1988, when I adopted a mostly vegetarian, organic diet, organic foods were difficult to find. I always had to seek out that one obscure health food store in my community. And even when I found it, the selection was limited. But now, you can find organic foods in many mainstream grocery stores such as Giant, Safeway, or Walmart. Even wholesale stores, such as Costco, have a growing choice of organic foods. Since the demand for organic food increased, the marketplace responded.

Twenty to thirty years ago, it was also difficult to find a place to practice yoga. You either had to live in an urban area or find a yoga teacher who taught at home. In recent years, it's become much easier to find a yoga class and many classes are offered with a gym membership. When enough people find that it's time for change and take action toward it, change does happen on a massive scale.

The Future of Healthy Living

It's my dream that in the future, there will be no more fast food chains. Healthier quick service restaurants like Sweetgreen or even Chipotle will become more of the norm. As a result of this expansion, we'll see the prices come down for healthy foods. In this same dream, health insurance companies will cover the preventive care costs of gym memberships, yoga classes, meditation courses, massage, acupuncture, and nutritional counseling. I would also like to see health insurance companies give vouchers to purchase organic food and give you discounts on your insurance plans if you get tested for blood pressure, cholesterol, blood sugar levels, and body fat every six months, and the tests come back with healthy results.

I would like to see employers financing stress management work-shops, paying for their employees to take vacations, and encouraging a year of family leave when an employee has a baby. I would like to see every American company making it mandatory for employees to take one hour of their workday for company-offered exercise, wheth-er in the form of a fitness class, a walk and talk meeting, or a gym workout. You might be inclined to think that businesses wouldn't be able to make their employees exercise. Yet certain professions do require that employees stay fit. This practice could be a program to incentivize employees.

A great business model I studied was with a startup company called Buffer. In 2016, this young social media company, a 100% re-mote company, paid their employees to take vacations. According to founders Leo Widrich and Joel Gascoigne, they started an unlimited vacation policy, but found that the employees almost never took va-cation. Intuitively, they knew that if their team members didn't take vacation, they would suffer burnout. In addition to a receiving a pay-check during vacation time, they gave an additional stipend to each employee to take a vacation. Buffer also encourages their team to move by giving them Fitbits. It's this careful attention to employee wellness that will help reverse the trend of chronic lifestyle illness.

In the end, if we place more focus on preventive health and there-by turn our health care system completely upside down, it will cost everyone a whole lot less in money, time, stress, and heartache.

10% on the Problem and 90% on the Solution

Buried under the corporate structure of Western medicine is a wealth of detailed, ancient, and legitimate knowledge. This knowledge of-ten takes on the form of Complementary and Alternative Medicine (CAM). If honored and applied, this knowledge can help our current generation of children and form a new medical structure for future generations. Yet many are the roadblocks in creating a new mainstream system. These obstacles don't necessarily come from lack of will, knowledge, or finances, but rather from bigger and more powerful voices who will feel threatened if the medical structure changes. These voices come most notably in the form of pharmaceutical companies. In this book, I'll address these artificial, yet seemingly impervious barriers that are keeping us from getting healthy.

Motivational life coach Tony Robbins teaches, that as a general rule, we should spend no more than 10% of our time on the problem and the rest of the time on a solution. To that end, the first part of this book will help you – the consumer, patient, or perhaps even medical worker – fully understand the problem. I'm quite certain that most people don't grasp the severity of the problem and the urgency with which we must find immediate solutions. In the second part, I'll offer solutions based on my knowledge and research on wellness and CAM. Finally, in the last section I'll help you explore how to live a balanced life in healing.

I can't pretend to have all the solutions. But for a small slice of time, I've taken the steering wheel to direct the conversation in another direction. Where we are now is not where we need to be. Everyone who has an interest in your wellness and in the wellness of future generations has the responsibility to keep the conversation going after this book.

A Last Note on Enjoying This Book

If you're not a medical professional, much of the terminology in this book will seem foreign to you. To that end I've included an extensive Glossary of Medical Terms in the back of the book. In section two, I've included chapters on healthy practices and healing modalities. Feel free to dive into whatever chapter speaks to you. As you become more intrigued by integrative medicine you'll find yourself referring back to those chapters time and again. Happy reading!

PART ONE

The Development of Modern Medicine and Where We Are Today

It is more important to know what sort of person has a disease than to know what sort of disease a person has. -Hippocrates

TO BEGIN, WE MUST delve into history to understand how and why modern medicine started in the first place. This knowledge will allow you to see how modern medicine grew into what we experience today. In this book, what we call "Western medicine" will be freely interchanged with the terms "modern medicine" and "allopathic medicine." When I speak of modern medicine throughout this work, I will be referring to the medical system formed and developed after the year 1850 in the United States. And once you understand where Western medicine came from, you will begin to understand its limitations.

Following the history, we will explore your role as a patient in the modern medical model. And finally, you will learn about your power as a consumer on all levels of health.

CHAPTER 1

THE HEROIC DEVELOPMENT OF MODERN MEDICINE

THE PRACTICE OF ALLOPATHIC medicine began before the nineteenth century but it wasn't until after the year 1850 – right around the start of the Industrial Revolution – that it began to grow by leaps and bounds. It's hard to believe how far we've come in the short span of one hundred and fifty years.

Like many of the technological advancements during the American Industrial Revolution, modern medicine also benefited from enormous discoveries. With the minimal tools they had to work with, it is frankly incredible how much nineteenth-century physicians were able to achieve. These modern medical pioneers worked fervently to not only save lives, but also improve the American quality of life with their findings. They are the true heroes of modern medicine.

HYGIENE – WHAT A CONCEPT!

Spread of infectious diseases as a result of poor living conditions and sanitation problems only increased as urbanization expanded. However, in this same period, medical pioneers like Hungarian doctor Ignaz Semmlweis were making strides: in 1846, Semmelweis brought down the death rate of childbed fever (also known as puerperal fever) among new mothers by insisting that doctors, midwives, and nurses wash their hands with chlorinated lime water before touching women in childbirth. While he was unaware of microorganisms, he accidentally discovered through deduction that a majority of physicians whose patients died of childbed fever had been performing autopsies before assisting with childbirth. To combat this, he asked these physicians to wash themselves with chlorinated lime water to remove any human body particles left behind from the autopsies, and his method worked.

Before Semmelweis's intervention 25-30 percent of new mothers who became infected died. Once the medical students began hand-washing the maternal mortality rate dropped to 1.27 percent. But even with evidence of his hand-washing success, he was still met with much resistance by the medical community in Vienna, Austria, and eventually fired from his post at the obstetric clinic where he worked until 1849 the year he was fired[23] Even though his medical students saw the value in his practices, his superiors did not understand them.[24]

In 1854, Florence Nightingale, a nurse who cared for wounded British soldiers during the Crimean War in Turkey, noticed that most soldiers were dying because of the poor hygiene practices in the hospital. Injured soldiers lay on the floor in their own blood and excrement. Shortly after arriving in Turkey, she got to work. She recruited the less sick patients to help her scrub the hospital from floor to ceiling. Her work in hygiene and sanitation reduced hospital death rates in Crimea from 42% to 2% by the time she left in the summer of 1856.[25] Based on her observations, Nightingale wrote Notes on Matters Affecting the Health, Efficiency, and Hospital Administration of the British Army, an 830-page report analyzing her experience and proposing reforms for other military hospitals operating under poor conditions.[26]

These early pioneers discovered that hygienic practices could stop the spread of infectious disease even before microorganisms were identified as the cause. Yet around the same time period, scientists in Europe were experimenting with the idea that something invisible to the naked eye might be the cause of many illnesses.

MILITARY MEDICINE: MEDICAL ADVANCEMENT OUT OF NECESSITY

Meanwhile, in the United States, the sanitary conditions during the Civil War (1861-1865) were simply inhumane. More men died from infectious diseases – like typhoid fever, pneumonia, mumps, measles, and tuberculosis – than from battle wounds.[27] Hospitalization systems during the Civil War era were haphazard. Poor sanitation, hygiene, and meager diets created breeding grounds for disease in military camps. The sheer numbers of wounded soldiers between 1861 and 1865 triggered advancement in medicine out of pure need.

Even though Florence Nightingale paved the way for women in a traditionally all-male medical field, it took the first two years of the American Civil War to introduce women nurses into military medicine. The exact number is not known, but it's estimated that between 5,000 and 10,000 women became nurses and treated wounded and sick soldiers during the Civil War.[28] After the publication of her books on nursing and hospital administration Florence Nightingale even gave direct advice to military medical personnel during the Civil War.[29]

Dr. Jonathan Letterman, the Medical Director of the Army of the Potomac, invented an ambulance system for transporting wounded soldiers and formed an efficient evacuation plan to quickly remove the wounded out of the battlefields. During the Battle of Antietam on September 17, 1862, Dr. Letterman's Ambulance Corp removed 23,000 wounded and deceased soldiers within twenty-four hours.[30]

In 1863, William A. Hammond, surgeon general for the Union army, designed new hospital layouts and wrote a handbook on hygiene for the army[31], and Clara Barton, eventual founder of the American Red Cross, brought medical supplies out to the fields[32]. Throughout the Civil War, doctors and nurses received training in the prevention and treatment of infectious diseases, anesthetics, and best surgical practices. As a result of these new medical practices, the hospital mortality rate fell to 8% in the last few years of the Civil War. Many of the accomplishments in early modern medicine can be traced back to the Civil War, since many of the practices from this era are used still today.[33]

BACTERIA, PASTEURIZATION, AND THE INVENTION OF MEDICAL CHEMICALS

Rapid advancements in scientific discovery after 1850 gave way to tremendous improvement in infectious disease control and quality of life for many patients. Scientists like Louis Pasteur, who popularized the Germ Theory of Disease, finally convinced the medical field that microorganisms exist and are the cause of infectious diseases. In 1862, Pasteur went on to invent a treatment process to kill bacteria in wine, beer and milk, known today as pasteurization. Experimenting with the Germ Theory helped Pasteur develop vaccines for chicken cholera, anthrax, tuberculosis, rabies, and small pox.[34] Around the same time period, advances were made in physiology, surgery, pathology, and cell theory.[35]

One of the most important discoveries of the period – that of drug isolation – paved the way for modern pharmacology. In the early nineteenth century, scientists discovered how to isolate drugs in their purest form and examine their effects on animals and humans.[36] Based on initial research in France in 1803 by J.F. Derosne and A. Seguin in 1804, Frederich Wilhelm Adam Serturner isolated morphine in 1806 in Germany. Serturner's discovery was an important one as it transformed pharmaceutical chemistry from a state of alchemy to a respected branch of science.[37] As researchers began to understand the chemical composition of certain drugs and what they did, they were able to start synthesizing them from basic units. Alkaloids and antipyretics (fever-lowering compounds) were the first drugs synthesized upon this discovery. By the late 19th century, German scientist, Oswald Schmeiderburg firmly established pharmacology by writing a textbook on pharmacology and founding the first pharmacology journal.

Up until the discovery of drug isolation, the medical discipline of pharmacology consisted of apothecaries who were responsible for preparing and prescribing drugs made from herbs. At the inception of modern pharmacology, this medical branch split between the apothecaries and those who wanted to uniquely study the development of medicinal compounds.[38] Hence this became the dividing factor between herbal remedies and prescription medications, as we know them today.

Heroic Medicine

"Heroic medicine" was the method of mainstream medical practice in Europe and the United States between 1780 and 1850, although the actual practices date back some 2,000 years prior. Doctors called "regulars" administered treatment of heroic medicine. The term separated them from alternative health care practitioners who administered gentler forms of therapy. Heroic medicine is based on the theory of the four humors, which attributes disease imbalances in the four "humors" of the body: blood, phlegm, yellow bile, and black bile. It also attributes to patients four bodily conditions: hot, cold, wet, and dry. These attributes correspond to the four elements: earth, air, fire and water.[39] The most common procedures in heroic medicine were bloodletting, intestinal purging, vomiting, profuse sweating, and blistering. Bloodletting, the initial treatment, consisted of venesection, opening up the vein, scarification, performing a series of small cuts, or cupping, placing a warmed cup over the cut and letting it fill with blood. Purgation consisted of administering large doses of mercury to the patient. Blistering involved placing hot plasters onto the skin to raise blisters, which were then drained.[40] This type of medical practice was called Heroic because of the enormous amounts of treatment administered to the patients.[41]

Regular physicians believed that all disease was due to overstimulation of the nerves and blood, and by using these harsh therapies, the body would return to its normal state.[42] They often employed high doses of mercury, quinine, and arsenic to treat patients. But even though many patients died from these extreme treatments, others got better. Some patients seemed to be encouraged by the very fact that the physician was doing something to cure their ailments and that this belief helped heal the body. In other words, historical literature shows that heroic medicine had more of a placebo effect than anything else.

The origins of the four humors can be traced back to Egyptian and Mesopotamian practices. The Greeks and Romans also employed these tactics. The theory equally has a connection with Ayurvedic medicine from India, which uses five elements: space, air, fire, water and earth and three mind body types based on these five elements.

It's important to note that modern medicine evolved directly from heroic medicine. The separation that took place around the 1850s divided medical practitioners into two categories; the Regulars or those who would become practitioners of modern medicine and alternative practitioners, who would be banned from practicing medicine in the United States.

Taking the Harsh, Leaving the Rest

The practices of bloodletting, purgation, vomiting, and sweating are still used in Ayurvedic medicine, but under careful observation, only in particular cases, and certainly not using toxic chemical compounds. Instead, Ayurvedic medicine is an example of a medical system that works to balance the body gently.

The primary methods of practice in the Western world prior to the mid-1800s employed only harsh therapies to try and cure patients. In fact, the biggest critics of heroic medicine were often the patients themselves. Regular physicians wanted to shock the body into wellness and dismissed all other forms of gentle treatment, including the use of non-toxic herbs, as pure quackery.[43]

Heroic medicine has direct lineage to modern allopathic medicine. The idea of shocking the body into wellness is one prevalent in today's medicine. Chemotherapy is an example of modern-day heroic medicine. The way we produce and administer pharmaceuticals today, using only the active ingredient, is reminiscent of heroic medicine's philosophy to jolt the body into wellness. Yet, the connection makes sense. Practitioners of heroic medicine were the ones who formed modern medicine.

While much of modern medical practice today is scientifically or empirically based, we cannot deny that there is a harsher edge to this type of healing.

Other Forms of Medical Practices and How They Got Pushed Aside

Heroic medicine was not the only medical practice at the time that modern medicine was emerging. Herbal medicine had already been in practice for centuries. In the 1790s, German physician Samuel Hahnemann (1755-1843) introduced homeopathy into the world. Homeopathy operates under the concept of "healing of the same," the term coming from the Greek words omeos ("similar") and pathos ("suffering").[44] The concept of homeopathy is similar to that of vaccinations. The patient is given a small dose of medicine that mimics the symptoms of the disease. In chapter eleven, we'll delve deeper into the origins and therapeutic uses of homeopathy. Other alternatives to heroic medicine in the 19th century included Thomsonianism (which used botanical remedies and steam baths), Eclecticism (botanical practice), hydrotherapy, and magnetic therapy.

Fierce competition existed between physicians practicing heroic medicine and practitioners of all other forms of medicine, especially homeopathy because it worked and most Americans were abandoning regular medicine for it. The regular doctors coined the term "irregulars" for all practitioners who did not practice heroic and later modern medicine. Hahnemann, in retaliation, called the Regulars "Allopaths," which meant "different from the disease." Hence, the medical community adopted the term *allopathy* and this term continues to refer to Western medicine today. Once the American Medical Association (AMA) gained the power to impose quality standards in medical schools across the country at the state level, hatred toward alternative medical practices only increased.[45] The Regulars insisted that alternative medical practitioners were imposters and quacks. Alternative practitioners were arrested, fined, and jailed for practicing medicine without a license. Yet they couldn't get medical licenses because the AMA refused to recognize any of the non-orthodox practices as valid.

Even though herbal medicines were the only real pharmaceuticals of the day, the 1807 Medical Practices Act's ban on alternative medicine left modern medical practitioners without reliable medicines for nearly a hundred years.[46]

And so the politics of medicine began.

EXPLORING THE REASONS FOR THE DEVELOPMENT OF MODERN MEDICINE

In order to understand where we find ourselves in 2018, we must explore why modern medicine has developed the way it has for the last one hundred and fifty years. Up until about the mid-1850s, allopathic medicine was extremely unpopular. It was unreliable, and it killed more people than it saved. Amputation was a regular form of surgery. Anesthesia included alcohol and chloroform. Treatment through heroic medicine mostly resulted in death. Even George Washington died a premature death through bloodletting treatments, blistering, and extreme doses of arsenic.[47]

In early America, barbers (yes, you read that correctly) were the first dentists and surgeons. You could go to get your haircut and have a tooth pulled, hence the white and red poles, which were formulated by the drying white bandages with washed out blood hanging outside of the barbershop.[48]

Disease epidemics ran wild in urban areas due to poor hygiene and poor sanitation. Thanks to late nineteenth-and early twentieth-century scientists, modern medical developments began to save lives and increase life expectancy, including but not limited to vaccines, anesthesia, advanced surgical practices, and synthetically-made medicines, such as insulin.

Thus, the reason modern medicine developed at the rate that it did was because of monumental problems in society: war, population growth, urbanization, and unsanitary conditions due to industrialization. Scientists and researchers of the nineteenth and the first half of the twentieth centuries had to troubleshoot problems that had never been properly addressed. And the explosion of scientific discoveries made for enormous growth in a short amount of time, given the length of time humans have been around.

And yet the modern medical model has always been about fixing something that is broken. Given the history of early modern medicine, it's easy to understand the need for this sort of model. The scientific heroes of this era wanted to save lives and improve the quality of life.

So we're left with the question: *Is that model still the ideal and necessary model to move forward?* The answer is important, given the fact that one-third of all diseases in the U.S. today are related to lifestyle. Since diseases of lifestyle are mostly preventable, I would suggest that the early medical model is outdated and needs modification.

As in most areas of expertise, plans need revision. If you look at any successful business, there are constant improvements, revisions, and if necessary, a complete overhaul in the business model to ensure the business continues to succeed in the future. The problem today is that the modern medical system came to prominence as a monopoly. There is no system of checks and balances. Elite medical societies, put into place starting with the AMA in 1848, pushed out any alternative practices. Those same medical societies made sure there were legal ramifications if anyone tried to practice any other type of medicine. Because of this, alternative practices were no longer acknowledged and by the 1890s the final push was given to homeopathy.

The business practices and political questions surrounding this issue run deep. Allopathic medicine's biggest competitor, homeopathy, nearly put allopathic doctors out of business up until the 1850s. Instead of medicine becoming a collaboration between both sides for the betterment of the patient, it became a brutal battle rooted in money, high society, and prejudice against German immigrants, women, and the less educated. And in the end, allopathic medicine won the battle. While I haven't written this work to go into a deep study of the history of medicine in the U.S., if it interests you a good book on the topic is *Divided Legacy: The Conflict Between Homeopathy and the American Medical Association* by Harris L. Coulter.

Let's fast forward to today. Allopathic medicine may have won the battle in the second half of the 19th century but patients being treated by this medical system are still searching for more. You see, the whole reason people searched for and adhered to alternative medical practices prior to 1850 is because allopathic medicine didn't provide lasting solutions. Mothers were among the most frightened by allopathic medicine in early America, because it killed their children. And today, Americans are still outraged by the inadequacies of modern medicine and its limited choices.

The Arrogance of Modern Medicine

In the preface, I explained how my mother revered the doctor like a god. By understanding the uprising of modern medicine, you will understand that we were conditioned to think this way. Modern medical physicians, scientists, and researchers were the heroes of the day. In the late 19th century, post Civil War, physicians were once again considered among the educated elite. Furthermore, Americans, at the end of the 19th century didn't have any other choices in medicine, as allopathic medicine had gained its monopoly. Fortunately, this fledgling system did begin to save lives – something medicine had rarely done in the Western world. As a result, the general public began to have blind acceptance of modern medicine as absolute truth and that trend continued.

Yes, modern medicine saves lives. I'm grateful for antibiotics, vaccines, modern surgical techniques, and anesthesia. Thank God we're not sawing off peoples' legs left and right, and thank God I don't have to go to a barber to get a tooth pulled. But this monopoly and arrogant attitude toward alternative healing modalities must stop.

We have come to an era where arrogance doesn't prove to be the solution in every health situation. More money and more research don't always equal healthier lives. Scientific studies don't equal absolute truth. In fact, we've begun to experience quite the contrary.

I need to emphasize that I'm not admonishing a singular person or set of people in the medical field. I'm referring to modern medicine as a whole. There are Western physicians who are open-minded and those who are closed-minded when it comes to integrative medical practices. But we must remember that physicians are formed by what they're taught in medical school and residency. If they've never been exposed to alternative medicine, healthy lifestyle courses, or other healing modalities, we can't possibly expect them to adopt these as part of a medical practice. Not to mention that most are fearful of medical malpractice if they do not follow medical protocol by the book.

If we assume that modern medicine is the best and only way to practice medicine, we might learn by taking lessons from history. Medical history is full of discoveries that were once refuted by respected scientists in the same field. For example, when Louis Pasteur proposed the Germ Theory in the 1850s, the medical community thought it was absurd. Another more recent example comes from Nobel Prize winners Barry J. Marshall and J. Robin Warren in 2005 for their discovery of bacteria as the cause for ulcers. Just five years prior to their award, scientists ridiculed them saying that it was impossible for bacteria to live in an acidic environment.[49] These small examples show that we are always making new discoveries.

Is it possible that there is a lot we still don't know about health and healing? Can we at least entertain the idea that this physical human body might not be an ailing unit that we must shock into health with harsh chemicals or unnecessary surgery? Is it possible that instead, it that can be healed over time in various ways?

Arrogance is a defense mechanism but it's not empowerment. When we stay arrogant, we close our minds to possibilities. With 150 million Americans sick with chronic lifestyle illnesses in 2018, it's time that we begin to question the importance of this arrogance and begin to let down our defenses. If we put modern medical education and indoctrination aside for a moment, we could perchance see human health and healing in a broader scope.

WHAT IN THE WORLD DID WE DO TO STAY ALIVE BEFORE 1850?

Still the question remains: if modern medicine is only 200 years old, and humans are 200,000 years old, how did we manage to survive as a species all this time?

Disease, germs, war, and poor hygiene existed long before we pinpointed these problems in the past two centuries. Yet humans survived. They even maintained lifespans of one hundred years or more. So, the more precise question is: how did they do it without modern Western medicine?

In studying different medical systems across the history of the world, I came to a general conclusion: there exists a common thread. To come to this end, I looked at Galen's system of medicine, Hippocratic Medicine, Islamic Medicine, Chinese Medicine, Ayurveda Classical Indian Medicine, and Native American Medicine. Hippocratic Medicine from 400 BCE – conventionally known as the predecessor of Western medicine – determined the cause of disease to be natural causes (rather than evil spirits, which was the common belief at the time).[50] Hippocrates believed in a more holistic approach to treatment. He placed a huge emphasis on the doctor-patient relationship and even referred to the physician as a "servant toward health." Keeping the body in balance through diet and other means was central in this medical system.[51]

I found that all these ancient systems of medicine prioritized closeness to the earth and its elements, closeness to plant life, and using the earth's energy in some way toward healing. Ancient societies that date back 5,000 – 7,000 years had advanced medical knowledge that somehow got lost throughout time. Two of the oldest medical systems, Traditional Chinese Medicine and Ayurvedic medicine, had detailed systems for: disease classification, complex herbal remedies, successful surgeries, and a wide taxonomy of medical specialties, including but not limited to pediatrics and gynecology.

I found a beautiful description of surgery done by a famous Chinese physician, Hua Tuo, who lived around the second century AD. He invented an anesthetic called Mafei San, which he boiled and gave orally to his patient. The anesthetic would knock the patient unconscious. He would then perform the surgery, cutting even through the abdominal wall if necessary to remove a tumor. He would stitch the area closed, apply a cream or salve to the area, and the patient would heal in four to five days.[52] And he performed this surgery without any of the medical technology that we have today.

Ayurvedic medicine has similar qualities to Hippocrates's theory of the four humors. Ayurveda, however, is a spiritual and scientific system of medicine. Ayurveda looks at the patient holistically and is concerned with balancing their doshas (or their mind-body types) based upon the five elements: space, air, fire, water, and earth. Balance is achieved through proper nutrition and healthy routines, both daily and seasonal. In Ayurveda, preventive measures like yoga, exercise, and meditation are key to one's health. Detoxification and purification of the body help prevent serious illness. In chapter seven we'll talk about how to properly detoxify the body and keep the body more pure.

In the early days of Islam starting from the 8th century, Islamic scholars debated on how to form a style of medical practice. Belief in the religious texts, the Quran and Hadiths clearly showed a duty to care for the sick. Yet scholars weren't convinced that physicians should use Greek, Chinese, or Indian medical techniques since many of these were rooting in paganism. However in the end Islamic physicians were given free rein to practice whatever type of medicine they saw fit. As a result the practice of Islamic medicine incorporated aspects of Hippocratic medicine, Egyptian medicine, and Ayurvedic medicine.[53] During the Islamic Golden Age (between the eighth and thirteenth centuries CE) scientific, economic, and cultural developments expanded, including medical knowledge. According to the Qur'an and the Hadiths, followers of Islam had a God-given duty to take care of the sick and maintain a healthy body and soul. The best description of Islamic medicine comes from the Father of Islamic Medicine, Al-Razi. He wrote primarily medical texts, many of which were translated into Latin and considered an undisputed authority in European medicine until the seventeenth century. Al-Razi believed that each patient must be treated individually with emphasis on hygiene and diet, a theory that also reflected the ideas of the empirical Hippocratic school of thought.[54]

The following quote outlines Al-Razi's philosophy on practicing medicine:

"In the beginning of an illness, chose remedies, which do not weaken the [patient's] strength. [...] Whenever a change of nutrition is sufficient, do not use medication, and whenever single drugs are sufficient, do not use composite drugs.

-- Al-Razi

Native Americans practiced healing with herbs, plants, and roots for thousands of years. Like in other ancient medical practices, they believed that health was a balance of body, emotion, and spirit in addition to living in harmony with the environment. Native Americans believed that if they lived in balance with the earth, they would stay well. Each person took responsibility for his or her health and knew that every thought and action had its consequence. Medicine men and women practiced healing the spirit and chasing away any bad spirits. When European settlers arrived to North America 500 years ago, they were astonished to see that the Native Americans were cured easily of many wounds and diseases that would be fatal to them. Native peoples' knowledge of herbal medicines and healing far exceeded the Europeans' knowledge at that time. The following quote by Mourning Dove, Salish demonstrates how Native Americans viewed illness and healing.

"...everything on earth has a purpose, every disease an herb to cure it, and every person a mission. This is the Indian theory of existence."

Mourning Dove, Salish, 1888-1936[55]

It's true that thousands of Native Americans died due to what they called "white man diseases" such as small pox and measles. But that's only because they didn't have the time to learn about these diseases and create remedies for them. Nonetheless, many European settlers learned and practiced American Indian medicine. They became known as "Indian Doctors" or "botanical practitioners" and strongly opposed the practices of the Regulars.[56]

One common thread in all ancient healing traditions seems to be reverence – not only reverence for human life in healing, but also reverence in considering the person as a whole and unique individual. Additionally, every ancient medical system indicates a connection to a person's environment and balance with the external world. But today, that balance is lost.

COMMONALITIES IN ANCIENT MEDICAL SYSTEMS

Western medicine is an infant in the history of medical systems. Technology has advanced Western societies in ways beyond what we could have previously imagined. But if you give a baby a computer and programming skills, that baby still needs to learn actual human skills. The baby still needs to learn about their environment and life around them. Therefore, I feel that technology has been a double-edged sword for modern medicine.

In our questioning, however, we must not underestimate the amazing advances in modern medicine, because many discoveries in

Western medical development are truly miraculous. We have precision diagnostic tools and surgical tools to decrease margin of error. But these are not enough. We need to incorporate the aspects of ancient medical systems that helped humans survive – not only for the last hundred and fifty years, but for thousands of years prior.

In studying ancient medical systems, here's what I found they most had in common:

- Treatment of the patient as an individual
- Spirituality as a contributing factor toward healing
- A holistic approach (treating the entire person and not just the disease)
- Use of plants in medicines
- A willingness to work with nature instead of against it
- Use of the biorhythms of the earth to help with healing

Below I will expand on each of these findings from ancient medical systems.

TREATMENT OF THE PATIENT AS AN INDIVIDUAL

Each person is different and unique. Therefore, we each require different treatment programs. No two treatment plans should look exactly alike. Western medicine has become very linear. Thus, the most common treatment programs include a diagnosis for symptoms and a prescription for each symptom. On the other hand, ancient medical systems took a rounded approach that encompassed many aspects of health, taking into account the body, the mind, patients' emotions, their family life, their spiritual practices, and their living situations.

SPIRITUALITY AS A CONTRIBUTING FACTOR TOWARD HEALING

With the exception of the Galen and Hippocratic systems, other medical systems mentioned in this work included spirituality as a means toward healing. In part two, I will discuss the undeniable power that prayer and other spiritual practices that contribute to healing.

A Holistic Approach

Many ancient medical systems used holistic approaches to healing. These medical systems didn't impose limits, such as sticking only to herbs and plants (which were a majority of the medicines prior to 1850) or to surgery. In general they realized the need for a combination of healing measures to completely heal the patient.

Plants Used for Medicines: Working with Nature Instead of Against It

Gentle approaches in medicine, with exception of acute cases, allow the body to heal naturally. Modern medical practices don't teach citizens of Western society to take gentle approaches, nor do physicians take the time to encourage and counsel to this end. Ancient societies didn't have the scientific knowledge we have today and perhaps that's the reason they relied heavily on nature's resources for healing.

Using Biorhythms of the Earth to Help with Healing

We're a part of nature. As an integral part of nature, we participate in the rhythms of nature. The rhythms that affect our bodies are called biorhythms. For example, the twenty-four hour clock is called the circadian rhythm. The rhythm of the moon is a twenty-eight day cycle and affects the gravitational pull of the earth. A woman's menstrual cycle is another example of a biorhythm. Also the seasons of the year affect us physiologically and psychologically as in the example of those who experience Seasonal Affective Disorder (SAD) in the winter. If we're connected and go with the flow of nature, we experience ease and wellness. On the other hand, if we fight the rhythms of nature we can experience disease and discomfort. If you eat during the night or sleep too little, you throw off your circadian cycle. Or a woman who suppresses ovulation by taking a birth control pill goes against her body's natural monthly cycle.

One aspect of connecting to biorhythms is spending time in nature. You may rarely immerse yourself in nature if you live in an urban area or especially if you live in a suburban area. I know people, in suburban areas, who almost never have to go outside if they don't want to. These people go from their garage to the car, to the office parking structure, to the elevator, to the office cubicle or conference room, back downstairs to grab a quick lunch inside the office building, back to the car in the office garage, and right back into to the garage at home. Whew! It's no wonder we can be disconnected with our biorhythms and those of nature. Yet, many ancient medical systems used the rhythms of nature to enhance healing. They used the earth's energy for healing through healing strategies like acupuncture, tai chi, qi gong, meditation, water therapy, or magnet therapy.

As you can clearly see, something has been lost in the translation of ancient medical practices to our current Western one. Let's explore the reasons and how we can get closer to a better solution.

CHAPTER 2

WESTERN MEDICINE IS NEITHER THE PROBLEM, NOR THE ENTIRE SOLUTION

You can't afford to get sick, and you can't depend on the present health care system to keep you well. It's up to you to protect and maintain your body's innate capacity for health and healing by making the right choices in how you live. -Dr. Andrew Weil

THE ARGUMENTS PRESENTED IN chapter one might lead you to think that I'm blaming Western medicine for all of America's health problems. Yet, the title in chapter two appears to be lifting that blame. What I mean by the title is Western medicine by itself is not the problem. Let's look at modern medicine objectively. By itself, it's composed of tools to diagnose and treat illness, as well as tools to discover advanced medicines and procedures to better treat illness and injury.

Take, for example, a breast cancer diagnosis. Women today are encouraged to get mammograms every two years after age fifty.[57] They can also get tested to see if they have the BRCA genetic muta-

tion, which puts them at a higher risk for breast cancer. Early di-
agnostics can mean early treatment. Early treatment may result in
a better survival rate. As of 2016, the five-year average survival rate
for breast cancer was 89%.[58] This includes an average of all stages of
cancer. If cancer is only located in the breast, the five-year survival
rate goes up to 99%.[1]

Normal procedures to remove the tumor include surgery: either a
breast-conserving surgery (lumpectomy) or a mastectomy for more
advanced stages of cancer. Doctors may also prescribe systemic
treatment, called adjuvant therapy, which can include hormone
therapy, chemotherapy, targeted therapy, and radiation therapy.[59]
Neoadjuvant therapy, or the above listed therapies may be prescribed
in certain instances prior to surgery. In the case of a mastectomy,
advanced surgical techniques for reconstructive surgery can make
the patient feel whole again. All in all, the prognosis for a person diagnosed with breast cancer is very good. Treatment of the disease is
varied and individualized. And because breast cancer is fairly common, new treatments are constantly being researched and always on
the horizon.

The only drawback with early detection is that many types of
smaller, non-invasive and slow-growing tumors never develop into
bigger tumors or put the patient's life at risk. One type of small non-
invasive early cancer is ductal carcinoma in situ (DCIS). This type of
cancer begins with abnormal cells inside the milk ducts in breast tissue.[60] Since 2009, research has shown that some tiny cancers, such as
DCIS, disappear without treatment. For example, cancer researchers now conclude that most DCIS will never become an invasive
breast cancer, even without treatment.[61] The other controversy surrounding early detection argues that exposure to radiation through
mammograms can actually cause breast cancer. But even given these

---

1 Five-year survival rate means the percentage of people in a study or group
who are still alive for five years after the initial diagnosis or treatment.

drawbacks, the conclusion is that early detection is advantageous, and statistically, the five-year survival rate for breast cancer patients has increased. But because the risk of yearly mammograms is high and can cause misdiagnosis and overtreatment, The American College of Obstetricians and Gynecologists now recommend that an average-risk woman can start mammograms as late as age 50 and can opt to be screened every two years until age 75.[62]

In reading through the process of diagnosing, treating, and curing such a disease with Western medicine, you might deduct that there is nothing inherently wrong with the modern medical model. In fact, statistics show that lives are saved with this model.

Yet herein lies the problem. In allopathic medicine, we treat the disease and not the person. We are constantly looking for ways in which the human body is malfunctioning versus building it up for optimal health. Even a routine screening becomes a scrutinous search for pathology. Still it's not the fault of the physicians that we, as patients, have become entangled in this system of over-testing and lack of trust in our bodies. It's the result of the culmination of the past 150 years of building our medical system into a business with the primary goal of turning a profit.

Good Doctors, Good Intentions

I've never met a doctor who said that they went into medicine for the paycheck. Certainly, good pay has its incentives. But it takes a lot of discipline, tenacity, and money to go through four years of undergrad, four years of medical school, and three to seven years of residency. On top of all the years of study and dedication, the average medical student exits school with about $183,000 in medical school debt.[63] So by the time they're ready to practice medicine independently, they're between 30 and 35 years old and already overwhelmed with debt.

Unless your doctor went into medicine through family pressure, they probably had good intentions going into medicine. If you ask, most doctors will tell you they went into medicine to help people. But the reality of medicine is often different than what they signed up for. Even if a physician wants to take the time to get to know a patient, they can't. How much time they spend with you is regulated, for the most part, by their medical practice, the health insurance companies, and the price of their medical malpractice insurance.

As I mentioned previously, physicians must almost always carry an active medical malpractice insurance plan whether they are practicing or not. One former client from my Ayurvedic practice, a physician herself, had decided to quit her pediatric practice because of the stress that came with the administrative work. While unemployed, she still had to pay her $30,000-per-year medical malpractice policy. She had to remain covered in the event that any past patient might decide to sue her for medical malpractice. And in addition to consistently paying for medical malpractice insurance, physicians must constantly take courses and workshops to keep their medical license updated.

This is why your physician must see four to six patients an hour just to afford staying in practice. Your doctor is trapped in this system, too. A physician friend of mine shared with me that he discouraged all of his children from going into medicine. "It's just not the same as it was," he explained. "We don't have the freedom to practice like we did, even twenty years ago." I know doctors who have become so dissatisfied with this lack of connection with their patients that they have started independent, integrative practices and take only cash, check, and credit cards for their services. They've broken away from the health insurance model to try and practice medicine better.

In a way, that's part of the solution. But these visionary doctors must now charge around $200 to $300 per visit because they're spending so much time with each patient. My endocrinologist, for example, operates his practice this way and spends about 45 minutes with me. I appreciate the trusting relationship with him, but I also understand that not everyone can afford this. As a result, unfortunately, even a physician who finds a way out of the system isn't able to cater to patients from all income levels.

DOES DOCTOR REALLY KNOW BEST?

To answer this question: yes and no. Doctors are well trained and very well educated. They understand anatomy, physiology, and pathology. Your doctor may be a specialist in their field – and an excellent one, at that. If you have heart disease, your cardiologist will know how to keep your heart ticking and increase your life expectancy through medications. They may suggest an angioplasty, a stint, a pacemaker, or even bypass surgery. Your doctor will know how to treat your illness or injury, certainly – but they may not know how to treat you.

Western doctors may know your health history based on what you disclose on a waiting room questionnaire, but they don't know much beyond that. Does your physician know the answers to the following questions?:

- What is your occupation?
- Are you married, single, dating, in a relationship or the status of that relationship?
- Are you happy with your current romantic relationship?
- Have you had any major life changes in the past year? (A move, a divorce, an adoption, a death in the family, etc.)
- Do you have children and are you the primary caretaker of those children?
- What are your passions and hobbies?
- When was the last time you took a vacation?
- What are your spiritual beliefs?

- What kinds of food do you like to eat, and what kind of diet do you keep daily?
- Do you feel safe at home?
- Do you struggle financially, or are you confident in your finances?
- Do you drink alcohol or take drugs daily? How much do you drink on the weekends?
- Are you happy most of the time?
- Do you love your job?
- Do you feel you are living your life's purpose?
- Do you have a strong family support system nearby?
- Do you have supportive and loving friends?
- Do you exercise daily and what kind of exercise do you do?
- Do you feel emotionally stable most of the time?
- Do you feel hopeful about the future?

I would bet that your primary care physician doesn't know the answers to most – if any – of these questions. So, given this: *Do you think your doctor knows best* –enough to treat you fully into optimal health?

You might think that these questions don't really matter. But they matter more than you think. Health is more than the absence of symptoms. And symptoms, when they are present, are often caused by more than just physical ailments.

There have been attempts to pull answers from patients with new and improved questionnaires. Yet I'm skeptical as to their effectiveness. The last time I was at an appointment for a physical, the intake nurse (who happened to be a student and not yet a certified nurse), asked me a series of new depression screening questions. First of all, she asked two simple questions inquiring whether I was feeling sad or having thoughts of suicide. And secondly, these questions were being administered by a person I didn't know and would probably never see again. So if I was depressed, would I be inclined to answer truthfully? These feeble attempts are not the same as actually knowing a patient.

LOOKING AT THE CUBAN MODEL

So let us keep entertaining the original question: Does the doctor know best? I thought it would be interesting to look at the medical model in Cuba, where government-sponsored health care exists with no out-of-pocket cost to citizens. While the system is not perfect, it's a great model for patient-doctor rapport and successful preventive medicine. Cuban health care is available for all citizens regardless of income level. Every person has a family physician responsible for a set number of patients. And the physician goes to each patient's home at least once yearly.

The main focus in Cuban medicine is preventive care. The physicians, nurses, and other health care workers are based in the community, meaning that each physician lives in the same area as their patients. A patient may be referred to a specialty clinic for tests or other procedures, but the patient's main physician provides all follow-up care. The patient is counseled in-home on preventive care measures like birth control. A patient's entire family is involved in discussions about the patient's health.[64]

And thanks to this, Cuban medicine has proven to be extremely successful. Vaccination rates in Cuba are among the highest in the world. The life expectancy of Cubans is 78 years, which is comparable to the United States, and infant mortality rates are less than five per one thousand live births – better than in the United States.[65] And because of the strict economic embargo between Cuba and the United States, Cuba has had to manufacture most of its own medicines. Thanks to limited resources, Cubans doctors have relied largely on herbal medicine, which has worked well over the past 65 years.[66]

However, if the United States government lifts the embargo, Cuban physicians fear that an influx of prescription medicines from the

United States and Europe will cause them to lose all the knowledge learned on natural medicines and healing. One such physician Umberto stated in an interview with NPR:

"I see my patients like a family, not as a sick person who I'm better than because I'm a doctor. We're just as human as the patient. We try to interact a lot with the patients. If the patient is unwell, he is the one in pain and he knows what he feels. Sometimes love cures more than medicine.[67]

In the example of Cuban medicine, "Yes, Cuban doctors know best- or at least, they know more than American doctors.

KEEPING US DEPENDENT

Prescription medications are one of the few resources that Western doctors have available to them. This has become a huge problem. As of November 2015, the *Journal of the American Medical Association* reported that 59% of Americans over the age of 20 were taking at least one prescription medication. And on top of that, 15% of Americans take five or more prescription medications – a number that has doubled since the year 2000.[68]

Once you start taking a prescription medication, it's difficult to stop. It can be dangerous to abruptly stop taking a medication. Anti-anxiety medications and anti-depressants have withdrawal symptoms. Pain pills and sleep medications are highly addictive. Your body adjusts to the medicine and changes physiologically in response to it.

Another problem on the rise with the prevalence of prescription medications is non-medical use of prescription opioids (Vicodin, Dilaudid, Demerol). In 2013, prescription opioids were involved in more deaths than all illicit drugs (cocaine, heroin, ecstasy, etc.) combined. As a consequence prescription opioid abuse has become a U.S. epidemic.[69] To make matters worse, consistent use of even one prescription medication may cause side effects, which can lead to additional prescriptions in order to offset these side effects. Each year, about 4.5 million Americans visit the doctor or emergency room because of adverse prescription drug side effects.[70]

When you take a prescription pill, you are a guaranteed repeat customer. You need to go to your doctor, get your blood drawn, make medical claims, and pay the co-pay or price of prescriptions. They have you hook, line, and sinker.

THE HYPNOSIS OF ADS

It would be easy for a foreigner to pinpoint the focus of our society today in the U.S. All they would need to do is turn on the radio or TV to see what is ruling the airways: drugs, drugs and more drugs.

The other day, I was jogging while listening to Pandora with the ads. It seemed like every five minutes I was hearing an ad for a medical center, medical lab, a new medical program, or a new cancer treatment. It was insane. As I ran, I thought, *the absolute last thing I want to think about is getting sick.* Yet here we are, day after day, bombarded with reasons that we might be or insinuations that we are sick.

In 2016, drug makers spent $6.4 billion marketing prescription drugs in Direct to Consumer (DTC) advertising – or almost double of what they spent in 2012 $3.5 billion, just four years prior.[71,72]

Let us put this number into perspective. In 2014, here is what the five most-advertised brands[73] spent on advertising in the United States:

- AT&T- $1.44 billion
- Verizon- $1.29 billion
- Geico- $1.6 billion
- McDonald's Corporation – $935 million
- Chevrolet- $888 million

Even if you combine all five of these companies' advertising expenses together, they don't even come close to $6.4 billion.

The question that remains for me is: why do drug companies need to advertise? Prior to 1983, when the first TV commercial for a prescription pill was aired, you would never see prescription pills advertised in the marketplace. If you were sick, you went to the doctor, who then prescribed something if necessary. But prescription pills were not household names. And you would certainly never think to ask your doctor about a certain pill. It's almost as if drug companies are desperate for you to be sick. With such a massive advertising budget, it's in the drug companies' best interest if you do stay sick. We are brainwashed into believing that we need prescription drugs to survive.

The buck doesn't stop there. You play your part in this downward spiral. In an effort to help you, I'm going to play devil's advocate here. Who is the one ultimately asking for the drugs? As the consumer, you are. And if you're not, are you taking responsibility for your health and wellbeing otherwise?

We're inundated with ads telling us why we should be sick or need prescription medications. But it's your responsibility to take charge of your own health. Until the health system changes to include a more integrative approach to health and wellness, it's the only medical system we have.

CORPORATE BLOCKING

Big corporate entities are cashing in on you becoming and staying dependent on them. This is absolutely no joke. Humans have struggled with illness since they first roamed the earth. There have always been waves of illness and epidemics throughout history, which in turn means that humans are guaranteed customers for the medical industry. Given that at some point in every person's life they will experience an illness of some sort, why in the world do we need to sell remedies as if customers were hard to find? And the more disturbing question is why have we in the United States now accepted this as commonplace?

For-profit medical establishments don't care about you getting better. If our current system cared about you getting better, there would be regulations in place to ensure your good health. Examples of such regulations include:

- Putting caps on costs of prescription medications.
- Capping costs for medical procedures including surgeries, MRIs, CAT scans, blood tests, etc.
- Setting limits on health insurance premiums and lowering deductible and out-of-pocket costs.
- Creating incentives for you to practice preventive health measures.
- Limiting the number of overused surgical procedures such as caesarian sections per medical facility. (In 1970, the caesarian section rate in the United States represented 5% of all live births and in 2017, that rate has increased to 33%.)[74]
- Rewarding physicians who perform fewer procedures.
- Cracking down on physicians who prescribe high numbers of pain-killing medications that are keeping patients addicted.

If we are to be informed consumers, it's important that we understand the conflict of interest in many areas of the medical field. You visit a doctor's office because you want to get and stay healthy. Your doctor's office, the pharmacy, the medical labs, and hospitals might be slightly concerned about you getting healthy, but what they want more than that, is to cash in on you being sick.

STOP ASKING AND TAKE STEPS TOWARD YOUR IMPROVED HEALTH

Even though ads tell you to "Ask your doctor," how about refraining until you hear a diagnosis? I've talked to frustrated physicians who are caught in the middle of the pharmaceutical crossfire because patients are asking for these drugs. For example: if you go to your doctor and say you're having trouble sleeping and you need (insert brand) sleep medication, how are they to dispute you? Or if you tell them you have anxiety, and the only way you can get well is by taking (insert the brand) anti-anxiety medication – because your sister Mary and your friend Mable take it, how is your doctor going to determine whether or not you actually have anxiety?

The problem with asking for these types of drugs, based on an ad you saw on TV or because a friend takes them, is that you're setting yourself up to become dependent on these highly addictive substances. Do you see how pharmaceutical advertising can work to your detriment? Physicians go to school for several years to understand the effects on chemicals on the human body and big business has given us, the consumers, the power to make risky medical decisions that we should never have the power to make.

Just because we have marvelous technology and advanced diagnostic tools doesn't mean you must insist on medical testing. There is such a thing as over-testing. No test is 100% accurate. In fact, many medical tests can bring about false positives, causing anguish, anxiety, and subsequently more testing.[75] Therefore patients who insist on excessive testing because they're worried that they might have a disease might be putting themselves unnecessarily in harms way.

When it comes to health, we must realize that quick fixes and Band-Aid approaches do not work and almost always backfire. Great health is established only through hard work and consistency.

In recent years, we've become used to having things at our disposal quickly. We want everything *now*. We want our coffee drinks fast, a rapid text message response, and an instantaneous answer from Google. Many of us don't want the hard work of therapy and workshops on communication or anger management. *No thank you, just give me the anti-depressant.* We want the four-hour energy drink so we can go, go, go. Then, we're so wired that we can't sleep, so we take some extra melatonin or a sleeping pill. Nothing can replace consistent and focused action to ensure your long-term health and wellbeing, not any pill, test, or quick-fix.

How the Internet Has Led to Self-Diagnosing

Are you addicted to WebMD?

Medical doctors have to go through eight years of college – plus three to seven years of residency – just to learn medicine. How is WebMD going to give you the equivalent of eleven years of medical education in a frantic one-night web search marathon? It can't.

But Michelle, you may retort, *you just told me that my doctor probably doesn't know best. Plus, you told me to take responsibility for my own health.*

Make no mistake: your doctor knows plenty about medicine. However, they don't know the nuances that make up you and your lifestyle. But that doesn't mean you should resort to Internet surfing to come up with a diagnosis for yourself and then present it on several coffee-stained sticky notes to your physician. Your energy would be much better served by taking preventive measures to make sure you don't get sick in the first place.

But this is symptomatic of our current medical system. Ultimately the thing that is causing patients to self-diagnose, self-treat, and insist upon unnecessary prescriptions, is a lack of trust in the health partnership.

And in the end, everyone comes out frustrated.

Conclusion: Be Informed

Instead of self-diagnosing or caving into the hypnosis of prescription medication ads, when you are, in fact, prescribed a treatment or test, learn everything you can about it – including your right to refuse it or ask for something different. That's being a smart consumer. And you are the consumer. You have choices in all personal medical matters, including not following the advice of your doctor and asking for a second opinion. If you're not assertive when it comes to asking your doctor questions, try to muster up the courage to ask until you have clear answers. A conscientious doctor won't mind you asking and will strive to educate you about your diagnosis.

CHAPTER 3

POWER AND TRUST BETWEEN YOU AND YOUR DOCTOR

THE WAITING ROOM AT Dr. Alfreda Jones' OB/GYN office is always full of women, young and old, sometimes sitting for several hours to see her. In fact, you learn from the first appointment with Dr. Jones that you should bring a lot of reading material, work, or crossword puzzles to keep you occupied, because she is perpetually running late. This charming Italian-American doctor sits down with you as if she were having coffee in an Italian piazza. She talks with you about your life and she shares her latest adventures with her husband and four kids. When you ask her a medical question, she explains the answer in such detail that even as a layperson, you understand it completely. You are so absorbed in conversation with her that you never even realize she's examining you, but she is. An average visit with Dr. Jones can take anywhere from 45 minutes to an hour – And that's from the time you're in the room with her. She wears her heart on her sleeve and you can tell that she genuinely cares.

When I was pregnant with my third child, I was dead set on having a natural childbirth. To that end, I was studying Bradley childbirth techniques (which focuses on natural childbirth). I shared with Dr. Jones my plan to have a Bradley birth, and to my surprise she answered, "Absolutely not!" Shocked and a little afraid, I asked why. She responded, "I have never lost a mother or a baby and I don't intend to. Bradley classes teach you to be confrontational in the hospital with your doctor, and I don't want to go there."

She then suggested she could help me find another OB/GYN. Dr. Jones had delivered my second baby, and I loved her personality, so I really didn't want to go to someone else. I asked her if she'd be willing to discuss each item on my birth plan with me the next time we met. She agreed, and we came to a consensus.

On the day I went into labor, the baby was taking a long time to come. At about 11 P.M., Dr. Jones showed up to my labor room even though she wasn't the doctor on call. She sat in a chair beside the bed and began talking to me and massaging my back. To my surprise, she stayed with me all night long, right up until my baby was born at 6:58 A.M.

Now that is a doctor who knows how to practice medicine from the heart! Did she go the extra mile because that is the type of doctor she is and the kind of person she is? That's certainly a large part of it. But I believe the other part is the bond of trust we had in our patient-doctor relationship, because I had the courage to speak up and assert my wishes.

Would you ever give your baby away to a stranger for an unlimited amount of time? We give our bodies away to Western medicine with full confidence that our physicians will "take care" of everything. But for all intents and purposes, under the current model, your doctor is a complete stranger. Try having your doctor look at your chart and tell you what your birth date is, or even what country or city you are from.

In part, it's your responsibility to communicate better with your health care provider. It's on you to let them know who you are as a person.

As both a patient and a consumer, you have more power than you think. Every choice you make in the marketplace has an impact on what products and services are offered. Taking responsibility for your health gives you freedom of choice. When you're fastidious about your healthy lifestyle habits on a daily basis, you'll have more choices and feel empowered when you have to make bigger health decisions. .

Here is an example: when I had thyroid cancer, I went through two surgeries and radioactive iodine therapy. As part of medical protocol for thyroid cancer treatment, I would have to withdraw from all thyroid medication for six weeks, watch my body slowly die, and get a full body scan to make sure no cancer cells were left.

For six weeks prior to the radioactive iodine treatment, I suffered greatly. It's a horrible experience to have no thyroid hormones for six weeks, as the thyroid governs many of the body's normal functions. The experience was so traumatic that I swore I would never undergo that process again. However for thyroid cancer patients, medical protocol dictates that patients must be scanned one year after the initial treatment, which includes the entire process of withdrawal of thyroid medication for six weeks and administration of a small dose of radioactive iodine.

So when the time came one year later for me have this full body scan again, I went to my doctor with a list. Luckily, I had found the right doctor – one who was willing to listen to me. I had armed myself with healthy practices and proved to him that I was a candidate with a very low risk for the cancer to return. I explained how I had gone vegan for the duration of all my treatments and that I continued to eat a 90% vegetarian diet of mostly organic foods. I was exercising five days a week, and I had done a lot of emotional healing. I finished by stating that I felt so strongly about not taking the test that I would rather experience cancer again. But ultimately, I left the decision open to him because I trusted this doctor. If he felt I needed the test, I would go through with it. In the end, he agreed with me. Because I had made long-term and consistent lifestyle changes, I was given the freedom to opt out of an otherwise very important medical test.

Taking responsibility for yourself means freedom. But it almost never means taking the easy way out.

Empowerment doesn't end there. Asking for more answers if you've been told you have high blood pressure or type 2 diabetes will help you be empowered in your health. Find out what lifestyle changes you can make or what herbs you can take to regain control of your health. Yes, there are people who don't want to change and who would prefer to take the pills and be told what to do. But the very fact that you're reading this book means you're not one of them.

Where you spend your money is also a form of consumer power. Are you supporting companies that contribute to making people sick with their products? Or are you spending your money on products and services that help people? A trip to the grocery store is a prime example of how you cast your vote. You can buy fresh, organic products and leave the processed foods on the shelves. Instead of heading to a fast food place, go to a salad place or make more meals at home.

The same goes for visits to the doctor. Do you spend way too much time going to the doctor's unnecessarily? Do you, like my mother, send your child to the doctor's at the first sneeze or cough?

In the following sections we'll explore how to navigate the relationship with your healthcare providers and how to give you perspective in your medical care choices.

THE PHYSICIAN-PATIENT TRUSTING PARTNERSHIP

I am far from suggesting we abandon the physician-patient relationship altogether. What I am suggesting is that we make it better. It's not just about your physician getting to know you better and developing a trusting relationship – It's also about your physician knowing other ways to help your body heal. We need an open dialogue with our physicians about alternative forms of healing that interest us. And truly, we need a vociferous and powerful uprising against the big corporations designed to keep us sick and tie doctors' hands, preventing them from recommending things like homeopathy and herbal medicine in lieu of prescription medications.

Physicians, too, need to empower their patients with positive reinforcement and kind words. I'm not suggesting they sugarcoat a diagnosis, but rather that they give a patient hope and encouragement and communicate that the human body is miraculous and that healing is possible on all levels.

I believe that doctors tend to become jaded over time. Fresh out of medical school, they start their medical practice with an air of optimism, but over time, that optimism wanes. They see sick people every day and so sickness becomes the norm. If all you see are elephants everywhere, you begin to think that the world is only populated by elephants. Another thing we must remember is that most physicians work for companies. And companies have a financial bottom line. When you add a financial factor to health, it's difficult to know whether the person treating you is working toward a financial goal, or if they are genuinely interested in you getting better.

Recently, I was at the dentist for a teeth cleaning. I tend to shy away from going to the dentist for the very reason addressed above. When I go to get my nails done at a nail salon, the kind ladies are constantly trying to upsell their services. They will suggest a sea salt scrub, high-grade nail polish, or body waxing. Since I don't get my nails done that often, and because the price isn't too elevated, I will agree to a couple of upgrades here and there. But I'm always skeptical when I'm at the doctor or dentist's office. At this dentist appointment, I was informed during my cleaning that I needed a deep clean.

My insurance only pays for a routine clean, and a deep clean is about $50 more. *Well*, I thought, *you only get one set of teeth in adulthood, so let's go for the deep cleaning.*

But during the deep clean, the hygienist explained that I should really get this upgraded fluoride treatment that lasts for three months, and that with the current state of my gums, I needed this treatment. The price of this upgraded fluoride was an additional $120 not covered by my insurance. She then asked me what toothbrush I was using. When I told her I used a fancy electric toothbrush, she suggested I buy (from the office) a $300 toothbrush with a lifetime guarantee. If I had followed all of her suggestions, in one office cleaning, I would have spent around $450 out-of-pocket, added to the $50 deductible I already had to pay. One visit would have set me back $500. And at the end, she said I needed to come back in three months – not the typical six months – because my gums really needed the deep cleaning.

As you can see, for-profit health companies tow a very fuzzy line between getting you healthy and meeting a financial bottom-line. It's also difficult to know whom to blame in a situation like this. Are the employees of a large dental office or doctor's office being pressured to upsell? Or are they being incentivized through commission for selling extra services and products?

Another potential conflict of interest is the fact that 75% of U.S. doctors get paid for prescribing name-brand drugs.[76] There are moral problems with this practice. Generic prescription medications must meet rigid Food and Drug Administration (FDA) standards and work just as well as brand name-drugs for a fraction of the price. Because they are compensated for it, these doctors are forcing their patients to pay a much higher price. And if a doctor is on the fence about prescribing a medication versus waiting to see if a patient's condition changes, that doctor is more likely to prescribe the medication if they know it will mean a bigger check at the end of the month. All of these practices erode the trust in the physician-patient relationship.

MAKING WESTERN MEDICINE NOT THE NORM, BUT THE EXCEPTION

Physicians who become speakers and consultants for pharmaceutical companies may truly believe they're helping patients with revolutionary breakthroughs. Indeed, there are health care providers who believe this wholeheartedly.

But these aren't the providers with the greatest vision, because they're not seeing the whole problem. Incremental increases in life expectancy or lowered mortality rates of a specific disease still don't address the real problem. There will never on this planet be a synthetic drug that will cure an illness completely, boost the body's immune response, and have zero side effects. It simply won't happen. But nature has many plants, herbs, and roots that do heal illness without side effects.

The true visionaries of medicine understand this and have started to educate themselves in alternative medical practices to complement their medical practice. They are the doctors of the future, because they understand the urgency to change.

Healing is a mystical reality that no one truly understands. Physicians do not heal. If they are good, they set up the right conditions to let healing take place. Even surgeons do not heal. Surgeons remove tutors, repair organs, replace arteries, or open veins to give the body a fighting chance to heal. You must keep in mind this idea of setting up the right conditions. With the knowledge physicians have acquired over years of schooling and continuing education, they guesstimate – with a certain amount of accuracy – what conditions they need to help create. They do nothing more and nothing less.

Through modern statistics, we can see that lifestyle illness is a rising trend. To respond, physicians must now shift their methods of setting up the right conditions for healing. If Western medicine and its practitioners wish to remain mainstream, they must adapt to the new realities in current Western societies. The current practices of Western medicine, in the case of chronic lifestyle diseases, must be pushed to the perimeter to make room for other practices. Apart from emergencies and acute medical conditions, the Western model needs to be the exception and not the rule. In other words, usage of Western medicine must become only the crust of your health and wellness pie.

Covering up symptoms with prescription medications and hoping that the seven deadly chronic lifestyle diseases will somehow stay away just doesn't work anymore.

Preventive Medicine: The Way of the Future

This shift is not a question of ego, pride, or arrogance. It's not an issue of who's right and who's wrong. We absolutely cannot look at the problem from that perspective. If we as a society – between alternative and complementary health care workers, healers, religious clergy, and patients – begin to point fingers, assess blame, and outsmart one another, we will accomplish nothing and our health will continue to degrade. What we need are solid solutions that will help everyone involved. This is no longer an academic issue, it's a societal and human rights issue. To that end, those of us with power in medicine and those of us who are consumers must do everything we can. We must work together to educate people about preventive health and educate ourselves about how we can create those optimal conditions for healing to take place.

In some modern societies, governments are finally listening. The Swiss government accepted five alternative therapies to be covered by insurance starting in May 2017, including homeopathy, acupuncture, traditional Chinese medicine, herbal medicine, and holistic medicine. These five therapies were included in insurance plans as part of a six-year study in 2012. They proved to lower healthcare costs, and initially proved to be more effective, even though a true measure of efficacy would take longer to assess.[77]

Another recent example is an Ayurvedic surgery performed in India on March 1, 2016. The group of doctors called it the world's first Ayurvedic surgery. They removed the prostate of an 83-year-old man without the use of antibiotics because of his allergies to allopathic medicine. Instead, they used Ayurvedic herbs. The man was observed for one month after surgery and is said to have recovered fully. "Conducting surgery with Ayurvedic support is the beginning of a new era," stated Manoj Kumar, director of the Orthopedics Department at Delhi's Maulana Azad Medical College.[78] This surgery is a beautiful example of the perfect integration of Western and ancient medicine.

Lifting Us from the Dark

Religions across the ages have often been accused of keeping their followers in the dark. The philosophy of many religious clerics, especially Catholic priests and bishops was that the more they kept scriptural knowledge away from the common man, the more control they had of the masses. In an article on the website, CatholicBridge.com, the author suggests that even though reading the Bible wasn't forbidden in Catholicism, priests worried that congregations would come up with conflicting interpretations of the scriptures.[79] Furthermore, for nearly 1,000 years, the catholic Bible remained in Latin, a language only the highly educated could read and understand.[80] As a result, those in religious power fed off of illiteracy, poverty, and war-torn conditions to keep people from the interpreting the truth.

The propaganda of Western medicine has kept us in this state of darkness, too. Even when things like herbs or homeopathic remedies are allowed in the marketplace, they are labeled with a disclaimer forced upon them by the FDA. These labels bring an air of skepticism surrounding herbal remedies.

It's time we brought light to the fact that alternative therapies *do* work. In order to help more people, we must work on accepting these alternative forms of medicine into the mainstream with society's blessing. One way we can lift the darkness is to help take away fear. In Old World religions perpetuating fear was one way to suppress an uprising. It was also a way to manipulate the general populace into following the whims of those in power.

In order to lift the veil, physicians can begin by being of service in love over fear.

Using the Power of Love versus the Crippling Power of Fear

I have just given you plenty of reasons to fear what's happening in the world of health. Hopefully, these will be used only to move you into action and not to cripple you. The authors of the book *Boundaries*, Dr. Henry Cloud and Dr. John Townsend, outlined a principle that I find insightful: "When you love someone, you might hurt them with the truth. But hurting them is not the same as harming them."[81] In illustrating the problems with contemporary Western medicine, I may have hurt you either directly or indirectly. But I've done this with love, because the truth is important for you and your loved ones to get and stay well. I've not harmed you by sharing this information, because in part two, I'll give you concrete ways for you to overcome the limitations of ill health.

Unfortunately, much of Western medicine's model today is designed to instill fear. When we're clouded with fear, it's difficult to make proper choices. Choices made out of fear are almost never the right ones, and leave us with regret once the fog clears.

Suppose you're a patient. You go to your doctor and discover you have hypertension or high blood pressure. Your doctor is obligated to offer a prescription to normalize your blood pressure. Fearful, you ask if there are other ways to do this. Your doctor might suggest reducing your stress, which in the end is not solid advice because stress is a relative term. You tell them that you don't want to take medicine, and they warn you what might happen if you don't take it.

Afraid of these potential consequences, you accept the prescription, get it filled, and start taking the medication. Once you take it, you experience a host of side effects, including dizziness, nausea, and headaches. You regret taking the medicine, but now you're afraid to come off of it.

Now, let's take the physician's perspective. The physician has a lot of fears, too. They know that if your blood pressure continues to rise, you will likely have a heart attack or stroke. They're paying through the roof for medical malpractice insurance, and they know that if they do not prescribe the blood pressure medication to you, they risk getting sued and possibly losing their medical license. On top of the fear of losing their livelihood and possibly costing you your life, the doctor knows that they cannot legally prescribe a healthier lifestyle for your high blood pressure, because there are no guarantees that you'll follow through.

Do you see now how this cycle of fear causes Western medicine to fail time and again? No one can make proper, compassionate choices when everyone is afraid.

As part of my profession, I teach prenatal yoga classes. I hear stories daily of healthy pregnant women being pressured into unnecessary medical procedures through fear. Let me emphasize that there are people with good intentions and poor intentions in every single career. But there is nothing more personal than the power to directly affect a person's health. The frustrations I hear daily upset me, because many of the things these women hear from their doctors are simply not true.

Here are some of the stories I often hear:

"My OB/GYN says I must schedule an induction, just in case, because the hospital might not have any openings when the time comes."

I answer, "Do you think they will actually turn you away at the hospital if you need an induction? Nonsense. That will never happen."

"My OB/GYN says that I must schedule an induction before my due date because he's afraid the baby will get too big and I'll need a C-section."

"Have you ever had a baby?" I retort. "Does your OB/GYN know you can't push a baby out?"

"My OB/GYN says I can't go past my due date because the placenta will break down."

I answer, "There is no evidence that shows the placenta breaks down until at least ten days past your estimated due date. And the due date is *estimated*, which means it may be wrong."

"My OB/GYN says I must schedule a C-section because the baby is too big."

"Too big by *whose* standards? I know a woman who's 4' 11" tall, and pushed out an eleven pound baby."

I will never argue if a pregnant woman I teach has a medical condition, or if her baby has a medical condition. But I will give the women the power to be assertive if they are healthy, have had a healthy pregnancy, and still feel they are being pushed by medical professionals to have pre-emptive procedures. These medical professionals are using fear tactics on these women to potentially harm them (because no medical procedure is completely safe), and that is simply not acceptable.

OUR LOVE OVER FEAR EXPERIENCE AT THE DOCTOR'S OFFICE

What if the doctor-patient relationship could thrive on love instead of fear? How different would the practice of medicine be, and how different would it be when and if you become ill?

Let's take the example of the patient with hypertension. Remember, *the focus here is love and not fear.*

You go to your physician's office for a routine check up. You know your doctor well, because every time you've visited in the past, he's taken the time to get to know you. He knows your children's names and ages. He knows your spouse and he knows what you do for a living. In fact, he walks into the patient room and gives you a hug like he's greeting an old friend he hasn't seen in a while. You smile feeling welcomed, and get the warm, fuzzy feeling that he cares. Deep down, you know he has your best intentions at heart. Your interaction goes as follows:

DOCTOR: Hey John, how's everything? The wife, kids?

YOU: Great, everything's good. Jimmy's growing up fast; he'll be graduating this year.

DOCTOR: Wow! Already? I can't believe time has flown by so fast. How's your law practice going?

YOU: Well, things have been a bit rough. We lost a partner and I've had to take on an extra load.

DOCTOR: I thought to ask because you're blood pressure is unusually high. It seems you're under a bit more pressure these days. Have you had time to exercise like we talked about last year?

YOU: You know, Doc, it's probably been six months since I last hit the gym. I've just been so consumed with work.

DOCTOR: Well, with high blood pressure, we can do a few things. But it's so high that we have to do these things fast. Do you agree? I don't want to have to put you on blood pressure medication because of the potential side effects. But you're going to have to make some changes. I'd hate to see Mary and the kids lose you to a heart attack. Do you get what I'm saying?

YOU: Sure, Doc. What do I have to do?

DOCTOR: First of all, lower your sodium intake. In fact, stay off salt altogether until you come back to see me in two weeks. I want you to get on the treadmill every morning and walk at a four-mile-per-hour pace for thirty minutes. My secretary, Sue, has the number of a lady who does mindfulness meditation. She's great, and she can get you practicing some meditation for 20 minutes a day. Do I have

your word that you'll do these things and come back with great results in two weeks?

YOU: Yeah. It's going to be hard with the practice and all, but I
don't want to risk losing my life. Thank you for caring. I'll see you in
two weeks.

DOCTOR: Give the wife and kids a big hug for me.

YOU: Sure thing, Doc.

I know there are physicians who practice medicine with love. I've
been lucky enough to meet a couple in my own life. But right now,
the current medical model does not support doctors who practice
medicine this way. Most doctors I know who practice with compassion, love, intuition, and integrative medicine cannot and do not
take insurance. Because they spend thirty minutes to an hour with
each patient, an insurance payment, which often reduces fees to $10-
$30 per office visit, would not keep their practice open.

I remember in 1986, encouraged by President Reagan, certain
school systems switched teachers to a system of merit-based pay,
meaning they began to reward teachers based on results of students'
performance.[82] The idea behind merit pay for teachers included
funding for professional development as well as encouraging increased staff collaboration to ensure student success. What if insurance companies rewarded physicians for keeping patients healthy?
Instead of simply prescribing a prescription pill, they would counsel the patient on preventive measures and actually reduce the costs
paid out by the insurance. An incentive-based system would put
more money into physicians' pockets and reduce the patient's need
for repeated doctors' visits.

PATIENT EMPOWERMENT

If we use love as a starting point to empower patients, we can make
obsolete many unnecessary medical procedures. Sometimes it can
feel as though physicians are not always advocates for their patients.

What we must remember is that we are all on the same team in trying to seek health against an illness, injury, or disorder. Physicians
may forget that they, too, are patients at some point. It's important
to keep in mind where your loyalties lie if the patient-physician relationship will evolve and work toward the greater good.

Suppose that your son wants to play soccer more than ever, but
he's not very talented at it. In this example, you were a star player
all throughout school, and you have the trophies to show for it. Now
your poor son, who isn't coordinated and doesn't have the technique,
has high ambitions. Would you brush him off and discourage him?
Or would you teach him the basics, spending time to explain and
cheering him on? Chances are you'll want to see him succeed. You're
not in competition to show him who's more knowledgeable about
soccer. And you most certainly aren't going to tell him that if he buys
the best shoes, ball, and shin guards that he'll get better quicker. No,
you're going to accompany him slowly through the difficult process
of acquiring skill after skill, with hours of practice and basic drib-
bling and passing until he gets it. You'll encourage him with kind
words and positive reinforcement. You'll urge him to practice even
when he doesn't feel like it. You will lovingly guide him toward his
goal.

Once we realize we are all headed for the same goal, we can easily encourage one another. We all want to be successful. All of us
– including health care workers – love praise. After Dr. Jones spent
the entire night with me before delivering my baby, I thanked her
profusely for months. I sent her thank-you cards and birthday cards
because I was truly grateful for what she did for me.

And to the physicians reading this: have you ever had someone
you admired and respected tremendously? If so, what wouldn't you
do for that person? When someone treats you with genuine love,
respect, and devotion, there is almost nothing you wouldn't do for
them. Your patients will shower you with praise when you operate

from this level of genuine interest. I will even go so far as to pay more for a doctor who is really good.

The physician-patient relationship is a precious and sacred one that shouldn't be intercepted by pharmaceutical companies, medical supply companies, or big corporate medical practices. Once we're able to embrace the intimate and empowering nature of this relationship, we will be able to move forward toward greater healing on all levels.

PART TWO

You Chose a Human Body

The moment I realize God sitting in the temple of every human body, the moment I stand in reverence before every human being and see God in him– that moment I am free from bondage, everything that binds vanishes, and I am free. -Swami Vivekananda

SOME TIME BEFORE YOU came into your earthly existence, you chose a human body. This human body is a vehicle through which you experience everything on earth. You need this human body to experience love through touch, sight, smell, and sound. You need your body to work and live out your life's purpose. You need your body to be of service to your Creator. In other words, there is no way out of this physical body in this human experience. You chose your body because you have a mission to accomplish during your time on earth.

So naturally, as spiritual beings choosing a human experience, we get cranky when real human stuff comes up. We get bothered when this body needs to eat, sleep or exercise.

Just imagine: you wake up in the morning and notice your stomach is growling. After using the restroom and brushing your teeth, you go to your fridge and look inside. You're confused about what to eat and know you don't have a whole lot of time before work. You close the fridge and look at the counter, where there's a bag of muffins. *That's easy*, you think. You grab a muffin, pour yourself a coffee, and bound up the stairs, eating and drinking your coffee as you get ready for work. For the most part, you don't even think about your body's needs. Those needs are just things that get in the way of doing other tasks. Don't we all behave this way to some extent?

The body is a gift that you chose. You *get to* feed, bathe, nourish, and exercise it. You get the *privilege* of taking care of it. The continual mindset should not be "Oh, I have to eat again. Do I *really* need to get more sleep?" Or "Do I *have* to exercise?" If you change your mind from "I have to take care of this body" to "I *get* to take care of this body," your life perspective will change drastically.

Through this body, you get to touch a loved one's skin, kiss your child, pet a cat, and caress a soft fabric. You get to see a beautiful sunset, a gorgeous smile, snow falling, or a butterfly's wings. Through this body you get to experience love, elation, joy, sorrow, grief, and frustration. It is only in this body that you get to play golf, hit a home run, play a piano, or sing a beautiful song. With your physical body, you get to do the work your Creator sent you to do by using your God-given talents. You have the privilege of seventy to a hundred years in this human experience, and in that time, you must honor this privilege by taking care of the body that is the temple of your soul.

Suppose a very kind and wealthy friend gave you a 2018 red Ferrari California T convertible to take care of for the year. Your friend says to you, "I'm going away for a year, but I just bought this car and I need you to take care of it. You can drive it and treat it as your own until I return." How would you take care of the Ferrari? Would you give it the best gasoline and oil? Would you keep it clean and waxed? Would you make sure the Ferrari stayed sheltered away from the rain and snow? Would you only park it in lots where you knew the attendants would take good care of it?

I know I would. If my friend lent me that car, I would care for it in the best possible way to ensure that it was in impeccable shape when my friend returned. I would leave no stone unturned when it came to that car. I would spare no expense to make sure it was well taken care of. I would be so grateful to my friend for lending me such a valuable vehicle. And I would feel privileged that they chose me over all of their other friends to take care of their brand new, expensive car.

Let's imagine that before you came to earth, your Creator said, "I'm giving you this body for a certain amount of time. Please take good care of it. Give it the best food and water. Don't feed it toxins or chemicals. In order for this body to work properly, you must exercise it and give it rest. Treat it with respect. Don't give it away to just anybody. This is a special gift I'm lending to you, and I'll be back to pick it up."

How have you treated your body so far? Have you treated it like a Ferrari? Or have you treated it like a fifteen-year-old Chevy sedan? If God came back today to pick up the body that he lent you, would He say you took care of it in the best way possible?

You are a Ferrari, my friend. You *are* THE Ferrari. And if cars don't resonate with you, you are a diamond. You are the most precious thing you can imagine.

CHAPTER 4

LOVE AND TRUST YOUR BODY

Your body has natural healing capacities that nobody in the field of medicine can pretend ultimately to understand. -Dr. Wayne W. Dyer

IN ORDER TO EMBRACE integrative medicine and to help you overcome chronic lifestyle illness or any other ailment, you must first change your perspective on your body. Right now you might not trust your body's innate capacity to heal. This mistrust can create a downward spiral of self-doubt and fear surrounding any symptoms you may be experiencing. Your body was meant for health. You must embrace this on every level in order to open yourself up to other forms of healing. You must believe you are a healthy, vibrant, and dynamic human being.

THE STATE OF DISEASE SHOULD NOT BE THE NORM

Disease is not normal, nor should it be. It's a deviant state. After all that we see, hear, and read, we might be inclined to think that our bodies will inevitably become ill one day. This is simply not true. Our bodies are not even supposed to degrade and break down as we get older. For the most part, this is a Western mindset that we've been conditioned to accept.

Your body's natural state is called *homeostasis*. Your body does everything it can to maintain a constant, healthy state regardless of the outside environment. Homeostasis controls your blood pressure, pH levels, body temperature, salt levels, and glucose concentration.[83] Your autonomic nervous system controls the functions of your internal organs, all without your help. Your body contains around 100 trillion cells, each with a different function and purpose.[84] Most of the time, these cells get you through life just fine, avoiding illness. Perhaps it's time you put a little bit of trust into your body's healing capacities.

TRUST YOUR BODY AS A HEALING MACHINE

Have you ever gotten a small cut? Once you do the necessary first aid – wash the area, apply an anti-bacterial cream, and put on a Band-Aid – do you have to do anything else for the cut to heal?

The answer is no. As soon as you cut your skin, your body stops the bleeding through hemostasis (the process during which blood coagulates turning from liquid to gel). As the blood clots it forms a barrier or scab so microscopic intruders can't come in. At the same time, three types of white blood cells make their way to the wound and consume any bacteria and debris left in the cut, at which point you may notice inflammation. Through the process of proliferation, your body rapidly creates new cells. Finally, during the maturation phase, your body continues to heal the wound and strengthen the area with strong collagen that creates scar tissue. All the healing is done without your direct intervention.

Now obviously, healing will precipitate if you stay hydrated and have proper nutrition, including a variety of vitamins, minerals, phytochemicals, and amino acids. But other than that, a small cut is often healed without our conscious effort. We tend to take this type of healing for granted.

THE POWER OF THE MIND AS A TOOL FOR HEALING

In 2005, I contracted a virus that made me extremely ill. I had a high fever and the mid-back area near my kidneys hurt like crazy. I went to the doctor looking for relief and was convinced I had some sort of bacterial infection affecting my kidneys.

The doctor took my urine and did some blood tests. I remember being so weak that I couldn't get up off the examining table where they left me to rest for twenty minutes. The urine came out clear, and they sent me home while they waited for the blood tests to come back from the lab. Two hours later, I received an emergency call from the doctor, who told me that my blood liver enzymes were extremely high and that I needed to get to a hospital immediately. He was convinced I might have hepatitis.

Shocked, I asked my husband take me to the emergency room. The hospital was busy and less shocked by my diagnosis, so we had to wait a couple of hours. I decided to meditate and visualize my liver cells as happy and healthy. I literally spent two hours imagining happy faces on all of my liver cells.

When I was finally called in, the ER staff gave me fluids and took my blood again. To my surprise I was feeling better, but tired. Several hours went by when finally they came back with my new test results. Amazingly, the results said that my liver enzymes were completely normal. They compared the blood test with the one taken earlier in the day and they were dumbfounded. In the end, they shrugged and let me go.

What was the possible explanation for this instantaneous healing? Could my initial doctor have used someone else's blood to determine my results? That might have happened, but it's unlikely. I attribute the miraculous healing of my liver blood enzymes to my constant, confident visualization that my cells were healthy, happy, and normal. It was at that moment that I experienced the power of the mind, and knew that spontaneous healing is possible.

The power of the mind is easily shown in the placebo effect. To define, placebo treatments are controlled medical interventions with no active drug ingredients. According to a May 2017 article in Harvard Health, how placebos work is still not entirely understood but involves a complex process of neurobiological reactions from the release of feel-good neurotransmitters like dopamine or endorphins, to an increase in brain activity associated with moods and self-awareness.[85] The placebo effect causes improvements in a patient's health, which range from changes in heart rate and blood pressure to perception of pain and decreased depression, anxiety, fatigue, and some symptoms of Parkinson's.[86]

One former Harvard Medical School faculty member, Dr. Ted Kaptchuk, performed clinical drug trials to study the effects of placebo treatments on trial patients. As he studied the outcomes, Kaptchuk noticed a direct correlation between the way placebos were administered and the patients' level of healing. For example, one experiment gauged whether patients would respond better to placebo treatment if the doctor was caring and if the room was calm and serene. After a study of 262 adults with irritable bowel syndrome, he got his answer: the group that received the placebo with a sustained, caring interaction with the doctor had much better results than the other groups in the experiment.

Placebo surgery has also shown to be effective. From December 2007 to January 2013, five orthopedic clinics in Finland conducted a study on patients, between the ages of 35 and 65, who needed knee surgery to repair the meniscus.[87] The patients were divided into two groups: one group received the actual surgery, and the other group received anesthesia, but did not receive the surgery while they were under. All patients were informed that they were a part of a clinical trial and that they may or may not be actually having the surgery done. And after twelve months, the results showed absolutely no difference in the recovery of the two groups.[88] When only a positive state of mind changes the body physiologically, we simply cannot deny our body's natural ability to heal.

STRENGTHEN THE MIND TO HEAL THE BODY

In order for your body to heal, you must believe healing is possible. A belief is nothing more than something we hold onto as truth. Right now, you might hold a superficial belief: "Yes, I know my body can heal. I've seen cuts heal, I've seen mosquito bites go away, and I've recovered from colds and flus." But I'm talking about an even deeper level of healing – healing right down the cellular level. That kind of healing comes from a mind that is strong and disciplined. Did you know that every word you say – spoken or unspoken – every thought you think, and every thing you believe has a potential effect on your health? In this section I'm going to give you a program to train your mind for healing.

LISTEN TO YOUR INTERNAL AND EXTERNAL DIALOGUE

You'll be surprised what you hear when you start to listen to yourself. I've already proven the power of a positive mind, but you can completely reverse the effect it has with a negative outlook. Setting yourself up for good health is as easy as your internal conversation.

What do you say to yourself as you go throughout your day? Perhaps you say things like...

- I am tired.
- I have no energy.
- I need a coffee to stay awake.
- I have allergies.
- My metabolism is slow.
- I'm just not flexible, and I'll never be flexible.

- I got the raw end of the gene pool.
- I always get the flu.
- I'm probably getting a cold.

The list goes on. My first response: No, no, and no! Stop telling yourself those things! Don't say anything that is potentially self-defeating about your health. Instead empower yourself with positive affirmations about your body, mind, and health.

In addition, refrain from engaging in conversation about your health with someone else that might bring about negativity. For example, when I'm with someone who brings up the flu season, I simply say, "I take good care of myself and I don't plan on getting the flu." I know what you might be thinking – *Michelle, how can you say you won't get the flu? Things happen. Nobody plans on getting the flu.* While on a conscious level people don't plan on getting a virus like the flu, when they constantly listen to news stories or talk about the latest flu strain or epidemic, they're subconsciously allowing the fear of illness to stay present in their mind.

Instead, why can't you make active plans to *not* get the flu? And perhaps take steps to stay healthy such as taking preventive doses of vitamin C, zinc, and echinacea, for example. It's all about your mindset. I don't even let the flu into my immediate energy field. Since I've kept this healthful mindset, I tell my kids that they're not getting the flu either. And they haven't.

If it's okay to say negative things, why isn't it okay to say positive things? Where did we learn this behavior? We have somehow been conditioned that it's safe to say negative and that it's superstitious to say positive. When someone says something negative like "I'll probably gain ten pounds if I eat this whole piece of cheesecake," everyone nods and laughs approvingly. But if you said "My son will get accepted to Harvard this year," people look at you disapprovingly and say things like, "Don't count your chickens before they're hatched." Why doesn't anyone say "Don't count your chickens" to the person who says they will gain ten pounds? Or, for example, have you ever seen someone "knock on wood" when they deliver good news so as not to "jinx" it? It's as if we're afraid to assume goodness. This is a poisonous attitude and it's time to let it go.

This is why you must change your beliefs first. It all starts with the words you use to talk about your own health. Adopt affirmations like...

- I am healthy.
- I am strong.
- My body is a fat-burning machine.
- I have perfect health every day.
- I have extraordinary energy.
- I'm energetic.
- I love my body.
- My cells are vibrant and strong.
- I'm free from addictions.

Reprogramming your brain isn't an easy thing to do. We're creatures of habit and most of our internal dialogue goes unnoticed for most of our lives. Positive affirmations, like the ones above, are great tools to reprogram your mind. It may sound ridiculous, but speaking them aloud is even more powerful and recording them with your own voice is the best. Negativity overrides positivity ten to one, so in the beginning you'll have to work extra hard to get the negative voice out.

I've made lists of intentions and desires for over ten years now. But doing vocal recordings of my affirmations and listening to them daily is relatively new for me. When I record them (which is easy to do on any smart phone), I actually sing them into the phone, almost like a commercial jingle. After all, commercial jingles are so difficult to get out of our heads because they're so catchy – and isn't that the idea? You want your affirmations to stick. One of my positive affirmations is "palm trees are in my front yard." I sing each affirmation at least five times before going on to the next one. Once I was going about my daily work, not listening to my affirmations when I started singing, "Palm trees are in my front yard." All of the sudden my 12-year-old son turned to me and said shocked, "Mom, you don't have palm trees in your front yard!" Blushing, I turned to him and said, "Oh, but I'd love to have palm trees in my front yard." I hadn't even noticed I was singing my affirmations.

Getting Rid of Body Shame

Like many people growing up, I had issues with body image. I felt my thighs were too fat and my breasts too small. I wanted straight hair and a flat tummy. As a teenager I constantly looked at other girls who were prettier or had better bodies and wished I could be more like them. Perhaps you can relate to some of these body insecurities. And even though we grow up and hopefully develop in our self-esteem, we still carry many of these body issues into adulthood. Many of us continue to berate ourselves because we're not more perfect.

A few years back I had an eye-opening experience that completely changed my view on body perfection. A friend had given me a voucher to go to a Korean spa. Unbeknownst to me, the jacuzzi section of the spa was single gender and required total nudity. Due to my body issues, I wasn't at all comfortable getting completely naked in front of hundreds of ladies, but I reluctantly complied for the spa experience. In the beginning it was difficult because of my insecurities. But after a few minutes I opened my eyes and was surprised to learn that every woman I saw had flaws, like me. In fact it was a relief to learn that no one has a perfect body. As a woman it made me feel more normal and less insecure.

Maybe you've always wanted to change something about your body. Or perhaps you were teased as child or even abused. Yet body shame can prevent you from treating your body well. Even if you know have a lot of weight to lose or if you've been told you're not attractive, you must love yourself no matter what. When we come from a place of love rather than shame, it's easier to make changes. Regardless of what you need to change, start from a place of blessing your body.

LOVE, AND NOT PUNISHMENT

For various reasons, we consciously and unconsciously punish our bodies. You may not even be aware that you're doing it. For example, overeating on a consistent basis is a form of body punishment. At times we use food to try to manipulate or control others, which in the end only hurts ourselves. For instance, some people binge on junk food as a way to "eat" our emotions when in conflict with others. Or sometimes children will refrain from eating or go on a food strike to establish control in an overbearing or chaotic family.

Addiction is another form of body punishment. Abuse of drugs, alcohol, and food degrade your self-image and do severe damage to your body. Furthermore, addictions also have psychological, emotional, and spiritual components. Healing from addictions can be complicated, but great 12-step groups such as Narcotics Anonymous, Alcoholics Anonymous, Celebrate Recovery, and Overeaters Anonymous exist to help you work through addiction and restore a healthy body image.

Even though it might not seem like it, neglecting to exercise can also be a form of body punishment. We all need to exercise. Overworking and getting too little sleep are other ways in which we unconsciously abuse our bodies. Through these examples, I hope you're beginning to draw connections to negative behavior that will inevitably affect your health.

The way you punish your body may be very subtle. It may be a good idea to take a look at behaviors or ideas about your body that no longer serve you. For example, if you know that coffee makes you jittery and dehydrated but you still drink three cups per day, stopping may make you feel much better. If you have a hard time stopping, cut back to one cup or slowly switch to decaf. Or if you notice that every time a colleague gives you a hard time you reach for chocolate, try to replace that behavior with something healthy like journaling your feelings. Loving your body and aligning your behavior to match this love are both necessary for healing.

YOU ARE WORTHY TO RECEIVE

When it comes to health, some people hold on to nonsensical beliefs, or worse: they take on suffering, in the form of illness, as a form of self-punishment. First of all, you don't need to suffer to make anyone else feel better. One of my favorite teachers, Dr. Wayne Dyer, used to say, "You cannot get sick enough to make one person on this planet better."[89] And he's right. Yes, there is suffering in the world. But you can't help change any of that unless you are healthy yourself. When you get healthy, it can inspire others to get healthy. In fact, that's the strategy in recovery groups like Al-Anon. According to their teachings, if you get healthy, your addicted loved one is more likely to get healthy, too.

Highly empathetic people will often take on the suffering of others. Compassion and empathy are necessary and revered qualities in humanity, but you must not take on someone else's suffering because you feel the need to share the burden. You are worthy to receive health. Worthiness for optimal health comes from your Creator. You were created in Divine image and likeness, and there's no reason why you can't have perfect health.

GRATITUDE FOR YOUR BODY

Hold gratitude in your heart for your body each and every day. Go through each body part and thank it for giving you wellness and health. Thank your feet for supporting you all day long. Thank your heart for beating every second of every day your entire life. Thank your liver, kidneys, bladder, lymphatic system, and endocrine system. Thank your eyes, ears, skin, mouth, teeth, and tongue.

I know it may sound a little ridiculous, but gratitude enlivens and heals. Often because of societal expectations, women especially tend to complain about their bodies. It can be easy to complain that your butt is too big, your thighs are too fat, or your tummy is too flabby. But statements like these tend to create internal animosity toward your body. Try instead to consider your body as your best friend. If you told a friend she was too fat and had a big butt, do you think *she* would lose weight and get thin? No. She would probably get discouraged and give up trying. When you consider that your body *is* your best friend, you'll be more motivated to get it moving more and to give it nourishing food.

Send your body love and encouragement. It's even more important to do this when you're experiencing illness. For example, if you have cancer, you can say to your body, "Thank you, cells, for being so strong and remembering your Divine purpose." According to Ayurvedic mind-body medicine, cancer cells are simply cells that have forgotten their purpose. You might think of cancer as an invader in the body, but this isn't entirely true. Talking to those cells is a good way to heal them; you must help them remember that they belong to you and that they need to come together for the good of your health.

FINDING THE HEALER WITHIN

We all have the power to heal ourselves. Your own belief in your potential to heal is what will determine your ability to do so. I believe I experienced healing from abnormal liver enzymes and potential hepatitis in a few short hours because I held onto the belief that I was already healed. In the examples with placebo case studies, patients get better because they fully believe they have been given the means to heal. The stronger the belief, the quicker and more profound the healing will occur.

The bottom line is this: if you don't believe you have a healer within, you will have a difficult time with alternative forms of health care.

Instead of placing your belief in a doctor, nurse, hospital, or drug, place your belief in your own body.

You can start with affirmations. Healing movement classes can get you in touch with your body as you feel the orchestration of the individual parts moving together as a whole. Yoga, qi gong, and tai chi allow you to access your inner healer. Meditation can also open you to your Divine healing power.

Let Go of Fear

When approaching health-related situations, try to stay centered and grounded. If you get an unfavorable medical report or if you're awaiting biopsy results, practice body gratitude, visualizations, and affirmations. I know it's difficult to do – especially with uncertainty about your health. Fear stops us in our tracks and won't help us find creative solutions. Now is not the time to search Google endlessly or to turn on the radio or TV. Stay away from situations that make you anxious and move toward nature instead. Go for a walk, take a hike in the mountains, or walk along the seashore. Use this time for prayer and meditation.

If you're ill, please don't get angry with your body or be fearful that it's betraying you. Know that your body is always fighting for your good. Even in the case of cancer, your body's cells are inundated with a lot of toxins making them unstable. The unstable cells are a result of poor lifestyle choices, weak genes, or environmental factors. Cancer, like any disease, takes a long time to form and isn't a result of your body malfunctioning. Embrace hope and faith in your body and put fear to rest.

Disease Messages

Every illness sends you messages. Your job is to receive these messages and learn from them. Sometimes, eruption of disease makes logical sense, like when someone smokes for twenty years and is diagnosed with lung cancer. The most natural consequence to smoking is the development of lung cancer. But other times, disease seems to make absolutely no sense, like when a child is diagnosed with cancer. Yet in both cases we can look for the deeper meaning. The more obvious lesson with getting cancer from smoking might be a wake up call to stop. The less obvious lesson, but perhaps just as important in the second example, might be for a parent to spend more quality time with their child or to use the experience to help raise money for cancer research or to donate to an organization like the Ronald McDonald House.

Since we already know that disease isn't the norm, we can deduct that by the time illness has erupted things have been out of balance in your life for a long time. Your body has been sending you subtle messages that you haven't been openly receiving or that you've refused to receive. For example, if you suffer from alcoholism or drug addiction and everyone around you has repeated time and again that you need to get help, but you've refused to acknowledge the problem and now have cirrhosis of the liver, you've missed clear messages.

Illness messages can be extremely powerful and life changing. Often, the universe has been nudging you in another direction in your life and experiencing illness can be the shove you need to get you on your right life path. As devastating as it may seem, illness may make absolutely no sense to you until you look at the root cause. At times, it may seem that there is no cause, but if you dig deep enough, there almost always is.

If I had not experienced cancer, I would never have been motivated to dedicate my life to holistic medicine and helping others learn how to heal through healthy lifestyle. Now, it's my passion and my mission.

Never blame your body. Instead look for the reasons *why* you fall ill, and look for what you can learn from your illness or the illness of a loved one. You and your body are a team and your body wants you to be healthy. Listen to its needs and tell it what you need. The more in tune you are, the less you will have to worry about getting sick.

CHAPTER 5

EAT CLEAN

The doctor of the future will no longer treat the human frame with drugs, but rather will cure and prevent disease with nutrition. - Thomas Edison

BEFORE MY TRANSITION TO healthy eating at age eighteen, I ate like any other typical American. As a teenager my meals consisted of pizza loaded with meat and cheese, hamburgers, and tacos. I didn't see any problem eating these foods until I was taught to eat differently. My journey began in 1989 but continued when I moved to France for college. Seeing the way the French ate and how they ate changed my perspective forever. I learned not only to eat high quality food but also how to appreciate food and mealtime. After my brush with cancer in 1999 my relationship with food changed yet again to include even cleaner eating. Now my diet is so different from the typical American diet that it shocks me when I realize how most Americans eat. I forget that people still do eat fast and processed food. While I feel that I'm missing out sometimes, I've accepted that my choices will pay off in greater health now and in the future. If you're not already eating organic whole foods or if this kind of diet seems foreign to you, I hope you'll soon be convinced that by shifting your eating habits your health will benefit in enormous ways.

The Power of Organic Food: More Than Just Food

While you may think about food a lot throughout your day, you might not necessarily be thinking about the quality and origin of your food and how it's impacting your body. I've never suffered from an eating disorder, but I think about food a lot. I love the sensual experience of good food. Once, on a college visit with my son, I realized that I was thinking about my meals in advance. Part of the reason is because I refuse to eat low quality food or typical fast food, but it's also because being in a new town gives me opportunities to taste regional flavors and see how the locals dine.

In reality, you needn't be as obsessed with eating as I sometimes can be, and of course, obsession is unhealthy. That said however, there are enormous benefits in being selective about the food you consume.

I recently saw a Tweet, intended to be funny, on how there are so many people allergic to so many things these days, that future wars will be fought by throwing peanuts and cat fur at the opponent. While food allergies aren't something to laugh about, I've had conversations with friends who agree that when we grew up in the 1970s and 80s, we hardly knew anyone with food allergies. Now, it feels like most people have at least some kind of allergy. According to a 2010 study by pediatric allergist Andrew Liu and the NIH, nearly 8 million Americans suffer from food allergies – and children suffer the most. The CDC reports that the prevalence of food allergy in children increased by 50 percent between 1997 and 2011 , and that between 1997 and 2008, the prevalence of peanut or tree nut allergy has more than tripled.[90]

It's my theory that the rise in food allergies is caused in part by genetically modified organisms (GMOs), pesticides, herbicides, antibiotics, growth hormones, artificial colors, and other chemical additives in food. While taken individually, one of these reasons might not be a singular cause for a food allergy, but the synergy of a few might compromise the body's immune response.

Because of this, I am a big proponent of organic and non-GMO food. I will even go as far as to say that eating organic most of the time is a must if you wish to stay healthy.

STUDIES AGAINST THE BENEFITS OF ORGANIC FOOD AND FARMING

In 2012, organic food received negative hits in the media. The first was publicized through results of a Stanford University study that stated there was virtually no difference between the nutritional value of conventionally-grown food and organic food.[91] The study did, however, state that organic foods have 30% lower pesticide residues than conventionally-grown food, and that organic milk and chicken have an overall higher omega-3 fatty acid content.

What this study didn't take into account were the cancer-and disease-fighting antioxidant phytochemicals much more present in organic foods.[92] Phytochemicals are what plants produce to fight off pests and severe weather. The advantage is that these same phytochemicals help humans fight off disease when we eat plant-based food. However, plants grown with the help of pesticides and herbicides don't have to produce as many phytochemicals to stay alive because synthetic chemicals do this for them. In addition, other studies have shown that organic foods also have higher levels of vitamin C, iron, magnesium and phosphorous.[93] Therefore contrary to the 2012 study, organic foods prove to be more advantageous when it comes to warding off disease.

The second hit came from a joint study between McGill University and the University of Minnesota in which they examined 66 cases of land use in organic versus conventional farming. They found that organic farming produces 25% less food than conventional farming on the same land area.[94] This particular analysis only told part of the story, however: for some crops, organic and conventional farms produce the same amounts of food. For other crops, one reason organic farms might have a more difficult time keeping up with non-organic farms is because of the availability of nitrogen in the soil. Nitrogen is essential for good crop yield. Plants absorb great amounts of nitrogen while growing and soil deficient in nitrogen can cause slow growth, low-quality produce, and inefficient water use.[95] While organic farmers must rely on decomposing organic matter (such as cow manure) to release nitrogen, conventional farmers can use slow-release synthetic fertilizer so crops can use nitrogen more efficiently. However, crop yield is but one factor in determining the future of farming and feeding the world. According to the U.S. National Academy of Sciences a farm must be productive, economically profitable, environmentally sound, and socially just. Moreover, these four metrics of sustainability must be managed well so a farm can have a solid base. Despite these guidelines, conventional farming has primarily focused on crop yield while forgoing the other three sustainability metrics.[96]

Organic farming is less expensive, more efficient, creates less waste, and is more sustainable for the environment than conventional farming. Conventional farmers must purchase fertilizers, pesticides, antibiotics, and growth hormones for their crops and livestock, resulting in an overall greater cost for crop production. Organic farming uses the land, crops, and animals to make farming more efficient. For example, sheep don't like asparagus. So when an organic farmer has trouble with weeds in an asparagus farm, he can get a sheep farmer to bring his sheep to feed on the weeds – and at the same time, the sheep's excrement will fertilize the soil. Instead of enriching the soil through such natural means, conventional farmers must add outside minerals to the soil. Most of these added minerals end up running off into waterways, which affects fish, frogs, bugs, and algae and also affects your drinking water. Consequently, water treatment plants must use extra chemicals to clean up the water from agricultural runoff and this extra cost is passed on to the consumer.[97]

Moreover most of the non-organic crops produced in the United States aren't designed to feed humans, but rather to feed livestock. Corn and soy are two of the biggest American crops. Ninety percent of corn and soy crops are used to feed animals and to produce ethanol (a grain alcohol that can be blended with gasoline and used in motor vehicles[98]), while only ten percent are intended for human consumption.[99] It takes roughly one acre of corn to feed one cow. Cows don't naturally eat corn – they eat grass and clover. As a result, they must take antibiotics in order to properly digest the corn they are fed, and if you eat cow or cow byproducts, these antibiotics wind up in your food. And on top of that, milk and other dairy products from corn-fed cows are lower in omega-3 fatty acids, while grass-fed cows yield much higher contents of these acids. Omega-3 fatty acids are essential for brain growth in children and help fight off heart disease in adults, yet our bodies can't naturally produce these fatty acids so we must get them from food. Few foods naturally contain omega-3 fats therefore getting them through grass-fed dairy products is helpful toward your overall intake of this essential fat.[100]

Hopefully, you now have a clearer picture of the inefficiency and harm of conventional farming. But in case you're still skeptical about switching over to organic food, allow me enlighten you about what exactly you are consuming when you eat non-organic.

TOXINS, ANYONE?

Maybe you've never thought about how your non-organic food is grown. And maybe you're hesitant to find out. In what follows, I outline the most common chemicals and products used in conventional food production. I leave it to you to decide if you want to continue consuming them.

Pesticides & Herbicides

According to a 2015 article in Consumer Reports, the CDC reported that there are traces of 29 pesticides in the average American's body.[101] Of these 29, three extremely toxic pesticides and herbicides used in non-organic crops are glyphosphate (also known as Roundup from Monsanto), glufosinate (also known as Basta) and malathion. All three are known to cause health problems and Basta is known to cause birth defects. Other pesticides, banned from the U.S., are also found in non-organic foods. Here's why. Sneaky chemical companies export the banned pesticides to countries outside of the U.S. for use on crops, then import the food back into the U.S. for sale and consumption.[102]

GMO or genetically engineered (GE) foods and plants are modified to survive large applications of herbicides. In fact, since GMOs were invented, the use of toxic herbicides such as Roundup has increased 15 times. And as a possible consequence, GMOs have been linked to increased food allergens and gastro-intestinal problems in humans.[103]

While many sources will explain that proof of the direct health impact of pesticides and herbicides are inconclusive, others have been consistently studying farm workers to see how frequent exposure affects their health. Multiple studies show farm workers and their children have increased rates of childhood ADHD, Alzheimer's disease, birth defects, breast, prostate, and other cancers, depression, fertility issues, immune system damage, low IQ, ovarian cancer, Parkinson's disease, and respiratory problems.[104] Even though most of us are not handling farm chemicals, we are indirectly impacted by food, water, and air exposure.

In 2015, one fascinating study was conducted in Sweden to monitor the effects of a pure organic diet on a family who didn't normally eat organic food. The experiment was designed to test five subjects – a father (age 40), a mother (age 39), a girl (age 12), another girl (age 10), and a boy (age 3) – on the levels of pesticides and herbicides in their bodies over a two week period of only eating organic food. Other measures were taken to decrease chemical exposure, such as changing their personal hygiene products and detergents.

For the first week, the family ate only conventionally-grown food, and for the second and third weeks, they ate only organically-grown food. Urine samples were taken every morning and analyzed for 12 different pesticide residues. The outcome was astonishing: while levels for 8 out of the 12 pesticides were high in every family member, by the seventh day of eating organic food, the levels had reduced measurably, especially in the children.[105]

But the most concerning effect of pesticides and herbicides in food is not finding traces of an individual chemical, but rather the effects of the resulting combination of harmful chemicals in the human body. This is known as the cocktail effect. Children are more susceptible to this effect than adults because they eat and breathe more in proportion to their body weight than adults do, which means that same exposure leads to a higher concentration of chemicals in their bodies.[106] Before 2016 the negative synergistic effect of the chemical cocktail on humans was difficult to prove. But in 2016 a new genotoxicity test by French scientist, Marc Audebert showed damage to human cell lines when five pesticides, mainly found in fruits and vegetables, were mixed together.[107] Critics of organic food argue that only trace amounts of pesticides and herbicides are found in humans when they eat conventionally grown food. Although this may be true, the new findings of the harmful effects of combined pesticides in the human body only strengthen the arguments of those who support organic farming and organic food consumption.

Contaminated Sewage Sludge: Do You Want Waste to Go with That Salad?

Yes, you read that correctly: the key word here is *contaminated*. Since the early 1990s, the EPA has encouraged the use of contaminated sewage sludge – renamed *biosolids* – to grow non-organic crops. In other words, farmers are urged to use human poop as fertilizer.

Poop is often used to enrich soil. However, the sewage sludge farmers use are mixed with industrial and toxic chemicals. The toxic sludge from waste treatment plants contains around 60,000 chemicals (Remember the example from the previous section, it's not necessarily individual chemicals that are the problem, but a combination of them that can be harmful).[108] Basically, anything you pour down your drain or flush down your toilet could also be used to grow your food, whether it's rinsed paint, pills, cleaning products, or car oil. Both the CDC and the NRC have criticized this practice, but the EPA has done little to regulate it. In a November 1990 edition of the *United States Federal Register*, the EPA had this to say of sewage sludge: "Typically, these constituents may include volatiles, organic solids, nutrients, disease-causing pathogenic organisms (bacteria, viruses, etc.), heavy metals and inorganic ions, and toxic organic chemicals from industrial wastes, household chemicals, and pesticides."[109]

Even though supporters of biosolid use claim it is safe to use, a U.S. government study reported in May 2014 in Environmental Health News found traces of prescription drugs and household chemicals deep in the soil as a result of a couple of decades of biosolid use as fertilizer. In 2014, after pressure from customers, Whole Foods Market took an active stance against the use of biosolids by their producers of conventionally grown flowers and produce. According to USDA Organic Standards, organic food cannot be grown with the use of biosolids.[110]

Still, the EPA claims that biosolids are safe for use in the production of crops for human food consumption when produced according to federal guidelines and regulations.[111] In spite of its claims for safety, in 2009, the EPA found over 100 toxins in its Targeted National Sewage Sludge Survey.[112] In conclusion, even former EPA scientist, David L. Lewis, who is a critic of the agency, agrees with environmental groups that the EPA's standards for regulating biosolids is extremely low and that there is reason to be concerned.[113]

Here's my take on the subject of sewage sludge. As much as I'd like to trust government agencies and believe that their policies are for the good of all Americans, I have a difficult time overlooking undeniable proof. To help you visualize what happens in plant growth, think back to a time when you or your child conducted this ever-popular Kindergarten-level science experiment. In this experiment you take either carnation flowers or celery stalks and place one flower or stalk in different glass vases filled with water tinted with food coloring. In a short amount of time the plant absorbs not only the water but also the food coloring and changes the color of the plant. The plant needs water and doesn't discriminate between clean or contaminated water. Now think about everything you consume or throw down the toilet: conventional food with its traces of pesticides and herbicides that come out in your poop, prescription medications that are processed out in your urine, and cleaning solutions that you pour into the waterways. Everything that goes down your toilet will now be spread out on crops and become new food. As a result we wonder why we have outbreaks of the E-coli bacteria on vegetables and fruits.[114] Clearly, through conventional farming practices we're contaminating and then re-contaminating ourselves.

Hormones & Antibiotics

If you're eating non-organic dairy, meat, and eggs, chances are you're also ingesting growth hormones, such as Monsanto's genetically-engineered bovine growth hormone (rBGH).[115] It is also likely you are ingesting antibiotics, which can compromise your immune system and create superbugs.[116] Plus, in the long-term, when you regularly consume non-organic dairy, you increase your risk for breast or prostate cancer.[117] You might see dairy products with the label "no rBGH" or "antibiotic-free." While it's a step in the right direction, if your dairy is not labeled USDA organic, you cannot guarantee that it's pesticide and herbicide free, because the feed for the dairy cows is probably not organic. Moreover, cows were not meant to eat grain and corn. Therefore, the most nutritious milk will come from cows that are grass-fed. Watch labeling for eggs and meat as well. Words like "natural" and "cage free" do not mean the same thing as organic.

.

Never Eat These Foods Unless They're Organic

According to the Environmental Working Group, a nonprofit organization that analyzes the results of government pesticide testing in the U.S., the following fruits and vegetables have the highest amount of pesticide levels on average:[118]

Apples Celery Cherry Tomatoes Collard Greens Cucumbers Grapes Hot Peppers Kale Nectarines Peaches Potatoes Spinach Strawberries Summer Squash Sweet Bell Peppers

Do your best to try and buy organic for the produce listed above, especially when you're buying for children or making homemade baby food. When possible, buy local at farmers markets and talk to the farmers about their farming practices. Many local farms can be spray-free farms (those who don't spray pesticides and herbicides on crops) but not bear the "USDA Organic" label, because obtaining this label can be costly.

Another option is to grow your own garden or to have a window box garden. Growing herbs, tomatoes, and peppers are fairly easy to do in small spaces. Many urban areas have community gardens where you get to take care of a plot and plant what you'd like. Or if you're like me and you don't exactly have a green thumb, you can opt to get fresh, in-season fruits and vegetables through an organic farm food co-op. For a reasonable price (on average $19 per week), you will get a box of produce weekly. The amount of food can be quite big. So if you have a small family or live by yourself, see if a neighbor wants to split the cost and take half. The great part about getting the co-op produce box is that you may encounter vegetables you don't cook with often.

To find a food co-op program near you, go to localharvest.org and search "organic food co-op." It will give you a great opportunity to look up new recipes and try new foods.

Join the Global Movement Away from Chemical Farming & Animal Cruelty

As far as I know, we get one earth. To date, we haven't yet found another planet that mimics ours. I'm not the extreme environmentalist type. That is to say, I'm not about to chain myself to a boat to protest tuna fishing, but I do care about our planet. When I was born on this earth, parts of it were given to my care. And just as I would borrow a friend's car or lawn mower, I will give it back in better shape than when I borrowed it. It's the right thing to do.

That being said, the choices I make every day impact not only my body, my family, and my life, but also the planet. Since we must eat food three times or more a day, what we consume has a monumental impact on the environment. Just as pesticides, herbicides, and antibiotics hurt your body, they also hurt animals and plants. You take your stand on this issue when you purchase products for consumption.

As I mentioned, a cow's natural diet is grass and clover, which their digestive system is designed to digest perfectly. They create beautiful proteins out of grass and make luscious, rich milk. But instead, farmers feed cows government-subsidized corn because it costs a lot less and makes a cow fatter quicker. A cow raised for meat can mature in fourteen months, whereas a cow fed on grass matures in four to five years.

However, raising a cow on corn comes at a great cost to both the cow and to you. Cows get sick on corn. It's too high in starch and they simply cannot digest it properly. This is why they need to be fed antibiotics from the moment they're taken off grass. They are also prone to liver disease and ulcers on a grain diet. The cows are suffering and sick. This cruel treatment of cows is what makes your nonorganic beef and dairy. And this is just one example; animal cruelty in feedlots doesn't stop at cows. Chickens are raised in horrifying conditions, and pigs, geese (for goose liver pate), or any other type of meat animal you can imagine are raised without considering the animal's welfare.

Because even organic labeling doesn't guarantee proper animal treatment, you can look for the Animal Welfare League label on your organic products. To see the Animal Welfare League's standards for specific animals, you can go to animalwelfareapporved.org and click on "standards."

You don't necessarily have direct power in influencing how food is grown or raised, but you do have consumer power. You also have the power to influence those around you and to educate them about the reality of food today. Most people have no idea about where their food comes from. And as a practitioner of enlightened medicine, you can teach, educate, and suggest better ways to consume.

Organic Food Makes You Gentle & Alive

The energy you consume, from the food you ingest, affects you on every level. Food that was made with harshness will create harshness in you. Everything we eat makes up the cells that keep us alive.

In the West, we don't have fully developed concepts to explain the energy field, so instead, I will use Eastern medicine to explain it. In Ayurvedic medicine, there are two concepts of energy that merge together to explain this phenomenon. The first is *prana*, or vital life force. There is prana in every living thing. Prana is the energy that makes things alive and vibrant. Another word to describe prana comes from Chinese medicine: *chi* or *qi*. The more prana or chi you have, the more energetic you will feel, the healthier you will be, and the higher you will function on every level. The disciplines of yoga, tai chi, qi gong, and the alternative medical practices of acupuncture, acupressure, and reflexology are examples of using prana or chi to open up blockages in the body and mind. The second Ayurvedic concept used in explaining energy with food and nutrition is *ojas*. Ojas are healthy chemicals that come from pure food, clean water, and positive experiences. Energetically, you want to accumulate ojas and prana to live in optimal health.

To follow this logic, food that has been processed, chemically fabricated, or dead for a long time has lost its prana. In addition, meat that comes from animals that have been mistreated, confined to small spaces, and deprived of sunlight, fresh water, and healthy live plants are also depleted of prana. In the same vein, ojas come from the freshest food with the most vitamins, minerals, and phytonutrients. Food that is leftover, frozen, canned, or processed doesn't have the same amount of ojas as food that has been freshly picked, locally bought, or made and served the same day. Another subtle nuance with ojas has to do with your emotional state when you eat your food (Incidentaly, in *The Wheel of Healing with Ayurveda*, I explain more about how you can enhance your eating experience to increase ojas).

Eating organic food also makes you gentler, less aggressive, angry, or upset. As I explained above, the mere cocktail effect of the pesticide and herbicide chemicals inside of you wreak havoc on your biochemistry. Your body has to work extra hard to purge out the toxins from non-organic food. This will drain your energy and also make you more susceptible to illness.

Furthermore, if you are not vegan, you're consuming animal products and by-products daily. As I mentioned, the food you eat, the water you drink, and the chemicals you ingest are creating every single cell in your body on physiological, psychological, emotional, spiritual, and subtle energy levels.

To understand the relationship between agitated energy and conventionally grown meat, dairy, fish, and eggs, imagine the following illustration: the chicken you eat has been genetically manipulated, artificially inseminated, and hatched. She is force-fed and slaughtered as a 42-day-old baby. During her 42-day life, your chicken has been stuffed in an overcrowded shed, where she is forced to sit on a manure-laden floor that is only cleaned every two to three years. Since your chicken is forced to grow 65 times faster than her normal growth rate, she suffers from painful leg problems, including lameness, because her body is too big for her legs.

In the dark of night, your chicken is captured by a "catcher" and forced into a crate stuffed with other chickens. In the process of being stuffed, she suffers from broken wings, legs, dehydration, or maybe heart failure. Your chicken is scalded alive after her throat has been cut. Since she has been raised in such unsanitary conditions, she is infected with salmonella, camphylobacter, E. Coli, and other bacteria, so she has to be soaked in a tub of toxic chemicals so you don't get sick when you eat her. Now, all of that negative, suffering, and toxic energy is what you absorb when you eat your chicken. Your cells become infused with "sick and suffering" energy.

While you can't guarantee that your animal-based food will be grown without cruelty, by eating organic and doing research on local organic farms, you can minimize exposure to negative energy in your food.

You Can Afford Organic Food

Organic food is expensive. There's no doubt about that. One of the reasons that organic food is so expensive compared to conventionally-grown food is because government subsidies lower the cost of certain foods, especially those related to corn, soy, wheat, and rice.[119] Since much of the non-organic prepackaged food is made with by-products of government subsidized corn and soy, those products are much less expensive than fresh fruit and vegetables. For instance, you can buy a family-sized box of breakfast cereal for about the same price as three organic apples. Because the cereal is probably sweetened with high-fructose corn syrup and has a government subsidized grain such as corn or wheat, the cost is lower and you'll feel like you're getting a lot more food.

The next reason that organic food is more expensive is because its demand is so high. In 2016 organic food only represented 5 percent of total food sales in the U.S., yet the demand for organic food increases each year.[120] More than 82% of U.S. households buy organic food on a regular basis according to a March 2017 survey published by the Organic Trade Association (OTA).[121] Because of the high demand in the U.S, much of the organic food that U.S. citizens consume is imported, which raises the costs of organic food overall.[122]

But you may still be wondering how in the world you can afford organic food. This is a real concern for many who want to change their eating habits and feed their families in a healthier way, but don't necessarily have the budget to support a 100% organic diet. For many years, as a low paid writer and yoga teacher, I had to be creative with my finances in order to buy organic food. I consider food to be medicine, and I'm fortunate enough to not have to go to the doctor's office except for check-ups and to have very healthy children.

So, without further ado, here are five ways in which you can afford organic food...

1. Organic food co-ops and local farmers markets

I mentioned this previously, but by participating in an organic farming co-op, you can get a lot of food for very little money. Depending on where you live, farmers markets can also be a way to get organic food at a lower cost than traditional grocery stores.

2. Buy less and eat less.

I'm going to be blunt: most of us in the United States – and perhaps in other wealthy Western countries – eat way too many calories. Many of us are filling up on empty calories with sugar and salt, which actually leave us hungrier without nourishing our bodies. We don't need a ton of calories to thrive. Women need an average of 1,700 calories daily, while men need about 2,000.[123] If you divide that number by three or four meals, you only need between 400 and 500 calories per meal.

Let me illustrate. A two-egg omelet, made with one whole egg and one egg white, a half a slice of cheese, ½ teaspoon of butter, one veggie sausage patty, and a whole wheat English muffin with butter is around 400 calories. Add one six-ounce glass of orange juice, and you are up to 450 calories for a small but nourishing breakfast. There is no reason why one person needs a ten-ounce, 570-calorie steak all to themselves. If you're eating a healthy, balanced diet, you're eating more vegetables and whole grains, and less meat, fish, chicken or poultry, which probably make up a big bulk of your food bill. And by eating less, you're spending less.

3. Refrain from buying processed and packaged foods (even organic ones).

If money is truly a concern for buying organic, you can save a lot of money by not buying packaged food. You can make healthy breakfast muffins at home on Sunday and use them for a few days out of the week. A kid-friendly snack can be made from celery or apples with nut butter, or a trail mix made with organic nuts, seeds, and dried fruit.

When it comes to buying organic grains, I've found that you can save up to 50% in price when you buy in the bulk food section at health food stores. For example, prepackaged organic basmati rice at Whole Foods runs around $5.00 for 16 ounces. But buying it bulk and filling the bag yourself can reduce the price to around $3.00. And sometimes, you don't even need the amount that is sold in the pre-packaging. If you need only a few organic walnuts for a salad, buying just a handful in the bulk section can save you a lot and reduce food waste.

4. Grow some organic herbs, vegetables, and fruits.
Even with little know-how you can grow many vegetables and herbs yourself. One year I planted mint, and now I have an abundance of mint every year. Growing organic mint takes virtually no mainte-nance and is great in salads or with cantaloupe. Basil, cilantro, bell peppers, hot peppers, tomatoes, and cucumbers are fairly easy to grow as potted plants and in window boxes.

5. Increase your organic food consumption incrementally.
You don't have to overwhelm yourself with an all-or-nothing ap-proach. Start by increasing your organic food consumption by 10% and add another 10% after a few weeks. See where you can save a few dollars in your budget to be able to make this change. It's important, however, to pay attention to the foods you buy on regular basis. Ask yourself if they are increasing prana and ojas into your life or if they are simply empty calories used to fill up a void.

It may seem like a big sacrifice to be able to eat more healthfully now, but in the long run it will pay off. You will spend much less on doctor bills, prescription medications, and expensive medical tests. You will have more energy to do the things you love and more vitality to contribute to your family, friends, and society.

DON'T BE AFRAID TO LEAVE THE PARTY

On the Oprah Winfrey Show I once heard Oprah say something about how most people gravitate toward 'bad' food because it's like a little party in your mouth. Overall we tend to have a lot of emotional connections to food. Advertisers have done a great job at convincing you that you deserve a break today, you deserve nothing less, and you deserve to super-size it. For a while, you'll feel like you've left the party, and this will make you feel quite lonely. Not only will your mouth feel lonely but it's also likely that your peers won't understand what you're doing. And they won't join you – at least not right away.

Think of yourself as the pioneer in the healthy eating movement. You're a visionary at the forefront of change. I've been looked at weirdly, teased, ridiculed, and criticized for choosing organic and mostly vegetarian food. My own mother recently told me she heard that vegetarians were more likely to get Alzheimer's. But most people from India are vegetarians and have been for centuries. And they are no worse off for being vegetarian than anybody else.

Your inner party animal will pout for a while and tell you that you deserve to eat fast food, drink those cans of beer, or eat a 24-ounce ribeye. In the beginning, you will need to constantly override that inner party animal. Your body will need to detox from the unhealthy food, the overdoses of caffeine or alcohol, and any other toxins or stimulants you give it. Eating clean will mean you have to clean up the after effects of the party. Give it time, and soon you will find that the switch to clean eating was worth it.

THE KARMIC CONNECTION TO ORGANIC FOOD

When you make the right choices, you're always rewarded. You might not see the results today or tomorrow, but in the long run, the universe always has a way to bring the goodness of your choice back to you. You can even talk to your higher self, God, or Mother Nature about your wish to purchase and afford organic food. You can connect to universal energy by affirming "I want to help myself and the earth by purchasing organic or locally grown food. Please help me with the necessary resources to be able to do this."

The universe pays attention to requests that help bring balance back to the earth. It doesn't matter that you're only one person. You can and will make a difference by choosing to help the animals, plants, insects, water and oceans, other human beings, and yourself.

CHAPTER 6

HEAL WITH HERBS

SOCIAL CONDITIONING CAN BE strong. Most of us have grown up in Western countries where the normal form of treatment for ailments is prescription medication. We have been socially conditioned to trust our doctors to know the safest and most effective brands. Yet you only need to read the lengthy drug descriptions on your prescription insert – or listen to a drug disclaimer at the end of a commercial – to learn that most conventional medicines aren't safe at all. In fact, many prescription medications do more harm than good.

On the other hand, the earth has given us an abundance of plants designed to help us heal most, if not all, ailments. But if you're not familiar with them, you won't know what to take. In the United States, we haven't been educated on herbal medicine and furthermore, many companies have fought hard and spent lots of money to make sure we stay in the dark on this topic.

It's time to bring herbal medicine into the light so you can increase your options.

Mother Nature's Pharmacy

Have you ever spent time observing animals in nature? They go about their day, living in the present moment without worry. They don't sit around worrying about where their next meal is coming from or what they might do if they fall ill. They go out, search, and trust that the earth will provide for them. They know this because it has always been the case.

We, too, were put on this earth as animals – thinking and consciously aware animals, but an animal nonetheless. So why have we evolved to mistrust the earth and its natural gifts? What sets us apart? And what made us forget that we, too, just like every other creature, have the earth's natural resources to give us everything we need?

It doesn't matter if you are an evolutionist or a creationist. If you evolved from microorganisms, then you would still have to believe the earth provides, as it provided for you as a microorganism. And if you believe God put you here, then why in the world would a Creator drop you here and not provide you with the food and medicines you need, but give those resources to every other creature? It's totally illogical. Yet here we are, in the Western world, walking around as if we have to "figure it all out." We spend tons and tons of money trying to invent medicines and technology to fight disease when we have everything we need in nature, and even more than we need to heal every ailment under the sun.

Mother Nature has an entire pharmacy, at low cost and it's all for you. Humans have used nature's pharmacy since they first walked the earth. Prior to modern medicine, every society on the planet had a way of classifying plants for healing. In fact, many prescription drugs today originated from plants and herbs. For example, one of the first medicines used in modern society, aspirin, comes from willow bark. Early practitioners of pharmacology learned how to extract the active ingredients from plants. With these active ingredients, they created synthetic drugs. The drug, which contains a high concentration of these active ingredients, forces the body into health. Herbs, which are gentle and holistic, coax the body into healing. This is the reason for accentuated and almost immediate side effects of prescription drugs versus their herbal counterparts. In addition, herbs are often used together synergistically to enhance their healing capabilities, but also to help reduce potential side effects. Furthermore, with herbal remedies you have more options for therapeutic use than with prescription medications. You can add certain herbs and spices to cooking or sprinkle them on top of cold food. Or you can ingest them with a carrier such as honey, oil, or ghee. Finally, herbs can be infused in teas, oils, or taken as an extract, capsule, tablet, or applied to the skin in a cream or ointment

Let's explore the increasing dangers of many prescription medications and uncover the mystery surrounding herbal medicine.

The Dangers of Prescription Pills

While prescription drugs were initially created to help patients heal from symptoms and diseases, these days, most cause more harm than good. In 1998, the Journal of the American Medical Association projected that 106,000 deaths resulted from patients taking prescription medications as properly prescribed by their physicians. However, a more recent analysis estimates that that number was closer to 128,000 in 2017.[124] And death by adverse reactions to prescription medications is now the fourth leading cause of death in the United States.[125]

Each prescription drug has on average seventy possible adverse reactions. For this reason adverse drug reactions are responsible for the hospitalization of between 1.5 to 2.7 million Americans per year.[126] What's worse is that an additional 770,000 people per year develop an adverse reaction once hospitalized.[127] Furthermore these numbers don't take into account the rising U.S. epidemic of death by prescription opioid overdose. The United States makes up only 4.6% of the world's population, but consumes 80% of its opioids and 99% of the world's hydrocodone, the opiate that is in Vicodin.[128] Other extremely addictive (and therefore abused) prescription medications include depressants, such as barbituates and benzodiazepines (Xanax, Klonopin, Valium), oxycodone (OxyContin and Percocet, Demerol and Darvocet), Codeine (commonly found in prescription-strength cough syrups), and Amphetamines or speed (Adderall and Ritalin).[129]According to the CDC, since 1999 overdose death involving prescription opioids has quadrupled. [130] In 2017, the CDC estimated that 91 Americans die each day from opioid overdose.[131]

Regardless of these numbers, pharmaceutical companies are still among the richest companies in the United States. Kantar Media, a consulting firm that tracks multimedia spending, reported that pharmaceutical advertising exceeded $6 billion in 2016 and is the 6th largest category of advertising in the U.S. up from 12th in 2012.[132] According to the Centers for Medicare and Medicaid Services (CMS), in 2015 Americans spent $325 billion on retail prescription drugs and that spending is estimated to increase by 6.3% per year through 2025.[133] As of the year 2000, the FDA has approved an average of twenty-four new prescription medications per year, many of which have harmful and long-lasting side effects.[134]

Pharmaceutical companies make a mint on keeping you sick and addicted. And much of the time, your doctor isn't helping. Physicians routinely get monetary rewards from writing brand-name prescriptions. Many doctors disapprove of this practice, but can't refuse the money. They wind up getting paid anyway, since many feel that the brand-name drug is superior in quality and effectiveness than the generic drug. Sometimes the generic version is not yet available and they have to prescribe the name brand. Other physicians literally make a salary off of pharmaceutical kickbacks. You can now go to: https://projects.propublica.org/docdollars/ to see if your doctors have received money from pharmaceutical and medical device companies.

In truth sometimes taking prescription pills is unavoidable. But if you can make your body as healthy as possible through many of the practices outlined in this book, your doctor may reduce or eliminate some of them. You can also help avoid the possibility of having to add new prescriptions in the future.

Keeping A Holistic Approach

A common misconception is that natural equals safe. If you take that as a blanket statement, it's false. Herbs come from the plant kingdom. Some herbs are completely safe, while others are safe only in small doses. For example, a few Senna pods can empty a person's bowels, while a lot of Senna could dehydrate a person to death.

In the United States, the FDA categorizes herbs as food and they are therefore not closely regulated for their effects as drugs. When choosing herbs, buy from a reputable source and select USDA organic whenever possible so you can ensure its regulation. Secondly, if you're currently taking prescription medications, you might aggravate or nullify the effects of your prescription drugs with any herbs you take. Please err on the side of caution and consult with your physician before taking any herbs or herbal formulas.

Finally, try not to think of herbal medicine as a one-to-one equivalent with prescription drugs. In other words, to practice enlightened medicine, you're going to look at the entire picture of your health and not simply treat each symptom. There's a root cause to your discomfort or disease. By masking the symptoms, you're not taking care of the underlying problem. Herbs, just like any other form of healing, can be used as a crutch to ignore what's happening in your life.

I'm emphasizing this principle in this chapter in particular because as a society, we've been conditioned and trained to look for quick fixes. I want to make sure you're not looking for quick relief in these herbal suggestions, but rather a complement to an over-all healthy living program. As an Ayurvedic practitioner, I'm slow to suggest herbal remedies for a quick fix. If I see an immediate problem that can be fixed with an herb, I'll tell the client. However, most of the time, a client's health issues can be fixed in another way: through diet, exercise, meditation, emotional and relationship healing, or even a career change.

A Wonderful Enhancement to Health

Now that I've warned you about taking herbs too loosely (no pun intended), many herbs – including kitchen herbs and spices – can be used easily to enhance your health. To help you get started on your journey to discovering the powerful healing benefits of herbs, spices, and roots, I'll describe the benefits of ten herbs you can use in your kitchen, and ten herbs commonly used as teas, tinctures, capsules, or tablets, but not used in food. Finally, I'll recommend herbalized oils and non-herbalized oils that you can use for various conditions. As mentioned with food, I highly recommend that all herbs, spices, and roots be USDA-certified organic products to ensure you the highest form of healing.

How to Take Your Herbs, Spices, and Roots

In the United States, we are used to taking vitamins and herbal supplements orally in the form of a pill or tablet. Taking an herbal supplement in a pill form is an easy way to take the herb, and a good way to ensure a consistent dose. In this way, it's easier to know whether or not a certain amount of the herb is working for you and if you need to increase or decrease the dose.

Ayurvedic medicine recommends using the powder form of the herb when you are able. You can take the herb on the tongue, hold it in your mouth for a second or two, and then drink some water. You can use a carrier for the herb, too. Common carriers are coconut oil, honey, and ghee (clarified butter) – you can mix the powdered herb or herbs with the oil, honey, or ghee and take them that way. The only downside of keeping a powdered herb is that the herb will lose potency on the shelf quicker than in tablet form.

Herbal teas are another way to take herbs. Teas are effective for quick use but may not be convenient for high therapeutic doses. Often, some herbal teas are useful for acute symptoms. One example is drinking tea with the Ayurvedic herb, *tulsi*, for an upset tummy.

In the following sections, I will give guidelines on how to take each spice, herb, or oil.

Ten Cooking Herbs, Roots, and Spices

Our wonderful plant kingdom is chock full of healing properties for every ailment. You might notice in the following list that more than one herb, spice, root, or plant can cure a same set of symptoms or disease. In these cases, you can pick one that treats the ailment and stick with it for a few weeks to see if it works for you before trying another one. Herbs also work together synergistically to hasten the healing process. For example, you can mix thyme and rosemary, or cardamom and cinnamon to enhance the effects of the individual herbs and spices.

The ten herbs, roots, and spices I've chosen are not an exhaustive list, but they will give you a glimpse at the healing potential in the plant kingdom, and will hopefully get you on board with using our earth's pharmacy.

1. Cardamom

- Best known for improving complexion, dental health, and treating digestive disorders.
- ***Effects on the body:*** Antiseptic, antibacterial, anti-inflammatory, antioxidant.

One of the loveliest smelling spices, cardamom has always been the most expensive spice in the world. In traditional medicines, cardamom has been used to treat heart disease, respiratory illnesses, and all forms of digestive problems. Cardamom is high in vitamin A, vitamin C, potassium, calcium, and iron. Chewing on cardamom pods helps with dental health and stimulates digestion. Cardamom also helps with stomach cramps, acid reflux, and gas.

Taking cardamom as a daily regimen for at least three months can help lower blood pressure and prevent blood platelets from becoming sticky. (Sticky blood platelets can be responsible for blood clots and strokes.) Cardamom has a delicious aroma and a sweet taste. It's good to add to teas, curries, and desserts.

Taking cardamom internally: Using the entire pod or powder, you can add cardamom to sweet and savory dishes. The best quality cardamom pods can be found in Indian or Middle Eastern stores and are lime green. You can use cardamom pods with hot water to make a tea and add powdered cardamom to naturally sweeten warmed milk, tea, and coffee. Powdered cardamom quickly loses its volatile oils after being ground. Therefore, you can grind cardamom seeds as you need them and add them to sweet dishes.

Taking cardamom externally: You can add cardamom oil to your skin care products to benefit from its high level of antioxidants.

2. CINNAMON

- Best known for balancing blood sugar and for treatment of type 2 diabetes.
- *Effects on the body:* Warming, antibacterial, antispasmodic, expectorant, analgesic, carminative.

Cinnamon has been used since the beginning of human history. For example, The Bible mentions cinnamon and the Greeks and Romans offered it to their gods.

Today with our current diabetes epidemic, finding solutions with diet and exercise can help alleviate suffering from the effects of diabetes. In addition, long-term studies have shown that taking one gram of cinnamon (about 1/4 of a teaspoon) once per day decreases blood sugar levels in type 2 diabetics. Cinnamon can also help with vaginal yeast infections, and can fight bacteria that cause stomach ulcers and stomach cancer.

Taking cinnamon: Whether via sticks or ground powder, you can add cinnamon to sweet or savory dishes. There are two types of cinnamon used for commercial purposes: Ceylon cinnamon – true cinnamon – and *cassia cinnamon*. Cassia cinnamon, which is lower in quality, is less expensive. You can purchase true cinnamon in Indian spice stores or online – just look for "Ceylon cinnamon" or "True cinnamon" on the label. For medicinal purposes, make sure you're taking Ceylon cinnamon, as taking therapeutic doses (1-6 grams) of Cassia cinnamon may cause liver damage.[135] When you buy ground cinnamon, make sure to use it within a few months, as it quickly loses its volatile oils. But cinnamon sticks, also known as quills, can keep for up to three years.

3. Fennel

- Best known for helping with gastrointestinal tract complaints and inflammatory diseases of the respiratory tract.
- *Effects on the body:* Cooling, stimulant, diuretic, carminative, antibacterial, expectorant, antispasmodic.

Fennel seeds are rich in oil and can help alleviate gas in infants and also help increase milk production in breastfeeding moms. It can help with nausea, morning sickness, and menstrual cramps. Fennel is often used for coughs. It can be used in a steam bath to clear skin problems and help acne heal more quickly.

Taking fennel: The best way to take fennel for medicinal purposes is to do an herbal tea infusion. Use one teaspoon of crushed fennel seeds and add to a cup of boiling water. Allow mixture to steep for ten minutes covered. Strain and sip tea slowly. You can also add fennel seeds to cooking to stimulate digestion and reduce heartburn. Chew on a mix of cardamom and fennel seeds after a meal to soothe indigestion.

4. FENUGREEK

- Best known for calming the stomach and digestive tract, stimulating the appetite, and lowering blood sugar and cholesterol levels. Fenugreek also increases milk production in breastfeeding mothers.
- **Effects on the body:** Heating, antioxidant, aphrodisiac, antirheumatic, pain reliever.

Fenugreek lowers blood sugar levels when taken with breakfast and dinner for insulin-dependent diabetics. Patients with coronary heart disease treated with fenugreek have seen lowered cholesterol and triglyceride levels.[136] Fenugreek has also been used to treat kidney stones.

Taking fenugreek: You can add fenugreek to food and drink fenugreek tea. You can also find fenugreek leaves and seeds in Middle Eastern or Indian spice stores. Health food stores sell fenugreek as capsules. You can safely take one gram daily to lower cholesterol and two to eight grams daily to improve breastmilk production.

5. FLAXSEED

- Best known as a natural digestive aid thanks to its high levels of polyunsaturated fats and omega-3 fatty acids, as well as its soluble and insoluble fiber. Omega-3 fatty acids protect the body from cardiovascular disease, rheumatism, and intestinal diseases.
- **Effects on the body:** anti-inflammatory, mild laxative.

Freshly ground flaxseeds can help alleviate constipation. Flax-seeds have been used to treat respiratory disorders, abdominal cramping, and urinary tract infections. Adding flaxseed to your diet may help lower serum cholesterol levels. Flaxseed is the highest natural source of lignans, which are a source of phytoestrogen. Consumption of lignans may help with hormonally sensitive tumors. Taking one tablespoon of flaxseed oil daily can help increase thyroid function and also enables the body to produce more sex hormones, which helps with fertility.

Taking flaxseed: You can eat ground flaxseeds. Mix them into food and include them in recipes. In addition, you can also drink flaxseed oil or mix it with food, such as yogurt or soy or almond milk. However, due to the high omega-3 fatty acid content in flaxseed oil, you should never heat the oil. Keep flaxseed oil refrigerated and consume it quickly as it has a limited shelf life.

6. GARLIC

- Best known for lowering blood pressure and cholesterol levels, garlic dilates blood vessels and improves blood flow. It also cleanses and calms the intestines. It can protect against heart attack and stroke with regular consumption.[137] Garlic is also known to prevent certain cancers.
- *Effects on the body:* anti-infective agent, anti-parasitic, anti-spasmodic, aphrodisiac, carminative, expectorant, rejuvenative, stimulant.

Garlic is a pharmacy on its own. It inhibits the stickiness of blood platelets, which reduces blood vessel clotting. It also helps prevent blood vessels from becoming stiff. Garlic has also been used in treatment of lung congestion, arthritic stiffness, and pain, and to calm mental turbulence.

Taking garlic: Add cooked or raw garlic to recipes. Chew on fresh parsley or basil to get rid of garlic breath. You can take garlic in powder form, tablets, and capsules. Garlic oil can be applied to skin infections and lesions externally.

Precautions: If you're taking blood pressure medications or blood thinners and you add regular garlic consumption to your diet, monitor the medications regularly to make sure you're not over treating.

7. Ginger

- Best known for its healing properties on the digestive system and treating nausea.
- ***Effects on the body:*** Warming, boosts the immune system, antioxidant, anti-inflammatory, antibacterial, antiviral.

Ginger is considered a universal wonder drug with many healing properties. It increases salivary enzymes when taken internally and therefore is good to reduce nausea and vomiting. Fresh ginger root is great for the treatment of morning sickness in pregnancy. It can also reduce the nausea associated with chemotherapy treatment. Ginger also helps with circulation and has been known to reduce blood cholesterol levels and reduce the stickiness in blood platelets. A ginger paste can be applied to the head for tension headaches and migraines. Ginger juice rubbed on the navel relieves diarrhea. Ginger is also a diaphoretic, which means it encourages perspiration to reduce high fevers. You can also apply a strong ginger tea on a cloth compress and use it on areas affected by rheumatism and arthritis.

Taking ginger: Ginger can be taken as a juice, fresh, dried, or in a jam or candy. You can add ginger to nearly any recipe. Ginger juice is best for colds, cough, and vomiting. For mental stimulation, sniff a few drops of ginger essential oil.

8. ROSEMARY

- Best known for relaxing the digestive tract, heart health, and boosting low blood pressure. Rosemary is also a muscle relaxant.
- *Effects on the body:* Heating, antioxidant, stimulant, anti-inflammatory, diaphoretic.

Rosemary is a fragrant herb originally from the Mediterranean region. It contains powerful antioxidants. These three antioxidants – rosmarinic acid, carnosic acid, and carnosol – make rosemary one of the most powerful antioxidants on earth. Rosemary boosts the immune system, and by inhaling the fragrance of rosemary, you can lower your cortisol levels and in turn reduce anxiety. Studies have shown that combined with citrus, rosemary can protect your skin against the sun's ultraviolet radiation.[138] Traditional healers used rosemary to treat diabetes, respiratory illnesses, arthritis, and dizziness.

Taking rosemary: Add fresh or dried rosemary to recipes. Breathing in the scent of rosemary can improve your memory and enhance your thinking. To prevent memory loss, including Alzheimer's disease and dementia, drink three cups of rosemary tea per day. For prevention of sun-related skin damage, add rosemary essential oil to natural sun block creams.

Precautions: Do not use therapeutic quantities of rosemary while pregnant or breastfeeding. However, using rosemary in cooking is fine.

9. THYME

- Best known for helping to fight off the viruses and bacteria that cause acute bronchitis.
- *Effects on the body:* Heating, stimulant, diaphoretic, anti-cough, anthelmintic, antiseptic, antioxidant.

A plant native to Provence, France, this fragrant herb is a staple in traditional French cuisine. Thyme contains the volatile oil *thymol*, which is one of Mother Nature's most powerful antiseptics. The thymol contained in thyme is also good to fight off bacteria on teeth and is therefore good in toothpaste and mouthwash. Thyme is anti-aging as it contains powerful phytonutrients and antioxidants. It also has anti-inflammatory compounds.

Taking thyme: You can use fresh or dried thyme in cooking. Dried thyme lasts longer – up to eighteen months in an airtight container. When using dried thyme, crush and crumble it in your hand before adding it to dishes to release the healing oils.

10. TURMERIC

- Best for reducing cholesterol, protecting the liver, reducing the risk of ulcers, reducing inflammation, and reducing pain and stiffness from arthritis. Turmeric soothes the digestive system and increases the protective mucous lining in the stomach to reduce the risk of ulcers.
- *Effects on the body:* Mildly heating, antibacterial/ antibiotic, anti-inflammatory, detoxifier, anthelmintic, carminative

Turmeric belongs to the same family as ginger. It has antibiotic properties and you can take it safely with almost no side effects. Found commonly as a kitchen spice, you can add turmeric liberally to soups or vegetable dishes. For a sore throat, mix a teaspoon of honey with enough turmeric to infuse into the honey then lick the spoon slowly to coat the throat.

Taking turmeric internally: As a kitchen spice, you can take the powdered form in many ways, including mixing it into recipes and with hot water or warmed milk. Turmeric capsules are sold in health food stores and can be taken to help lower risk of heart attacks or reduce blood cholesterol levels. You can also buy turmeric root and use it in cooking.

Taking turmeric externally: For pimples and blemishes, mix turmeric with water to form a paste. Apply to the lesion at night and wash it off in the morning. For other skin conditions, mix turmeric with coconut oil or ghee and rub on the affected area.

Ten Healing Herbs

These healing herbs are not ones you would typically find in the kitchen, but they have been used to cure ailments for thousands of years and are worth a trip to the store. Tried, tested, true, and most importantly pocketbook-friendly, don't hesitate to try these herbs to assist you in your healing.

1. Ashwagandha

- Best known for boosting the immune system, improving brain function, and enhancing reproductive health.
- *Effects on the body:* Heating, adaptogen, analgesic, aphrodisiac, astringent, rejuvenative, anti-inflammatory.

Native to India and referred to as "Indian ginseng", ashwagandha – or winter cherry – has many uses. It's known especially for enhancing the nervous system and brain function. It also helps boost reproductive organs in both men and women but is especially known to increase semen production. Ashwagandha has also been used to reduce side effects from chemotherapy and radiation in cancer treatment. Studies show that ashwagandha also increases the sensitivity of cancer cells to the effects of radiation therapy and protects the healthy cells.[139] Ashwagandha is frequently used as a mind tonic to help with mental turbulence, anxiety, mild depression, lack of focus, and insomnia.

Taking ashwagandha: Take twice daily in a powder or tablet form. Mix 1/4 to 3 teaspoons of ashwagandha powder with ghee or oil to take internally. You can also mix a teaspoon with warmed milk sweetened with honey or sugar.

2. Calendula (Marigold)

- Best known for skin treatment and wound healing. Calendula is also known for reducing inflammation in the body produced by ailments from hemorrhoids and ulcers to cancer.
- *Effects on the body:* Antimicrobial, antiviral, anti-inflammatory, antioxidant, astringent, emollient.

Native to Western Europe, Southeastern Asia, and the Mediterranean, calendula comes from the same family of flowers as the bright yellow marigold. Traditionally calendula has been used for external use, but the flower is so gentle and effective that it can be taken both internally and externally. One of the best herbal antivirals, calendula stimulates growth of new cells. High in antioxidants, flavonoids, carotenoids, and the phytochemicals, lutein and beta-carotene, calendula has anti-inflammatory properties and protects cells against free radial damage. Many childhood ailments can be healed with calendula from diaper rash to ear infections. Calendula improves skin firmness and hydration and has been used in cosmetics for centuries. The antiviral and antimicrobial effects of calendula are enhanced when mixed with sunflower oil, and calendula can even fight off antibiotic resistant bacteria.[140]

Taking calendula externally: Calendula has been traditionally mixed into creams and ointments. Oil of calendula is usually mixed with olive or sunflower oil.

Taking calendula internally: The dried flowers can be made into tea. The fresh flowers can be added to cooking or salads. Calendula is popular as a homeopathic remedy.

3. Chasteberry (Vitex)

- Best known for relieving PMS symptoms by stabilizing and regulating hormones. Chasteberry relieves breast tenderness, bloating, headaches, constipation, depression and inner tension.
- ***Effects on the body:*** For women, increases luteinizing hormone, modifies prolactin, and aids in the inhibition of the follicle-stimulating hormone, which helps balance out the progesterone to estrogen ratio.

Chasteberry has been used for over 2,500 years to treat various conditions, especially symptoms and ailments related to gynecology. In Europe, chasteberry has been used over the past fifty years for premenstrual syndrome (PMS), cyclical breast discomfort, menstrual cycle irregularities, and dysfunctional uterine bleeding. Chasteberry can also clear up hormone-related acne and help treat endometriosis. The transition into menopause can cause all kinds of symptoms from vaginal dryness to hot flashes, but taking chasteberry during perimenopause can ease these symptoms. Chasteberry can also help diminish uterine fibroids, has been known to reduce the size of an enlarged prostate, and can even help prevent prostate cancer. Traditionally, chasteberry was used to lower libido in monks, but there doesn't appear to be any scientific evidence that the herb has this effect.

Taking chasteberry: Take one or two 225-milligram capsules every day for three to six months. Chasteberry acts as a reset button for your system. After you see premenstrual symptoms subside, stop taking the herb. My favorite brand of chasteberry is Nature's Plus Herbal Actives. For treatment of endometriosis, the therapy is longer term, 12-18 months with two capsules daily.

4. Echinacea

- Best known for treatment of upper respiratory infections and for enhancing the immune system.
- *Effects on the body:* Antibacterial, antiviral, anti-inflammatory, detoxifier.

Native to North America, echinacea is one of the most popular herbal medicines in the United States. Native Americans used echinacea for upper respiratory infections, snake bites, and toothaches.

Studies have shown that echinacea stimulates the immune system by increasing the production of immune-stimulating chemicals and white-blood cells. Other studies have shown that taking larger doses of echinacea at the start of cold or flu symptoms shorten the duration and intensity of these diseases. However, taking echinacea over the long-term is not recommended, as it may lose its effectiveness. For maximum efficiency, take echinacea for short durations.

Taking echinacea: Most preparations involve taking echinacea internally. You can easily find the dried herb in tablets and capsules. You can also find it in teas, cold remedies, and throat lozenges. Take between 500 milligrams to 1 gram divided into 2-3 doses throughout the day. As a liquid tincture – usually mixed with other herbs, such as goldenseal – take 25-60 drops two to three times daily.

5. Gotu Kola (*Brahmi* in Sanskrit)

- Best known in India as a mind tonic and wound healer. Gotu kola is used to help heal skin injuries, traumatic injuries, and surgical wounds. It has also been used to improve memory and to treat insomnia and anxiety.
- *Effects on the body:* Cooling, mild laxative, diuretic, blood purifier, detoxifier, nervine, rejuvenative.

Gotu kola, known in Sanskrit as *brahmi*, has been used in India to treat a wide array of ailments. For thousands of years in ancient

Eastern societies, gotu kola was known as the longevity herb. Increasing memory is one of its greatest uses; you can take gotu kola while studying for a test or exam. You can also take gotu kola if you're over the age of fifty so memory loss doesn't become an issue. In addition, gotu kola helps reduce anxiety and improve mental clarity. Gotu kola is also used to reduce fever. One of gotu kola's main rejuvenative effects comes from its ability to improve circulation and blood quality. Ayurveda considers gotu kola to be the herb of enlightenment due to its unique cerebral effects. Gotu kola supplements are safe to take long term.

Taking gotu kola externally: You can apply gotu kola in a cream or ointment to wounds to hasten healing and to help strengthen scar tissue. Herbalized gotu kola oil can be applied to the skin as well as inserted into the nostrils to help with mental clarity.

Taking gotu kola internally: Take gotu kola internally for leg edema and pain, cramping, and swelling of varicose veins. Steep one teaspoon of dried gotu kola leaves in hot water, mix with honey and take before bedtime. To improve memory, take 1 to 2 grams daily in a tablet or capsule. Make sure the capsules contain 40 percent *asiaticoside*, the active ingredient in gotu kola.

6. Licorice root

- Best known for helping the upper respiratory tract, duodenal ulcers, and chronic gastritis. Licorice also stabilizes blood sugar levels.
- *Effects on the body:* Cooling, anti-inflammatory, antibacterial, immune enhancer.

Licorice root is native to Asia, Europe, and the Mediterranean. Although it has a similar flavor to anise or fennel, it is related to neither, and licorice is in fact fifty times sweeter than sugar.[141] Licorice root has traditionally been used to reduce pain and fever. Studies have shown that licorice appears to reduce elevated cholesterol levels and prolong the clotting time of blood, so it may be beneficial to patients at risk for coronary heart disease. Licorice has a long history of helping to mobilize mucus, as an expectorant, in coughs and colds. For women in menopause, licorice can help reduce hot flashes. Licorice can also soothe inflammation in the digestive tract caused by stomach ulcers and chronic gastritis. You can use licorice extract as a mouthwash to freshen breath and kill bacteria. In 2012, The American Chemical Society found that the two antibacterial chemicals in licorice root, *licoricidin* and *licorisoflavan A*, inhibited growth of the bacteria that cause tooth decay and gum disease.

Taking licorice root: You can take licorice root as a tea and drink one cup 2-3 times per day. In capsule form, take one or two 300-milligram capsules twice daily. Mix licorice root with ginger root into a tea to loosen mucus in the chest. Do not take licorice root therapeutically for more than six weeks.

Precautions: Be moderate in your consumption of licorice root for therapeutic uses. Excessive doses (50 grams daily) may have adverse side effects, such as elevated blood pressure due to sodium retention. Do not take if you have diagnosed high blood pressure, kidney, or liver disease, or if you are pregnant or breastfeeding. Licorice may interfere with several prescription medications, check with your physician before taking licorice.[142]

7. NEEM

- Best known for treatment of skin infections, inflammatory skin conditions, joint pain, and muscle aches. Neem is also known as a nontoxic insecticide.
- *Effects on the body:* Antifungal, antibacterial, antimalarial, detoxifier, blood purifier.

Neem's leaves, seed oil, and bark all contain many healing benefits. Neem oil can be used in shampoo to help fight off head lice. Neem is a gentle detoxifier and can be used with people who want to detoxify from overeating, drug, and alcohol abuse, antibiotics, steroids, or cancer chemotherapy drugs. Neem bark has been traditionally used to clean teeth and is good in toothpastes to fight off cavities and gingivitis.

Taking neem internally: You can purchase neem leaves at a Middle Eastern or Indian spice store. Add leaves to recipes to help reduce toxins in the body. You can find neem powder at a health food store. Add a half a teaspoon of the powder to juice as a detoxifying agent.

Taking neem externally: Make a paste with neem powder and water and apply it to the skin and scalp for athlete's foot, psoriasis, eczema, dandruff, or hair loss.

8. SHATAVARI (INDIAN ASPARAGUS)

- Best known for enhancing immune function and the female reproductive system. It is also effective in improving feminine fertility.
- *Effects on the body:* Cooling, antidiarrhetic, diuretic, antidysenteric, tonic, aphrodisiac, antispasmodic

Known as wild asparagus, shatavari grows in the jungles of India. Shatavari is used to help increase breastmilk production and for problems with fertility. It also helps to increase semen production, has anti-inflammatory properties, and strengthens the immune system for chemotherapy. Shatavari has been used to suppress uterine contractions. It is effective for reducing heartburn, irritable bowel syndrome (IBS), and reducing the symptoms of PMS. Wild asparagus is also effective in treating urethritis or cystitis. For men, who have a history of heartburn and indigestion, shatavari was found to be as effective some pharmaceutical agents.

Taking shatavari: You can take shatavari in both a powder and a tablet form. Add 1/2 to 1 teaspoon of shatavari powder to organic warm milk and brown sugar to aid digestion, otherwise, mix powder with ghee or oil. To treat PMS or menopausal symptoms, you can take 500-milligram capsules twice per day.

9. VALERIAN

- Best known for curing insomnia, inducing sleep, reducing anxiety, and calming an overactive mind. Valerian has also been used to treat muscle spasms and hypertension.
- *Effects on the body:* Natural sedative.

Valerian has been used as a natural sedative for thousands of years. Aromatherapy with valerian essential oil has proved to have a calming effect. According to studies by the NIH, Valerian appears to influence neurochemical activity in the brain by increasing levels of gamma amino-butyric acid (GABA), which is the function of benzodiazepine drugs such as Valium and Ativan.[143] It also appears to increase dopamine and serotonin levels. The FDA considers valerian to be safe and to have minimal to no side effects.[144] That said, due to the drowsiness it causes, you should not drive a vehicle or operate machinery while taking valerian.

Taking valerian: Valerian comes in tablets, capsules and teas. A good dose for inducing sleep is 450-milligrams. You can also get valerian essential oil and use it in an aromatherapy diffuser.

10. WITCH HAZEL

- Best known for healing minor skin injuries, skin and mucosa inflammations, varicose veins, and hemorrhoids.
- *Effects on the body:* astringent, mild antibiotic, antioxidant, anti-inflammatory.

American Indians depended on witch hazel for thousands of years to fight swelling, sores, and infections in the skin. Witch hazel is an astringent, which means it constricts swollen blood vessels and therefore makes it one of the best acne medicines. Witch hazel is also effective in reducing insect bites, blisters, and poison ivy inflammation. Its antioxidant properties help prevent skin cell damage and signs of aging.

Taking witch hazel externally: Witch hazel can be applied as an ointment, cream, gel, or suppository. It is also prepared in liquid form in a water or alcohol compound. Liquid witch hazel is the most economical form of the herb, costing around $2.50 per bottle, and can be applied to the skin with a cotton ball.

For acne, apply witch hazel several times per day. You can increase the effectiveness of witch hazel as an acne treatment by combining it with organic apple cider vinegar. You can also mix it with tea tree oil and organic coconut oil.

For hemorrhoids, apply witch hazel water using a cotton pad to the sore area six to eight times per day.

For insect bites, rub witch hazel cream to prevent irritation and inflammation.

Taking witch hazel internally: Witch hazel tea can be used as a mouthwash or for a sore throat.

Ten Healing Oils

The skin is the largest organ in the body, comprising about sixteen percent of your body weight with a total area of about 20 square feet. It's also the fastest growing organ. The epidermis, the top layer of skin, is reproduced every thirty days. And your skin is porous, so it absorbs everything you put on it – for better and for worse. Ultimately, it's a great way to administer herbal medicine. But you must also be careful what you are putting on your skin, for any chemical you put on your skin makes its way to your blood and lymphatic system. So when you choose oils, make sure they're certified organic.

I've divided the healing oils into two categories: carrier oils and herbal oils. The carrier oils can be used therapeutically by themselves and have many healing benefits. Herbal oils, on the other hand, tend to be more expensive and have some of the qualities that are enhanced with carrier oils, so mixing the two makes a little go a long way and speeds up healing.

CARRIER OILS

1. SWEET ALMOND OIL

- Best known for its gentleness and for its high levels of the skin protecting vitamin E.
- ***Effects on the body:*** Antioxidant, anti-inflammatory.

The name "sweet almond oil" separates it from bitter almond oil, which can be toxic. Sweet almond oil comes from edible almonds. Almond oil is mildly hypoallergenic and can be safely applied to everyone, even babies. As such, it's the best massage oil for infants. Almond oil is rich in vitamins A, B-Complex, and E, and in minerals like calcium, magnesium, and zinc.

The light texture of almond oil makes it useful in cleansing the skin and removing makeup. You can use almond oil on chaffed skin, and to treat skin rashes. There is no need to mix the oil with anything else – just apply it to the skin and allow it to absorb. Rubbing warm almond oil on the scalp can prevent hair loss. Almond oil also nourishes hair and nails. The antioxidants in almond oil make it great for anti-aging, and thanks to its gentle and hypoallergenic properties, it is good to put on skin irritated with eczema and psoriasis. Make sure you purchase the highest-grade organic sweet almond oil you can find.

Taking sweet almond oil: You can safely take sweet almond oil both internally and externally. External use is for the skin and as a carrier-oil for other essential oils. Internal use can reduce the risk of heart disease and regulate cholesterol levels. For internal therapeutic use, take one to four tablespoons of warmed sweet almond oil.

Precautions: Do not use almond oil if you have a nut allergy.

2. COCONUT OIL

- Best known for a multitude of purposes from a natural sunscreen to improving digestion.
- *Effects on the body:* Cooling, antioxidant, anti-aging, anti-microbial, anti-fungal, antibacterial, anti-inflammatory.

Coconut oil is one of the most versatile oils on the planet. A high-grade organic coconut oil has an aroma of coconut, but is mild enough to work well as a carrier-oil. When coconut oil is warmed, it is a clear liquid, and when it's cold, it's white. Coconut oil does not oxidize at high temperatures and therefore is great for cooking, as well as in smoothies, as a natural coffee creamer, and to replace butter.

For the skin, coconut oil is a great moisturizer, a good sun block with natural SPF, and can be used as a lip balm. In India, coconut oil has been used to keep hair from turning white and to prevent hair loss. Coconut oil can be used to heal wounds, like you would use antibacterial ointment. You can also use coconut oil as a face wash. Add a few drops of tea tree oil to coconut oil to help with acne prone skin. It's also for massage and can be used as a shaving cream.

Taking coconut oil: To get the maximum benefits of all the medicinal qualities in coconut oil, it is imperative to only get organic, unrefined, virgin coconut oil. Look for oils that have been through the "wet-milling" process and made out of fresh coconut meat. Never use coconut oil that has been hydrogenated or partially hydrogenated, for these are harmful to your health.[145]

3. SESAME OIL

- Best known for nourishing the skin and hair and for gently detoxifying the body.
- *Effects on the body:* Heating, anti-inflammatory, antioxidant, antibacterial, antiviral, emollient.

Sesame oil has been used for over 3,000 years in India as a carrier-oil for Ayurvedic medicine, as well as in China for other medicinal uses. There are two types of sesame oil: light oil from raw sesame seeds, and dark oil from toasted seeds. For therapeutic application, use only light organic sesame oil. In Ayurvedic medicine, sesame oil is used in 90% of herbal-based remedies and is known to strengthen and detoxify the body. It's a great carrier-oil especially in the cooler months of the year. Sesame oil contains the minerals magnesium, copper, zinc, and calcium, and is therefore good for bone growth. Sesame oil can also boost your mood and lower anxiety and depression thanks to its high content of the amino acid tyrosine (tyrosine is related to the release of serotonin in the brain, the mood-lifting hormone).[146]

Taking sesame oil: You can take sesame oil internally and externally. Use it for massages, for oil pulling (as a mouthwash), and for nasal lubrication in drier seasons. It's also a great lubricant for sexual intimacy and for vaginal dryness in menopausal women. For thousands of years, Ayurvedic medicine has also used sesame oil in herbal enemas to help detoxify the colon.

HERBAL OILS

The following oils can be mixed safely and easily with any of the carrier oils.

4. CASTOR OIL

- Best known for alleviating constipation, treating skin infections, and boosting immunity.
- *Effects on the body:* Anti-microbial, antibacterial, antiviral, anti-fungal, anti-inflammatory, analgesic, purgative

Used for thousands of years, castor oil is derived from the castor plant. The oil is squeezed from the castor seeds or beans, which date all the way back to Egyptian tombs from 4,000 B.C.E. Castor oil is a common remedy in Ayurvedic medicine, and for centuries, grandmothers and mothers were known to give children castor oil to boost their immune systems.[147] It's actually proven that castor oil increases white blood cells and the count of T-11 cells, which are a type of specialized white blood cell.[148]

Castor oil is a strong purgative (or laxative) and can clear the colon due to *ricinoleic acid*, the fatty acid that makes up 90% of the oil. One of the most beneficial properties of castor oil is its ability to improve lymphatic drainage. It also has the capacity to balance hormones and improve circulation. Castor oil is well known for inducing labor, especially in women who are past their due date. It also helps alleviate the symptoms and inflammation from arthritis.

Taking castor oil internally: For constipation, take 1 to 2 teaspoons on an empty stomach. You will see results in about 2-8 hours, so it's best to take it in the early morning. As daily maintenance, take one teaspoon daily.

Taking castor oil externally: Apply the oil directly to the skin for corns and skin wounds. Mix it with sesame or coconut oil to use as an acne face wash, then massage these oils into the face and rinse with water. To stimulate hair growth, massage castor oil into your scalp and hair, wrap your scalp with plastic wrap, and put on a shower cap. Keep the castor oil in your hair for several hours – or overnight – and then wash it out. For lymphatic drainage and uterine health, see chapter seven on castor oil packs.

Precautions: While taking castor oil is relatively safe, according to the FDA, it can cause cramping or diarrhea. Never take castor oil during pregnancy unless post-term or using it to induce labor at term. Castor oil will also permanently stain clothing and towels, so make sure you're careful when applying externally.

5. Clove Oil

- Best known for use in dentistry to treat pain, inflammation, and halitosis.
- *Effects on the body:* Warming, anti-inflammatory, antioxidant, antibacterial, antifungal, analgesic, antiseptic, aphrodisiac.

Cloves and clove oil have been used for thousands of years in China and are common components of homeopathic medicine. Clove oil contains high levels of manganese, as well as potassium, magnesium, and calcium. Its antibacterial properties are good for fighting the bacteria that cause acne.

Taking clove oil: Clove oil is potent and should be mixed with a carrier oil before application. A few drops of clove oil mixed with coconut oil and tea tree oil can be used to spot-treat acne, or as an acne wash. You can also mix a few drops of clove oil in raw honey to apply to blemishes. Leave the mixture on for an hour or two then wash the mixture off with water. Mix clove oil with tea tree oil and a carrier oil to make a great mouthwash; you can swish with a few drops for one minute, then spit. Clove oil is also high in antioxidants and can protect you against colds and the flu. If you feel you've been exposed to these viruses, rub your neck and chest with a mix of clove oil and coconut oil and leave it on. Clove oil also has a numbing effect and you can use it for teething babies by rubbing a diluted mix of clove oil with a carrier-oil on baby's gums.

6. Eucalyptus Oil

- Best known for helping with the common cold and infections of the respiratory tract.
- *Effects on the body:* Anti-inflammatory, antibiotic, antiseptic, antispasmodic, decongestant

Native to Australia, the leaves of the eucalyptus tree were used by aboriginal peoples to heal wounds. You can use eucalyptus oil plus a carrier oil to heal the scalp and fight off lice. Eucalyptus oil is also a great addition to home cleaning products: it helps remove odors, it kills mold, and it has anti-microbial properties. Make a homemade chest rub for asthma, bronchitis, pneumonia, and Chronic Obstructive Pulmonary Disease (COPD) by mixing eucalyptus oil, peppermint oil, and coconut oil.

Taking eucalyptus oil: You can apply eucalyptus oil externally or as a vapor inhalation. To take it internally, place 3-6 drops in a cup of warm water several times per day until symptoms subside. To apply it externally, mix a few drops with a carrier-oil and rub on the affected area. To ingest it as a vapor, place 2-3 drops in hot water and inhale the steam.

Precautions: Keep doses of eucalyptus oil to a minimum and always dilute before use. Eucalyptus is extremely toxic if ingested, so keep out of the reach of children.[149] Since eucalyptus can lower blood sugar, consult with your physician if you're taking diabetic medications.

7. LAVENDER OIL

- Best known for alleviating restlessness, anxiety, insomnia, loss of appetite, nerves, and stomach complaints.
- *Effects on the body:* Anti-bacterial, anti-fungal, anti-depressant, anti-inflammatory, antimicrobial, antiseptic

Native to the Mediterranean, lavender goes back to the early days of civilization. Evidence shows that the Egyptians used lavender oil in the mummification process. In the Bible, lavender is mentioned in the Old Testament book, the Song of Solomon. The word lavender comes from the Latin word *lavare*, which means "to wash". This name was appropriate since the Romans used lavender to scent their baths, beds, clothes, and hair. Lavender is a member of the mint family and has been used for centuries for food preparation and medicinal purposes. It has also been traditionally used as an insect repellent. Many studies show that lavender essential oil can be beneficial for medical conditions such as insomnia, alopecia (hair loss), anxiety, stress, and postoperative pain.[150]

Taking lavender oil internally: Place 1-4 drops on a sugar cube. Tea can be made with organic dried lavender flowers to help ease anxiety and depression.

Taking lavender oil externally: You can fill lavender essential oil in a roll-on container and apply it to your wrists or temples to help alleviate migraines and headaches, as well as to improve concentration. To use lavender oil in the bath, mix a few drops first with an emulsifier such as cream, milk, or honey and then add the mixture to your bath water. New moms can take sitz baths (a warm shallow bath that cleanses the perineum) with lavender to soothe irritated tissue after childbirth. For coughs and bronchitis, rub some lavender oil on your chest. Lavender can also be added to a homemade mouthwash to help heal gums.

8. PEPPERMINT OIL

- Best known for alleviating cramps of the upper gastrointestinal tract and the biliary ducts. Good for soothing irritable colon and healing the upper respiratory tract.
- *Effects on the body:* Cooling, antifungal, anti-inflammatory, anti-microbial, antiseptic, carminative.

Peppermint oil has many medical uses. Its calming effect can ease nausea, especially after chemotherapy treatments, and as it is a natural pain reliever, it can help soothe sore muscles. Keep a small bottle of peppermint oil with you and sniff it when you're feeling fatigued or need to improve your concentration. Smelling peppermint oil also helps people with ADD or ADHD to focus. Peppermint oil can be added to shampoo to strengthen and thicken hair, or it can be mixed with coconut oil to soothe your skin after sunburn. It has also been traditionally used in dentistry and is often added to toothpastes to freshen breath and fight off bacteria.

Taking peppermint oil: Peppermint oil can be taken internally, externally, or as a vapor. For gastrointestinal problems, take 6-12 drops of peppermint oil daily. For skin problems, rub a few drops on the affected area. For respiratory problems associated with the common cold or cough, add 3-4 drops in hot water and inhale.

9. TAMANU OIL

- Best known for treating hair and healing skin, especially fading scars.
- *Effects on the body:* Anti-aging, antibiotic, anti-inflammatory, antioxidant, anticancer, emollient, skin tonic, vulnerary.

Native to tropical Southeast Asia, tamanu oil comes from the fruit nut of a tamanu tree. The nuts used for the oil are only gathered once they fall off the tree, making it an environmentally friendly cultivation process. Tamanu oil works wonders for skin irritations, rashes, bruises, scars, stretch marks, and wrinkles. In fact, I have personal healing experience with tamanu oil: I once bought some to mix with other oils for my son's acne problem, then decided to use it on my face nightly as well. Prior to this, I had a bump on my face near my eye for over three years. It started out as a pimple, but had turned into a callus. When I went to my doctor, he suggested I used a corn Band-Aid with acidic solution in it. I was nervous about using a strong product so close to my eye. But after using the tamanu oil nightly for about 30 days, I noticed that the bump had completely disappeared. It was amazing. I was sold on the power of tamanu oil.

Tamanu oil works by penetrating all three layers of the skin: the epidermis, dermis, and hypodermis. In all my research to date, tamanu oil is the best anti-aging oil I have come across. Unfortunately, the oil itself is a little pricey – about $16 for three fluid ounces – but it's well worth it. My favorite brand, Leia Naturals, can easily be found on Amazon.

Taking tamanu oil: Tamanu oil is for external use only. It can be mixed with carrier and essential herbal oils. You can apply tamanu oil directly to an affected area. For acne treatment, you can mix a little tamanu oil with coconut oil and add a few drops of tea tree oil, lavender oil, and clove oil.

10. TEA TREE OIL

- Best known for treatment of fungal skin infections, minor burns, candida infections, and for dental hygiene.
- *Effects on the body:* Cooling, antiseptic, antifungal, antibacterial.

Historically, tea tree oil was used as an antiseptic to reduce surgical infections. The essential oil of the tea tree leaves can be used to treat many skin conditions. You can apply tea tree oil to your head with shampoo for dandruff, as a suppository diluted with a carrier-oil for vaginal yeast infections, or as part of a mouthwash for oral candida infections. Tea tree oil is also active against the bacteria in acne and can be effective in treating blemishes. You can add tea tree oil to diaper creams to treat diaper rash.

Taking tea tree oil: Tea tree oil is safe to use externally and can be applied directly to the skin. Ten percent tea tree oil cream can also be used to reduce or eliminate athlete's foot.

Precautions: Less than ten percent of people may have skin sensitivity to tea tree oil.

INTEGRATING HERBS INTO YOUR HEALTHY LIFESTYLE

While all these herbs will enhance your health, you still need to take precautions as you begin to integrate them into your diet and lifestyle. If you have a prior medical condition and are taking prescription medications, consult with your healthcare practitioner before adding in herbal remedies. Most prescription medications are made with the active ingredients already in plants, therefore adding an herbal remedy can either magnify or nullify the effects of the medicine, which can be dangerous. This is important to remember, even when only adding therapeutic doses of kitchen herbs to your life.

When using herbs as preventive medicine, it's best to incorporate only one for a few weeks at first to see how your body reacts. Or, if you're using a formula of several herbs for a certain ailment, try not to add or change anything else about the formula until you're sure you're not experiencing any side effects.

Most of all use your common sense. If something doesn't feel right, don't take it. As with any therapeutic substance, start small and increase dosage as needed. With practice, you'll become more sensitive to your body and understand what herbal remedies work best for you.

CHAPTER 7

DETOXIFY YOUR BODY

No matter how much it gets abused, the body can restore balance. The first rule is to stop interfering with nature. - Dr. Deepak Chopra

DETOXIFICATION OF THE BODY is not something we often think about in the Western world. Health magazines and blogs often mention a body detox, but with no real direction on how to detoxify the body on a regular basis. But a detox program will help you get rid of toxins, such as heavy metals, pollutants, excess minerals, and fats that can build up in bodily tissue. Ayurvedic medicine largely focuses on detoxification. The Ayurvedic program *panchakarma* – or "five actions" – has been used for thousands of years and is still used in spa and wellness programs throughout India.

When you use anything, it needs regular maintenance and cleaning. Several months ago, while using my favorite vacuum cleaner, I noticed my vacuum wasn't picking up dirt as effectively as usual. I cleaned out the portable canister and emptied it frequently, then bought a new filter. But it still wasn't working as it had before. Finally, after much frustration, I unplugged the hose and discovered that there was a blockage. All of the other things I had done to maintain the vacuum didn't work because the main system was clogged. Once

I removed all the debris from that hose, the vacuum worked even better than before.

The same goes for your body. You can give it plenty of water, feed it organic food, and take loads of vitamins. But if you don't remove the debris, at least a couple of times per year, your body can't work as well as it should.

The idea of doing a detox is to give your body space to relax and repair. When you're constantly overeating or eating the wrong kinds of food and drink, the body has to work extra hard at eliminating toxins. There are many different kinds of detox diets you can do, but my advice is to not go overboard. Just because something is good for you doesn't mean that more is better. I once had a client so addicted to colon cleansing that it created a lot of health problems for her. She couldn't eat, could not gain weight, and had a lot of anxiety. But when I mentioned that she might need to taper off the colon cleansing, she would have none of it. It can be easy to let a detox become as much of an addiction or unhealthy behavioral pattern as abusing food.

What Are Toxins?

Toxins are substances that your body cannot digest and integrate into healthy cells. They are everywhere in food and in the environment, and obviously, some toxins are more avoidable than others. The toxins your body ingests from conventional or non-organic food come from pesticides and herbicides. But in addition to pesticides and herbicides, you might also be consuming antibiotics and growth hormones. Plastics found in water bottles, food containers, and cookware contain harmful chemicals such as bisphenol A (BPA) and perfluorooctanoic acid (PFOA) that can cause cardiovascular disease. Pollutants in the air from chemical plants and cars are toxins. Then, there are toxins in municipal water supplies from rusty pipes or excreted pharmaceuticals. Most household and personal care products contain hundreds of harmful chemicals and can therefore create toxins in your body.

Then there are classic lifestyle choices that bring toxins to the body, such as alcohol, drug, and tobacco use. Even some prescription drugs can be considered toxic. Excess weight and stress are two other lifestyle choices that cause stored toxins in the body.

Given this list, you might be inclined to forget all about trying to detoxify your body. Let me assure you that detoxifying is one solution to improving your health, but not the whole solution. The whole solution includes changing your diet and way of living. Yo-yo detoxification – like yo-yo dieting – won't work. I know people who consistently eat horrible stuff and abuse their bodies by taking drugs or drinking alcohol, then go on a three-day juice fast to try and rectify the damage. In cases like these, the occasional juice fast might be the thing keeping you alive, but not by any means keeping you healthy.

ELIMINATE UNHEALTHY FOOD AND DRINK

You don't need fancy detox products, powders, or pills to improve your health. You need a gentle form of detoxification to encourage the body to work at its best. Then you need to ensure your daily health by making better choices. If you want to live in optimal health and avoid excessive visits to the doctor, put all chances on your side and eliminate unhealthy food and drink from your life.

1. Eliminate processed food.
You don't need processed food. It may taste good for about five seconds, but think about what it does to your body. Most processed food includes high fructose corn syrup and hydrogenated fats, both of which are cancer-making factories. Even natural and organic processed foods bring in way too many calories, offer too much sodium, and are generally devoid of the antioxidants and phytochemicals your body needs to fight off disease. If you need to snack, grab

a piece of organic fruit, cut up raw vegetables, munch on raw nuts and seeds, or eat some dried organic fruit. Think about why you're snacking in the first place. Are you not eating enough at mealtimes? Are you bored or stressed? Once you realize why you're snacking you can fill the void with a healthier habit or healthier food.

2. Throw out leftovers after twenty-four hours.

Food begins to decompose quickly after it's picked or slaughtered. When you cook food, you create a chemical change. The nutrients begin to leave the food, and you're left with calories but not vital vitamins and minerals. For example, when you cut into an apple, it starts to turn brown immediately as it starts to oxidize and lose its nutrients. To maximize your health, eat fresh fruits and vegetables and throw away food that has been in the fridge for too long.

3. Chuck frozen food.

For the same reason you would throw out leftovers, frozen food quickly loses its nutrients. The act of freezing does preserve nutrients a little longer as in the case of flash-frozen vegetables. But one thing you want to think about is the nutritional value of food that's frozen for a long period of time, for example over four to six months. While the frozen food might still be edible, it won't necessarily be as nutritious as fresh food.

4. Check your cooking oils.

Oils go rancid fairly quickly. I would recommend using only extra virgin organic olive oil, cold-pressed organic coconut oil, organic sesame oil, and organic expeller-pressed canola oil. Extra virgin olive oil is similar to a cold-pressed fruit juice in that it's very fresh. Store your opened olive oil away from heat sources, light, and use it up within a couple of months. Cold-pressed pure coconut oil will last longer since it has slower oxidation. You can keep coconut oil on a shelf for up to twenty-four months as long as crumbs or food do not contaminate it.

Organic sesame oil can be stored on the shelf for six months once it's opened, but preserves well if you put it in the refrigerator, too. And if you use canola oil as a neutral-tasting oil for cooking, make sure it's organic and expeller-pressed. The high heating process in the cheaper brands can destabilize the healthy fats and make them unhealthy. Opened expeller-pressed canola oil will last for up to one year.

5. Stay away from artificial sweeteners, artificially-colored foods, and chemical substitutes.

Products like Coffee-Mate are one of the worst things you could possibly ingest. Your body has a hard time knowing what to do with artificial chemical substances. Artificial sweeteners trick the body into releasing dopamine by offering a sweet taste without the calories. But because the calories don't come, the body still craves the high caloric sweet foods and incites you to eat even more.[151]

6. Eliminate soda, sports drinks, alcohol, refined sugar, and bleached and enriched flour.

Consuming these quick sugar foods can quickly lead to disease. As far as liquids go, the only thing your body needs is water. Soda and sports drinks are silent killers; they're full of sugar, caffeine, high-fructose corn syrup, and artificial colors. And there are more studies confirming alcohol's harmfulness to the body than its potential benefits. In fact, alcohol-related injuries and diseases are the third leading preventable cause of death annually in the United States.[152]

Type 2 diabetes has become our number one health problem in the US, with 30.3 million Americans diagnosed with diabetes and 84.1 million Americans over the age of 18 with pre-diabetes as of 2015.[153] Eliminating quick sources of sugar is one way to reverse this disease.

Many food sources in the American diet contain refined sugar and enriched white flour. Try to eliminate both.

7. Run away from deep-fried foods.

Even though French fries are an all-time American favorite, the oils used in fast food and restaurant-style fried foods clog your arteries and can cause diseases like strokes, heart attacks, diabetes, and Alzheimer's. In fact, one 25-year study conducted by the Department of Nutrition at the Harvard School of Public Health found that participants who ate fried foods 4-6 times per week had a 39% increased risk for heart disease and type 2 diabetes.[154] The oils from fried foods aren't able to break down properly in the body. So instead, they remain in the kidneys, liver, intestines, prostate, and colon for a long time. Try a healthier version of your favorite fried food. Use organic extra virgin olive oil for your freshly-cut organic potatoes with the skin on or for your homemade organi c fried chicken, and eat these things only on occasion.

8. Ditch tap water – and even most bottled water.

It's important for your health to drink at least half of your body weight in ounces of water daily. For example, if you weight 150 pounds, strive to drink 75 ounces of water daily. But tap water contains a lot of impurities and harsh chemicals. And water from plastic bottles can contain harmful chemicals that have been leached into the water from the plastic.

So how will you know which water to drink? When making your choice, there are three types of water you might want to consider...

1. **Artisan water**: Artisan water is bottled at the source such as Evian, Vittel, or Fiji water. These waters are from natural springs and contain natural-occurring minerals. Be wary of cheaper bottled water with pictures of mountains and nature.

If you read the label closely, many of these brands are not spring water, but purified tap water. On the flip side, spring water can contain contaminants such as coliform, arsenic, and phthalates.

2. **Distilled water**: Water is distilled by boiling it and capturing the steam. The resulting steam is free from impurities like metals and contaminants, but this process also removes helpful minerals. Normally your body gets about 15% of its necessary calcium and magnesium from water, which you can still get through food or mineral supplements. On the positive side, distilled water can effectively flush toxins from your body, and you can be certain that all pesticides, herbicides, and chemicals have been removed from distilled the water.

3. **Reverse osmosis water:** Like distilled water, reverse osmosis water ensures purity through an interesting process of filtration. Water flows naturally toward other water with a greater amount of salt. In the reverse osmosis process, pressure is applied to the more salinated water to push it through a semipermeable filter (like a screen door) and remove dissolved salts, minerals, bacteria, and other organic and inorganic solids.[155] Reverse osmosis water has the same purity as distilled water but has the extra step of eliminating fluoride and residual chemicals from prescription medications like birth control pills and anti-depressants that made their way into water supplies through toilet flushing.

Since pesticides, herbicides, antibiotics, and heavy metals are much more dangerous to your health than a lack of magnesium and calcium that you can get mostly through food, I would suggest imbibing a hybrid between distilled and reverse osmosis water with the occasional bottle of high-grade spring water. However, for your detox program, whether it lasts three days or ten days, I would encourage you to drink only distilled or reverse osmosis water.

9. Eliminate street drugs and tobacco, and reduce or eliminate over-the-counter pills and unnecessary prescription pills.

Tobacco use has no place in a healthy lifestyle, and that includes recent fads like vaping and hookah smoking. Nicotine, whether in the form of tobacco or the chemical components found in e-cigarettes, is harmful to your health; it's highly addictive and creates a compulsive behavior associated with other addictive substances. It also causes inflammation in lung tissue and has an effect on the lungs similar to that of smoking.[156]

Street drugs also do not belong in a healthy lifestyle. When you suddenly stop drugs taking drugs like alcohol, heroin, anti-anxiety medications (Xanax, Ativan), antidepressants, or pain killing opioids (Vicodin, Dilaudid), you can experience extreme withdrawal symptoms including tremors, grand mal seizures, or possibly cardiac arrest. It's best to go into a detox program at your local hospital or rehab center to get off of these drugs under medical supervision. If you suffer from addiction to substances, there are many places you can go to for help. Alcoholics Anonymous and Narcotics Anonymous meetings are free. These groups exist virtually everywhere in the world and have meetings several times a day, every day. To find a meeting in your area, go to aa.org or na.org.

Over-the-counter pills can be just as harmful to your health as some prescription medications. Many nighttime cold medications or sleeping medications are not only highly addictive, but can also interrupt normal sleep patterns. Even acetaminophen (the drug in Tylenol) can do severe damage to your liver when taken in high doses or over the long term, and can be fatal when taken with alcohol.

What are non-necessary prescription medications? Sleep meds heartburn medication are prime examples of these. As you begin changing your lifestyle by eating better, exercising, doing meditation, and breathing more, you'll be able to handle everyday life better and will naturally improve these processes. There are many natural ways you can ensure a restful sleep without taking sleep medications. For better sleep, you can put an essential oil diffuser in your bedroom and add organic lavender essential oil to the diffuser at night. You can make sure all of the lights are off, turn off all electronic devices, and make sure these devices away from the bed. You can also get to bed between the hours of ten and ten-thirty in the evening to ensure you're catching your body's natural sleep hormones. The same goes for indigestion. If you go back to chapter six, you can see how to use fennel, fenugreek, and cardamom to lower the natural acidity in your body. As you shift away from eating processed and fried foods, your stomach will naturally heal.

Eat Foods High in Antioxidants and Phytonutrients

Once you've cut out all of things that are harming your body, you can shield your body against attack by giving it healing weapons. An easy and healthy way to help your body is by eating foods with plenty of antioxidants and phytonutrients.

But first, what are antioxidants and why do we need them? Antioxidants are free radical scavengers. Free radicals are unstable atoms or molecules that have lost an electron and try to steal one from healthy atoms or molecules. Antioxidants help fight against oxidation, a normal chemical reaction that creates free radicals when a material is combined with oxygen. You can see the oxidation process when you cut into a fruit or vegetable and it begins to turn brown. The rust on your car is also the result of oxidation. When an atom is oxidized, it loses electrons and becomes unstable. As these atoms or groups of atoms lose electrons, they go around to healthy atoms and try to steal electrons thereby destabilizing them too. Free radicals are produced during the normal cellular process, but are also formed when we're exposed to environmental pollutants, alcohol, tobacco, and by eating an unhealthy diet. Our bodies produce a certain amount of antioxidants to help stabilize these free radicals, but over time, they cannot handle large amounts of oxidative stress. An overload of free radicals can cause illnesses such as cancer, heart disease, and Alzheimer's disease. Antioxidants stabilize free radicals and can therefore improve your health.

A phytochemical – or phytonutrient – is a chemical naturally found in plants that helps your body defend against disease. Examples of phytonutrients include lycopene (found in tomatoes, pink grapefruit, red peppers and watermelon) or lutein (found in collard greens, kale, spinach, broccoli, and Brussels sprouts). Phytochemicals help the plant fight against invaders, such as insects or harsh weather conditions. For example: what happens when you cut into an onion? A chemical called sulfide is secreted into the air and makes your eyes water. This is an example of a phytochemi cal designed to try and protect the onion. As such, when we eat these plants, the same phytochemicals help our bodies fight off infection and diseases.

Plants that have to fight harder for their survival produce greater amounts of phytochemicals. Organically-grown plants have larger amounts of phytochemicals than plants sprayed with pesticides and herbicides. Eating whole plant foods high in antioxidants and phytonutrients is the best way you can assimilate them into your body.

Each color fruit and vegetable brings a different variety of support for the body. Different antioxidants and phytochemicals protect against different diseases. For example, the phytochemical mentioned above, lutein, is good for eye health, cancer, and heart health. When choosing what plant foods to eat, select a variety of colors to maximize your healing potential: for example, when you're on your detox diet, select red foods in particular, such as cranberries, raspberries, red cherries, beets, and tea made from manjistha root. Red vegetables and fruits contain phytochemicals that are blood purifiers and liver cleansers.[157] Other examples of natural colors in food and their phytochemicals are...

- Green vegetables provide carotenoids, indoles, isothiocyanates, and glucosinolates, which may inhibit cancer cell growth.
- Orange fruits and vegetables provide beta-carotene and lutein, which may inhibit cancer growth and improve immune function.
- Dark blue and purple fruits and vegetables provide polyphenols, which may prevent cancer formation and prevent inflammation.[158]

THE LYMPHATIC SYSTEM

The bodily system mainly responsible for detoxifying the body is the lymphatic system. For the most part, it's a system that not many people are aware of or talk about until something in it goes wrong. How often do you hear someone talking about their spleen or thymus gland? Do you even know what these are and what they're designed to do?

Only second in importance to your circulatory system, the lymphatic system is comprised of tissues and organs that help the body get rid of toxins, pathogens, waste, and other unwanted materials. This system transports lymph, a colorless fluid that contains white blood cells, throughout the body. Lymph cannot travel on its own, as it has very little pressure and counts on the pressure from muscles to circulate. Therefore, any movement you make, such as deep breathing, walking, or other forms of exercise will help move this lymph through the lymphatic vessels. As the lymph is carried through the lymphatic system, it's cleansed and pathogens are removed so the lymph can return to the circulatory system.

Breaking Down the Lymphatic System

What follows is a basic explanation of the lymphatic system. It is important for you to understand how this system operates in order to appreciate its importance in your overall health.

Lymphatic Vessels and Lymph Nodes

The lymphatic vessels are where lymph is carried. They are similar to the veins and capillaries in the circulatory system. Lymph itself is fluid that leaks out of the circulatory system. Lymph nodes are connected to lymphatic vessels where the lymph is first filtered. The lymph node's job is to trap bacteria, viruses, cancer cells, and other unwanted material and make sure they're efficiently eliminated from the body. Once the lymph travels through the lymph nodes, it goes to the larger lymphatic vessels. There are hundreds of lymph nodes in the body, most of them deep within the body close to the lungs and heart, and others are closer to the surface of the skin such as under the arms and in the area of the groin.

Lymphatic Capillaries

Lymphatic capillaries are the vessels where lymph travels. These capillaries are located within the circulatory system and are designed to catch the fluid that fails to return to the circulatory system and therefore becomes lymph. Once captured, the lymph is filtered and cleaned through the lymph nodes before it returns to the circulatory system.

Lymphatic Vessels

Lymphatic vessels closely resemble veins, but instead of red blood cells, these vessels contain lymphocytes, a type of white blood cell. Large lymphatic vessels will combine together to form lymphatic trunks where lymph drains into the two lymph ducts which in turn return lymph to the blood.

Bone Marrow

Bone marrow is the spongy tissue inside of some of the bones including the hip and thigh bones. It produces 200 billion new red blood cells per day as well as white blood cells and blood platelets. Lymphocytes, immature white blood cells, begin their lives in bone marrow and the B-lymphocytes mature there. A B-lymphocyte cell must be able to recognize antigens and mount an immune response.

Thymus Gland

The thymus gland is a small organ at the center of the chest above the heart. This organ is most important in childhood through the end of puberty and functions as an endocrine and lymphatic organ. It's responsible for holding lymphocytes until they are mature and can turn into T-lymphocytes for the immune system. T-lymphocytes or T cells are responsible for directly attacking foreign substances such as bacteria, viruses, or other foreign tissues, for increasing the function of B-lymphocytes, and for producing cytokines that turn on other T cells.

Lymphoid Nodules

Lymphoid nodules are concentrations of mature lymphocytes, and are mostly composed of B-lymphocytes. After lymphocytes mature, they leave their primary site of maturation (bone marrow or thymus gland) and go out into the body to find other mature lymphocytes. They will then accumulate in various locations, such as the small intestine, to be able to quickly and effectively encounter pathogens and mount an immune response.

Spleen

The spleen is the largest lymphatic organ in the body and is situated on the left side of your body right above the kidney. It has two functions: the cleaning, destruction, and removal of red blood cells, and producing white blood cells for the lymphatic system. The spleen is divided into two sections: the white pulp section and the red pulp section. Its lymphatic function is found in the white pulp section where it produces and matures white blood cells.

Tonsils and Adenoids

Tonsils are clusters of lymphoid nodules. Three sets of tonsils exist in the body, one of which is located in the pharynx (in the back of the throat) and called *palatine tonsils*. The location of these tonsils is perfect for detecting pathogens entering the mouth and nose. *Lingual tonsils* are located on the lateral borders of the tongue and are much smaller. Finally, *pharyngeal tonsils*, or commonly known as adenoids, are positioned higher in the pharynx.

Peyer's Patches

Peyer's patches are small masses of lymphoid nodules located in the final portion of the small intestine, the *ileum*. They monitor intestinal bacteria and prevent the growth of pathogenic bacteria in the intestines.

STIMULATING THE LYMPHATIC SYSTEM

As I mentioned, the lymphatic system doesn't operate with the same kind of pressure as the circulatory system. Therefore, lymph has a hard time moving on its own and counts on your bodily movement to circulate throughout the lymphatic vessels. Here are some of the ways you can help your lymphatic system detoxify your body and improve immune function...

1. Practice deep breathing.

Full diaphragmatic breathing helps to squeeze muscles and organs and pushes lymph out into the lymphatic vessels. In the next chapter, we'll go over different methods of yoga breathing.

2. Move your body.

Any kind of movement will do. You can walk, run, stretch, vacuum the house, or mow the lawn. Get moving for better health overall.

3. Get massaged.

Many lymphatic vessels lie close to the surface of your skin, especially the top layer, or the dermis. Massage stimulates these vessels and can be helpful in moving lymph. One method of self-administered massage, dry brushing (with raw silk gloves), is an excellent way to stimulate your lymphatic system.

4. Wear loose-fitting clothing.
There are many lymph nodes around the chest and thoracic region. Make sure you're allowing your body to breathe properly by avoiding constricting garments in the upper body.

5. Drink plenty of water.
Lymph is mainly comprised of water. Make sure you're drinking water throughout the day. Fill up a large water bottle at the beginning of the day and finish it by the time you go to bed.

6. Perspire.
In the United States, we live in such a climate-controlled society that we don't have to sweat if we don't want to. But sweating is actually good for you. Sweating helps to detox the body, but it also does so much more. When you sweat, your body releases endorphins, which are your body's natural painkillers. Sweating also causes natural antibiotics to surface to the skin and helps heal cuts or bug bites. You are also inclined to drink more water when you sweat. This not only helps to keep you hydrated, but also flushes out the kidneys.

DETOX GUIDELINES

You don't need a fancy budget or a spa membership to do a detox. There are many ways you can detox at home and without spending a load of cash. Even though methods differ, there are a few similarities you will generally follow. Here are the main three rules of a detox program...

1. Simplify your diet.
During your detox, you want to choose whole foods that are easily digestible, such as clear broth soups, lightly sautéed vegetables, and

simple whole grains like organic basmati brown rice or organic qui-
noa. Reduce your consumption of all proteins, but if you need a little
protein, stick with lentils and beans. For snacks, you can eat fresh,
ripe organic fruit, and soaked almonds with the skin peeled off.

2. Hydrate.

You'll need to drink even more water and caffeine-free beverages.
Detox herbal teas are a good choice. You can also use a juicer to juice
fresh vegetable and fruit juices.

3. Rest.

Your body will require more rest when detoxing. You will feel more
fatigued as your body releases toxins from your organs and fat cells.
Be sure to select a period of time when you have the luxury to take
naps, meditate more, and sleep longer at night.

METHODS OF DETOX

You can find hundreds of different ways to detox online, in books,
and in magazines. It can be difficult to know which one is right for
you. As you select a detox program, think about the key goals for your
detox...

- Your primary goal is to remove toxins, including heavy
  metals, environmental chemicals, pesticides, herbicides,
  antibiotics (from animal food products), alcohol, drugs,
  and fatty deposits from your arteries and other circulatory
  channels.
- You want a detox that is gentle on the body.
- You want a detox that will stimulate the lymphatic system
  and help clean out the colon, liver, bladder, and kidneys.

In doing research for this book, I tried a three-day juice cleanse
from a reputable source. The detox program seemed logical and had
adequate research to back it. It also didn't require me to fast. The
smoothies, juices, and homemade nut milks were designed to keep

me full throughout the day. Everything I drank was fresh, and most were tasty, too. However, my body did not react well to this raw food juice fast. I felt fatigued, depleted of energy, and had headaches. For the first few hours, I attributed the symptoms to caffeine withdrawal, but as the day went on it didn't get any better. I felt nauseated and spent most of the day on the couch. I decided to continue on the second day. But by 11 AM, I had to stop.

If I had honored all the principles in Ayurveda that I've practiced over the years, I wouldn't have attempted it. Ayurveda teaches you to be gentle on the body and also to honor your mind-body type. My main Ayurvedic mind-body type usually doesn't respond well to extreme fasting or cold foods. But I thought that if I tried it, it might make me feel fantastic. It didn't work for me because my body responded with extreme fatigue, shakiness, and brain fog, but I know people who have tried juice fasts and have felt great afterward.

Based upon my experience, here's what I recommend you think about before starting any detox program.

- Do the claims of the detox program sound too good to be true?
- Does the program ask you to eliminate an entire food group, or two, or three?
- Does the program promise tons of weight loss in just a few days?
- Does the program require you to fast for more than a day or two?

Next, it's important to know your body. Know what you can handle and what you can't. For example: I've run two half-marathons. I trained for them and ran them with little to no problems. I know, however, that a half-marathon is probably the most my body can handle. I could attempt a marathon, but I don't think it would be enjoyable or healthy for my body and my body type. I also know that I can't give blood. The first and only time I gave blood, I nearly passed out and was weak for days. The same goes for extreme fasting or with this more recent experience a juice cleanse.

Knowing and honoring your body's limitations doesn't make you weak. Each of us has strengths and weaknesses. Use knowledge of your body to select an appropriate detox program for you. Perhaps you're one of the people who can fast or do juice cleanses with no problem. If it works for you, that's great. But if you're not sure, try to stick to the simple techniques below, along with a simplified diet of whole organic foods for a few days instead.

> **One note of caution:** If you're addicted to alcohol, street drugs, or prescription drugs such as opioids (Vicadin, Oxycontin, etc.), sleeping medication (Ambien, Restoril etc.), and anti-anxiety (Xanax, Ativan, etc.) medication, do not try to detox on your own. It can be dangerous and even deadly to go cold turkey. Instead, work with your doctor to get into a hospital detox program or wean off the prescription pills with medical supervision. If you are pregnant, breastfeeding, undergoing chemotherapy, or are suffering an active virus or bacterial infection, do not under any circumstances start a detox program. You must only detox the body when you're feeling strong and healthy.

EASY AND GENTLE DETOXES

Easy detoxes are little things you can do on a regular basis when you want to take a day to reset your digestive system. Often what happens is we tend to wait until we have the stomach flu or another gastrointestinal illness to purge out the toxins and reset our digestive system. You can opt to do this on your own so you don't have to get sick. Start with the simplified diet and eliminate all processed foods. Select organic whole foods and drink pure water. In addition, you can try the following techniques.

HOT WATER THERAPY

The concept is simple: think about what you do with a greasy pan. You scrub it with dishwashing soap and hot water. If the pan is your veins and arteries, then the grease is the fatty deposits and plaque that pollutes them. Hot water therapy will help loosen the plaque and fat and wash out your system. Drinking hot water also raises your body temperature, which means your body must work hard to bring your temperature back down, thus making your blood pump harder and burn more calories.

To do this, fill a thermos with water hot enough to make tea or coffee. Sip the hot water throughout the day. The effectiveness is in the frequency of drinking and not in the quantity. Aim to take a few sips of hot water every 15 minutes throughout the day. Meanwhile, you will be following the three main rules of a detox program listed in the Detox Guidelines: simplify your diet, drink plenty of water, and rest. If you practice this for a couple of days, you will notice your tongue becomes coated with a sticky white film. These are toxins being released.[159] Use a stainless steel tongue scraper to remove this film. With your tongue scraper in hand, gently squeeze the ends and insert the rounded part into your mouth toward the back of the tongue closest to the uvula. Gently press the tongue scraper down on the tongue as you move it forward toward the tip of the tongue. Repeat this action 7 to 14 times. Normally, you will use a tongue scraper once a day in the morning. But during your detox, you can use it whenever you feel the film on your tongue. My favorite stainless steel tongue scraper is found at Banyanbotanicals.com.

DETOX TEAS

A great homemade detox tea I first learned about at The Chopra Center is a fresh ginger tea. To make this, get some fresh organic ginger and scrape off the peel. Mince the ginger finely. Cut fresh organic lemon wedges and add some organic honey – raw organic honey is even better. Fill a large mug with hot water, add about a tablespoon of the minced ginger, a squeezed lemon wedge, and a teaspoon of honey. Stir well. Cover and let it steep for about 5-10 minutes. Drink the whole thing and eat the ginger bits at the end. Since ginger is rather strong, you can also steep it in more hot water before chewing on the ginger. Drink four to five cups of this homemade ginger tea daily during your detox.

Liver and kidney teas are great for your easy detox, too. In most detox formulas, you will find dandelion root, milk thistle seed, and lemongrass leaf. You should steep these formulas for 5-10 minutes with a lid on, too. When you're ready to drink the tea, squeeze the bag into the cup to get the maximum benefit of the herbs. During your detox, you'll be replacing your normal coffee and tea with these detox tea formulas.

BODY SCRUB WITH GARSHANA GLOVES

The basic principle of detoxing the body includes loosening and dislodging toxins from fat cells and from the entire lymphatic system. One way to do this is to scrub the body vigorously with raw silk gloves. Also known as dry brushing, using raw silk gloves to stimulate and drain the lymphatic system is an easy practice you can do a few times per week.

Try garshana massage on yourself right before your shower so you can use the heat to rinse the skin and continue to release toxins. Put the gloves on and begin rubbing in long strokes from the feet moving upward toward your heart. Massage your entire body. Use long strokes on the long parts of your body and use circular strokes on the stomach and joints. Apply light pressure where your skin is thinner and more pressure where the skin is thick. Massage for about five minutes.

After your garshana massage, take a shower – with hot water at first, then switch to cold after a few minutes. Cycle back and forth a few times from very hot to cold to stimulate your blood circulation, which will further enhance detoxification._

INTERNAL AND EXTERNAL DETOXES

For thousands of years medical systems across the globe have used both internal and external methods of to detoxing. The idea of the internal detox is to loosen and move the toxins inside the body toward its orifices and skin. Then in the external detox, the toxins are drawn closer to the skin and orifices to be purged out.

An internal detox is none other than consuming herbs or special foods to help move toxins through your digestive system. For example, you could eat ground flaxseeds or psyllium husk to help move your bowels and clean out the colon. A simplified diet with an increase of fruits and vegetables can also help move things through the digestive tract. You can also take suppositories via the rectum, or do an herbal enema, such as those prescribed in an Ayurvedic detoxification program.

External detoxes might include herbal oil massages, sweat therapy through saunas or steam rooms, dry brushing, or even herbal masks. Usually, a good detox program will include both internal and external methods.

INTERNAL DETOXES

Besides the teas mentioned earlier in the chapter, you can try one of these during your time of simplified diet...

- Take 1 to 2 tablespoons of ground flaxseeds in your food daily.
- Take 500mg of Triphala tablets2 morning and night.
- Take 2 teaspoons of Chawanprash (Indian gooseberry jam) morning and night. (Do not take Chawanprash if you are diabetic, pre-diabetic, or pregnant.)

---

2 You can find Triphala tablets at www.banyanbotanicals.com

EXTERNAL DETOXES

In this chapter, you've already seen descriptions of tongue scraping and dry brushing. In addition, you can try a self-administered oil massage from Ayurveda and a castor oil pack detox.

Abhyanga Oil Massage

Abhyanga is a traditional oil massage from India and has been performed for thousands of years as one part of a complex detoxification process. You can perform this massage at home with little cost. To see a full demonstration of an abhyanga oil massage go to my YouTube channel:MichelleFondinAuthor.

For your Abhyanga massage, you will need a base oil, such as organic sesame or coconut oil, and an herbal Ayurvedic oil. If you don't know your Ayurvedic mind body type (or dosha), then pick an Ayurvedic herbal oil for a Vata type. You will want to mix 3 tablespoons of your base oil to 1 tablespoon of your herbal oil. Place the oil in a plastic or glass bottle and warm the oil under hot tap water.

Do this massage in your bathroom before a bath or shower. Place a towel on the floor so you don't slip. Get undressed and sit on a stool or the toilet. Pour a little oil in your hands and rub together. You can begin at the soles of your feet rubbing oil into the feet and in between the toes. Move upward circling around the joints and performing long strokes on the legs and arms. Keep adding oil if your hands get dry. When you get to your abdomen, rub in a circular clockwise pattern around the tummy, and in circles around the breasts (if you have them). You can rub the oil into the face and scalp.

The whole massage will take between five to ten minutes. When you're finished, you can take a shower or bath. Be careful stepping into the tub or shower, as you will be slippery! Let warm water run over your body. As your body heats up, the herbal oil will infuse into your pores. You don't need to wash the oil off, but if you prefer to be less oily when you exit the shower, use a light natural soap. The oils will continue to detoxify the body after your massage.

Castor Oil Pack for Detoxification

Use a castor oil pack to help detoxify the area of the abdomen. The heated oil will infuse into the skin and enter the lymphatic system. Castor oil packs are good for non-cancerous uterine fibroids and ovarian cysts. Castor oil also helps detoxify the liver, gallbladder, and helps with inflamed joints.

To Prepare a Castor Oil Pack:

- Gather a bottle of organic castor oil, an organic flannel cloth, a bowl, plastic wrap, an old towel, and a hot water bottle or heating pad.
- Place the flannel cloth into the bowl and pour the organic castor oil until the flannel is saturated.
- Place the old towel on the place where you will be sitting or lying. Make sure you are wearing old clothes that can be stained (castor oil stains permanently on fabric).
- Place the saturated flannel on your abdomen and place the plastic wrap over it to hold it in place. You can also place a thin cloth on top of the plastic.
- Put the hot water bottle or heating pad on top of the plastic wrap.
- Relax fully with the castor pack for at least an hour.
- When you're finished, store your castor oil pack in a Zip-Loc bag in the refrigerator. Pour 1 tablespoon more of the oil with each subsequent use.
- Wash any excess oil off your skin with baking soda and water.

Repeat the castor pack application at least four days per week for four to six weeks while detoxifying the body. And as with any method of detoxification, make sure you're drinking plenty of filtered water.

Conclusion

Since detoxifying the body is a somewhat lesser-known topic in American society, it can be easy to either overlook or take to an extreme. My advice is to give it some thought and set aside two to three days to focus on a light detox before seeing how you feel. Taking a gentle approach to healing is always better than going to extremes. Plus, in order to keep a biannual healthy detox on your agenda, you'll want to have a good memory of your experience. And that can only be accomplished if you ease into your body detox by setting up the conditions for healing and letting your body do the rest.

CHAPTER 8

MOVE YOUR BODY

Life is like riding a bicycle. To keep your balance, you must keep moving. - Albert Einstein

NOT SO LONG AGO, we didn't have to think about movement. It was a natural part of our existence. Most jobs were labor intensive. Travel wasn't as easy as it is today and many relied on walking or biking to work or to the store. Even something as simple as getting up to change the TV channel is long gone. Our sedentary work and lives of convenience have made it so that we must make movement a conscious choice.

After reading the chapter on the necessity of detoxifying the body, hopefully you're convinced that you need to move more. Our human bodies haven't evolved to be sitting for long periods of time. Incorporating movement doesn't have to be complicated. If you a pair of shoes, you can move. Take a short walk after every meal. Vacuum your home for twenty minutes. Take the stairs. Ride a bike to work or park at the back of the parking lot. There are more ways to move than you can probably imagine. But unless you love exercise, I'll bet you're really sick of people telling you to do it, right?

One of the major excuses I hear in my practice comes from people who have been injured, have recently had surgery, or who suffer from a chronic illness. That major excuse is, "I can't exercise or move my body until..." And the object that fills in the blank is usually something like, "until I finish physical therapy" or "until I lose more weight" or "until I start to feel better." But that magic moment doesn't ever seem to come. The way through pain and illness is to start moving your body now, even a little bit. Do anything you can do to move. Program your mind to accept that movement is good for you. Even in hospital beds, nurses have patients move so they don't get bedsores. The more you can circulate your blood, the better your chances of healing. My oldest client is 91 years old. She has severe osteoporosis and a breathing tube in her nose attached to an oxygen tank, but she still does chair yoga with me every other week. Even with all of her aches, pains, and limitations, she moves for 55 minutes straight. If she can do it, you can, too.

A couple of years ago, I had a young female client in her early 20s who told me she had to stop doing yoga because of a condition called adrenal fatigue. Medical science has not found this to be an actual disease, as there is no proof that it exists.[160] In 1998, a naturopath coined this term. The condition is said to be triggered by large amounts of stress setting off the fight-or-flight response; in other words, caused by a classic case of burnout. The theory is that the adrenal glands stop working because of a constant release of cortisol. This young lady, because of the diagnosis, had stopped exercising altogether. She even quit school and work. And when one year later, she decided to join yoga once again, she stopped after two lessons because she said her body was too fragile to handle yoga. She added that she couldn't move at all. I explained to her that by not moving, she was causing her body to be even more fatigued. She didn't believe me. I see this happen all too often.

Disease itself can cause anxiety and depression, which are exacerbated by inactivity. One of the antidotes to these disorders is movement. When you move your body your brain releases serotonin and dopamine, two neurotransmitters that improve your mood and help combat depression.[161] Dopamine also improves your long-term memory, appetite, and helps regulate your sleep cycles. In addition, sustained cardio activity helps your body release endorphins, the feel-good neurotransmitter that is often associated with the "runner's high." Endorphins are known to help with stress and pain relief.[162] So as you can clearly see, your body has a natural mental health pharmacy at its disposal and to access it, all you need to do is get regular exercise.

GIVE YOUR MIND COMPELLING REASONS FOR MOVEMENT

When it comes to change, people are typically motivated one of two ways: either through fear, or through positive motivation. Unfortunately, most people react out of fear, and then motivation comes only later. Fear is a poor motivator, because the feeling of fear will not keep you going long-term. You have to have other compelling reasons to change.

In my teens and early twenties I I smoked off and on. However, when I got my thyroid cancer diagnosis at age twenty-eight, I stopped smoking completely and haven't touched a cigarette since. It was instant motivation based on fear. But if fear was my only motivator, I probably would have smoked the occasional cigarette after a few years. Eventually, however, I came to understand that smoking was bad overall, and moreover that it was a disgusting and horrible habit. I reasoned that if I wanted to guarantee that I would feel great and never get sick again, I couldn't even entertain the idea of smoking.

Whatever reasons compel you to exercise, allow them to motivate you. Perhaps you want to stay away from getting type 2 diabetes like your mom or grandmother. You might want to lose or maintain your weight. Or maybe you want to have more energy or sleep better.

Ideally, you need to aim for at least thirty minutes of cardiovascular exercise per day. You can even break those thirty minutes into two 15-minute increments, but it is best if you have a sustained elevated heart rate for at least twenty minutes at a time. You can achieve this by walking at a brisk pace or doing any other sustained cardio activity. Add in a stretching session at least once a week and weight training at least three times per week. The weight training can be something as simple as taking 12-ounce water bottles in each hand and doing some bicep curls, tricep extensions, extended arm circles for the shoulders, and squats or lunges.

The problem is that we tend to have an all-or-nothing approach. There is no reason why you can't watch a 10-minute YouTube video on arm exercises with dumbbells. You can find many phone apps demonstrating yoga poses, and even some offering full yoga classes. You can go for a walk. You don't need a gym membership or a fancy spa, just yourself and your motivation. You don't have to get cancer or have a heart attack to find your compelling reasons. You can think of them right now. Think of the most disgusting ailment you can dream up, and say to yourself, "I'm going to move my body so I never get that."

When I was young my mom used to tell me all kinds of stories of what it was like to get old. She used to tell me how older women get sagging arms, flabby tummies, and drooping breasts. And at the time she was referring to women over the age of 35. I was so horrified by her acceptance of these notions as reality for every woman that I thought, *No way! I will never old age take over my body.* It disgusted me enough to motivate me to lift weights so I would not get that way.

If you're having a difficult time finding your compelling reasons, hire a personal trainer or join a workout group. Let others motivate you into movement until you can find the reasons within yourself.

WAYS TO SNEAK IN EXERCISE

The words "exercise" and "workout" make many people cringe. Try not to focus on words – just move your body! Below are some tips to sneak exercise into your life so it doesn't seem like a workout.

1. Get it before your body realizes what is going on.

Let's be honest: you have had the best intentions many times to get in a workout at lunchtime or at the end of the day, and it just doesn't seem to happen. You even pack your gym bag ahead of time or put your yoga mat in the car. Yet every night at 10 PM, you wonder where the day went. You got busy or your mind thought up many excuses not to do it. Your body may have been cranky, and your mind confirmed that crankiness with, "Oh, that's okay, I'm not feeling well today. But tomorrow, I'll feel well enough to exercise." And guess what? With that mindset, tomorrow never happens.

It's been my experience that if I get out of bed early and go exercising shortly thereafter, I don't have time to make excuses, to get tired, or busy. By going out before you're fully awake, you trick your body and mind into exercising. It's a sneaky trick, but it works.

2. Get up every hour and a half to two hours and run stairs or pace the halls for ten minutes.

Don't head to the coffee break room. Instead, go to the stairwell and go up and down a few flights of stairs. Put your timer on for ten minutes and don't stop until it chimes. Walk the hallways or go outside and walk around the building. If you honor the time, you'll be getting in about forty minutes during an 8-hour day. Take a colleague with you if you need to "talk shop". Use movement time to hash out details of the latest proposal or transaction. If you work from home, get up and clean something for 10 minutes. Run laundry up and down the stairs. Vacuum a room.

3. Get your call time in or catch up on your latest shows.

I reserve my family phone calls for my walking time. Whenever I need to call my sister or mom, I grab my shoes, a phone belt, a pair of headphones, and head out for a walk. I know my conversations with my sister are never under an hour, so I am at least guaranteed an hour of exercise. Get hooked on a TV or Netflix show and only watch it when you're exercising. Download it to your phone, device, or stream it at the gym. I have even exercised extra because I wanted to watch another episode!

4. Try something you've always wanted to try.

One downfall of a workout program is that they tend to get boring. If you're always doing the same thing, you'll have a tendency to quit because you're bored or not seeing progress. Cross-training is the best way to keep your workout interesting and to use muscles in a new way. Anyone who knows me well, for example, knows that I love to dance Salsa and Bachata. I could do Latin dance for three hours straight and not get tired. Have you tried different classes, lessons, and formats? For example, you could try Acroyoga, ice-skating, or barre fitness. What is your passion?

When I get a client who says, "I hate working out!" it's usually because he or she thinks working out is being stuck at the gym on a treadmill or weight machine. Explore new ways to include variety in your workout.

5. Sign up for a fitness goal.

Grab a friend and sign up for a 5K or mud runner. If you commit to a goal, you're likely to train for it, especially if you're accountable to other people. I myself have run two half marathons, both with other people. I'm not a fast runner, so I knew I had to train so as to not disappoint my running mates. The human body is capable of so much, if you trust it and push its limits. Achieving your fitness goals is extremely rewarding. Those half-marathon medals are anchors for me when times get tough. When I get frustrated with other areas of my life or when I feel the odds are against me, I remember how I finished those half marathons, and I'm reminded of my potential. Let your new fitness goals be your anchors for future endeavors once you accomplish them.

LET MOVEMENT BE YOUR ESCAPE

Since the 1950s, when TV sets became a staple of the home, we have mastered the art of escape through electronics. It's true that we sometimes need downtime from intellectual pursuits. Watching a movie or chatting with someone on Facebook might be a good way to do that. However, it may be useful to ask yourself, "How much time am I actually spending on social media, text messages, video games, emails, and television?" Be truthful with yourself and calculate the total time for each day. Could you possibly take some of that time to exercise and move your body?

Think about the reasons why you need to escape. Are you running away from a problem? Are you denying an issue you don't want to face? Or are you procrastinating on a task you must accomplish? Movement increases blood flow to the brain, stimulates your imagination, and helps with creative solutions to your problems. And when you come back to them after your workout you'll be better able to deal with life's challenges.

PROPER BREATHING WILL HEAL YOU AND HELP YOU MOVE

When was the last time you thought about breathing? Breathing is, of course, something we do naturally. But have you ever thought about mindful breathing? Besides eating food and drinking clean water, breathing is an action we can directly influence, to enhance or harm our health.

You might have noticed that if someone scares you, your breath stops. When you're nervous, your heart beats faster and your breathing increases. When you're sad, your heart beats more slowly – or at an irregular rhythm – and you may forget to breathe regularly. If your mind is racing with worry, your breath is shallow and you might even pant, making yourself light-headed.

Breath is linked to your physical health, to your emotional state, and to your overall feeling of wellness. The quality of your breath will dictate the quality of your life. Let me give you an example: if your posture is poor and you're slumped forward, your breathing will mimic your body. It will be slow and irregular. But if your posture is tall and your breathing is full, you will have a more steady and powerful breath. As a result, you'll feel more powerful. You will have greater self-confidence, feel more alert, and make better choices.

Through the practice of yoga, I teach many different breathing techniques to get students into a better state. We've already addressed the role of breathing to help you remove toxins from your body by stimulating the lymphatic system. Proper breathing can also help lower blood pressure, lower anxiety and the fight-or-flight response, normalize heart rate, and stimulate improved brain function. It doesn't cost anything and all you need are a few simple techniques to practice daily.

Since stress-reduction is one thing my clients seek out most. I have three favorite breathing techniques I teach to help relieve stress. You can view a demonstration of all three of these breathing techniques on my YouTube channel: MichelleFondinAuthor.[3]

1. The Three-Part Breath

In yoga, the three-part breath is referred to in its Sanskrit term, *dirgha*. I also refer to it as the balloon breath. The three-part breath is a diaphragmatic breathing technique, in which you use your entire abdomen and chest to breathe fully. Most people are afraid to use their whole belly to breathe when they learn this. They don't want to puff out their belly as required. They feel afraid of looking fat. Don't

---

3 https://www.youtube.com/c/MichelleFondinAuthor

worry about how you look – you will feel a million times better when you master this.

- To begin, sit on a hard chair with your spine tall and feet flat on the floor. If your feet don't comfortably reach the floor, prop them up with a couple of yoga blocks or stack of books.
- Place your hands on your lower abdomen right below the belly button. Close your eyes so you can feel your belly.
- As you begin, start the inhalation through your nose with the lips closed. You will push out your lower belly as you inhale, extend the inhalation to the mid-belly and finally some air goes into the chest.
- As you exhale reverse this process, starting from the chest, to the mid-belly, and finally, the lower belly. As you finish the exhalation you should feel your belly button pressing inward toward your spine, as your belly gets "skinny".
- Repeat the flow with the next inhalation and continue breathing in this pattern. The whole time you will be breathing with your lips closed and through your nose only. You can slow down your breathing and count to help you along. For example, you can inhale to the count of four and exhale to the count of four. You can, of course, extend the count to five, six, or seven.
- You will find that the more you slow down your breathing, the calmer your mind will be. It's impossible to have a hysterical mind with a slow, even, and steady breath.

Repeat this breathing pattern for five minutes and use it as frequently as you like.

2. The Ocean or Darth Vader Breath

Once you've mastered the three-part breath, you can add a subtle sound to it. In yoga, the ocean breath – or Darth Vader breath – is called *ujjayi*. This breathing technique is practiced by partially constricting the back of the throat. The easiest way to produce this constriction is to imagine you're fogging up a pair of eyeglasses to clean them: You would hold the glasses up to your mouth, open wide, and say the word *HA*. The glasses would get foggy from the steam and you could then wipe them off with a cloth. You will reproduce this same *HA* sound – but with the mouth closed – to do the ujjayi breath.

Using the same technique as the three-part breath, inhale through the nose and begin saying the sound *HA* with your lips closed. As you exhale, you will also say the sound *HA* with the lips closed. It might feel a bit bizarre in the beginning but with practice the sounding breath becomes easier. My kids even call it the "angry breath" because it sounds a little like blowing off steam when you're upset. But instead of exhaling forcefully to blow off steam, the ujjayi breath is slow and controlled.

3. *Nadi Shodhana or Alternate Nostril Breathing*

Alternate nostril breathing, or *nadi shodhana*, has several functions. This breathing technique helps to calm down the central nervous system and synchronizes the hemispheres of the brain so they work together harmoniously. Doing a few rounds of nadi shodhana before meditation can better prepare you for the meditative state, and practicing nadi shodhana daily can also help alleviate insomnia.

- Begin by sitting with a straight back and your eyes closed.
- Place your left hand on your lap with the palm facing up. Take your right hand and place the index and middle fingers on the third-eye in between your eyebrows. Your right thumb will gently rest on your right nostril. The inside of your folded ring finger will rest on your left nostril.
- To begin, inhale through both nostrils and exhale through both with your lips closed. Block your right nostril with your thumb and inhale through the left nostril for the count of two. Block both nostrils and hold for six. Then, exhale through the right nostril for the count of four. In-

hale through the right, hold both, and then exhale through the left.

- Keep the same counts as you alternate. You can repeat this breathing pattern for two to five minutes. With practice you can increase the counts for each part of alternate nostril breathing to increase your stamina.

A Great Sex Life Will Keep You Healthy

While this might be an unexpected topic in a chapter on exercise, think about it for a moment. Sex is considered to be mild to moderate exercise. It feels great and creates intimacy. In addition, it provides a whole host of health benefits from lowered blood pressure to improved sleep. Most studies on the health benefits of sex conclude that many of the health improvements come when a couple has sex on average one to two times weekly.

1. Improved Immune Function

A study at Wilkes-Barre University in Pennsylvania showed that couples in committed, long-term relationships, who had sex once or twice weekly were least likely to get colds.[163] Immunoglobulin A is the body's first defense against colds, and by the end of the study, the students in the study had 30% more immunoglobulin A (IgA) in their saliva than the students who didn't have sex or those who had sex three to four times weekly.

2. Increased Libido

Just as moving your body increases your desire for exercise, having sex makes you want to have more sex. Women who have frequent sex find increased vaginal lubrication and elasticity. So if you find your mood for sex is low, try a romantic night with your partner and keep the momentum going for a couple of weeks. See if the increased frequency helps you get your vibe back!

3. Improved Cardiovascular Health

The Massachusetts Male Aging Study studied men from ages 40 to 70 with no prior cardiovascular problems over the course of 17 years. Researchers found that men in committed relationships who had sex more than twice per week were 45% less likely to develop cardiovascular disease than those who had sex once per month or less.[164] The reason for this is that frequent sex decreases build-up of the chemical *homocysteine*, which is linked to potentially deadly blood clots.[165] The study didn't show, however, any significant change in the levels of homocysteine in women. The improved heart health due to frequency of sex might also be due to an overall sense of health and happiness in the relationship.

4. Improved Bladder Control in Women

I teach prenatal yoga, and I'm always telling the expectant moms to do their Kegels. Unfortunately, part of being a woman and a mom is decreased bladder control. Weight gain and weak abdominal muscles can cause prolapse of the bladder and urinary incontinence. Fortunately, frequent sex with your partner can help. The contractions of an orgasm help to strengthen those muscles.

5. Good Exercise

It may sound like a stretch (no pun intended), but sex is actually quite good exercise. If you have the good fortune of having a partner who goes for one hour, you'll burn about 150 calories. Even if your normal time is only thirty minutes, you'll burn 75-85 calories. Apart from the calorie burn, sex keeps you limber and lubricates your joints making you less prone to injury. Consider it your yoga class in the bedroom. Plus, you have a natural workout partner.

6. Improved Sleep

Sex and orgasms raise levels of oxytocin, the bonding hormone.[166] Oxytocin lowers blood pressure and also reduces levels of the stress hormone, cortisol. In addition to all of those wonderful benefits of feeling good, oxytocin also relieves pain and induces sleep. That could be one of the reasons why men tend to fall fast asleep after having an orgasm.

TAKE A VACATION, FOR GOODNESS' SAKE

You don't need a scientific study to know that taking a vacation can make you feel better. On vacation, you generally unplug from daily routine, change scenery, and do things you don't normally do on a day-to-day basis. This change in perspective can improve your health and sense of wellbeing.

However, a July 2016 study on the workplace and health conducted by the Harvard T.H. Chan School of Public Health, the Robert Wood Johnson Foundation, and NPR showed that about 50% of Americans who work around fifty hours per week don't take all – or even most – of the vacation time they've earned. In addition, 30% of Americans stated in the same study that they worked while on vacation. When study participants were asked why they didn't take vacation, their answers varied: they did not want to give the workload to a co-worker, or they wanted to advance their career and be productive instead of taking time off. Maybe some of these reasons resonate with you.

Yet several studies show that taking a vacation, even a short-term vacation, can be beneficial to your health and wellbeing. And the longer the vacation, the longer the benefits last after returning to work. Getting away broadens your worldview and helps you see the bigger picture. Your mind becomes more creative. Life doesn't seem so heavy.

If you're among those who don't take vacations because you're worried about what might happen at work while you're gone, try to change your perspective for your own sense of wellbeing. While your work adds value to your place of business, the business can and will function without you. Many people get wrapped up in a controlling mindset and believe that their company can't function without them. Others feel threatened that someone else might furtively take their job while they're away. Both of these perspectives can create a lot of anxiety and unhappiness. Instead, take a moment to reflect. If someone really wants your job, they could pursue it whether you're at work all the time or not. And if decisions are made in your company while you're away that are detrimental to the company, you can troubleshoot when you return. Do you see how fear of things you can't control can get in the way of living a healthy life?

I live and work in the Washington, D.C. area. Many of my clients give their lives to their work and sacrifice nights, weekends, and vacations, only to be laid off a few years later when the company downsizes. I see this happen often. And what do those people have in exchange for all of the overtime spent? A much better salary? A solid promise for lifelong job security? No. These benefits don't happen often. Instead they have years – and sometimes decades – of their life wasted for hope of something unattainable: complete security.

Now is the time to start thinking about the bigger picture. Think about what truly matters in life. At the end of your life, you're not going to be patting yourself on the back for the number of hours you put in at the office. You're going to be thinking about how you contributed the world and how you've made a difference in others' lives. You'll be thinking about your relationships and how you enjoyed and invested in them. You'll be thinking about memories you created with those you love. You'll be thinking about times of laughter and quirky events that tickled your memory.

Work will always be there. But people, opportunities, and events will not be. Unless you actively work at it, you might not always have your health and the energy to throw a ball to your son or climb a jungle gym with your daughter.

Ask yourself this question, "Is work making me stressed, fatigued, and sick?" If the answer is yes, then you're either not taking sufficient breaks, or you're in the wrong line of work. But once you get honest with yourself about what really matters to you, then go ahead and take all the vacation and sick days you've earned. And once you do, notice how your mental and physical health improve.

CONCLUSION: A PERSPECTIVE ON MOVEMENT

Because exercise requires a lot of physical effort, many of us try to focus on singular goals for example – losing ten pounds, getting more buff, etc. – when back on the dating scene. But realistically, if you want to stay healthy, exercise needs to become a part of your daily routine for life. If you're able to adjust your mindset to this simple fact, it might become easier to integrate movement and exercise into your every day and to make it a priority.

CHAPTER 9

AWAKEN YOUR SPIRITUAL SELF

It is through gratitude of the present moment that the spiritual dimension of life opens up. - Eckhart Tolle

THERE IS A NON-PHYSICAL component to healing that most people have a hard time explaining. Studies have shown that a mother's kiss and compassionate embrace on the site of her child's injury speeds the process of healing and helps the child to experience significantly less pain[174]. A prematurely born infant in a neonatal intensive care unit gains more weight and thrives better overall – even up to age ten – when they receive skin-to-skin contact from their mother daily.[175] Those who have faith that they will be healed or have faith that a healer can heal them actually do heal. The placebo effect works similarly to faith healing. In each of these cases, there is no well-defined explanation as to why non-physical healing works, but it does.

DEFINING SPIRITUAL

"Spiritual" refers to anything beyond the physical, and most of the time, it also refers to something that science cannot readily explain.

It can allude to your individual spirit or soul, or to metaphysical phenomena such as the Divine, magic, miracles, coincidences, or the unexplainable aspects of Mother Nature. Many equate the word with religion, but while there is spirituality in religion, spirituality itself exists without religion.

We all experience spirituality in various ways. You can't possibly live your life without experiencing the spiritual realm regardless of your religious beliefs. If you've ever done anything that was nearly impossible for you, you operated on the basis of faith, which is a form of spirituality. I was talking with a friend who recently completed a marathon. He's not a runner or a serious athlete. He began training for the marathon just a couple of months before the race. I've trained for and run half-marathons, and told him I couldn't imagine running twice that amount. "How did you feel going into it?" I asked him. "Did you think you were going to finish?" He answered, "I didn't think. I *knew* I was going to finish. I had no doubt in my mind, even though my longest run was only fourteen miles." That is true faith.

You can experience spirituality when you are moved to tears by a piece of music. You can feel it when falling in love. You can find it in the awe and wonder of a beautiful sunset, or in a baby's laugh. But while we crave the spiritual essence of life, we've become far removed from it. Noise, distractions, media, devices, chaotic schedules, and social demands keep us from growing this aspect of ourselves. Yet if we listen carefully to our inner voice and the wisdom of silence we are constantly called to grow in our spirituality. We can either engage in this growth freely, or we can wait and sometimes the universe gives us a little push (or a big push) to expand and appreciate our spiritual selves.

REPLENISHING WHAT YOU'VE GIVEN AWAY

In the Western world, we are often running on energy depletion. At some point, we fill our lives with too many things (responsibilities, commitments, or even material items) and keep adding more until we run out of energy to give or to accomplish. Then we reach for caffeine, energy drinks, or protein bars in hopes that we can run for just a few more hours. Other times, we try to regain energy with escapism like watching TV, playing video games, or some other activity designed to forget our commitments.

But the only real way you can quickly regain inner energy is through your spiritual practices. It takes something bigger, higher, and more powerful than yourself to fill you with the vivacity you need to continue your journey in a healthful way.

Think all the activities you perform throughout the day. If you're responsible for other people, you have even more obligations. Many people live a life of mindless routine. They wake up, spend a short time getting ready, fix and eat breakfast, maybe feed some family members and get them ready, commute to work, spend around eight hours in the workplace, sit in traffic to get home, attempt to do some other activity that doesn't involve work, make dinner, clean up, wash some clothes, watch a little TV, and go to bed. Often there is little room to include a spiritual practice into an already jam-packed day. But when you do take the time to fit it into your schedule and follow through, you'll see the enormous benefits of replenishing the energy that you're constantly giving away.

I have clients who claim that they're able to replenish their energy through running, walking, gardening, or some other sport. All of these are immensely helpful in keeping you fit and healthy and are a must for a completely balanced life. Yes, you're getting much in return in the way of increased oxygen and blood flow, a higher metabolism, removal of toxins, and perhaps fresh air and a little healthy competition. But in all of these examples, you are still actively doing. In addition to receiving through exercise we need a silent receptive spiritual practice for optimal health.

I've often heard the expression "We've become human doings instead of human beings." Our Western world model has transformed our activities from a more balanced life of doing *and* being to a life of *only* doing, going, achieving, and increasing.

THE CONCEPT OF DUALITY

To help you further understand this concept of balance let's start with the basics. Everything in the physical realm has its polar opposite. There exists good and bad, light and dark, male and female, hot and cold, wet and dry, and so forth. As humans, we work on creating balance between these opposing forces.

In Eastern medicine, there exists the concept of yin and yang, or female and male energy. In yoga, the same dichotomy is also referred to as lunar and solar energy. The idea is to keep balance between these energies to stabilize yourself as well as your world around you. In our human bodies, we are bound by these energies. Our spirits, however, transcend these dualities. The spiritual realm has no polar opposites to balance. Everything is perfect balance, unconditional love, and pure light.

Thus, when you honor your spiritual practices, you are doing two things: one, you are rebalancing your human body, and two you are receiving all the good qualities of spirit or universal energy, which help you to transcend the confines of this world. As a result you are happier, calmer, more compassionate, and relaxed.

For example, when you're working non-stop, you're increasing yang or masculine energy. The more you move, compete, and heat up the body, the more solar energy you create. Since all of us need a balance of masculine and feminine energies, you'd need to balance the solar energy with a more passive, lunar feminine energy. If you're on the go all the time, you're not allowing an influx of yin or lunar energy into your life. Women need to be especially mindful of this concept. By nature, women are givers and nurturers. So when a woman is in the workplace, not only is she exhibiting the qualities of yang and masculine energy to compete with others at work, but she's also likely to take on extra work because her natural tendency is to nurture. This can create a whole host of health problems in women such as breast problems, infertility, and irregular menstrual cycles.

Hopefully by understanding the dual dynamic of the physical world, you can begin to accept the need to live in balance on all levels.

LOOKING AT ILLNESS FROM A SPIRITUAL PERSPECTIVE

Illness is complex and often involves many different factors. Disease is not formed overnight, and most illnesses are up to 100% preventable. A small portion of illness is due to genetics or birth defects, and an even smaller percentage is due to inexplicable causes: fate, bad luck, or what I call "Divine awakening."

Many ancient medical systems, such as Ayurvedic or Chinese medicine, can help you get to the root cause of the problem. Much of my book, *The Wheel of Healing with Ayurveda* is dedicated to helping you get to the root cause of illness, which is essential for complete and total healing. Most often, illness is a nudge from the universe telling you to do something different. Have you ever noticed that in illness, you tend to get quieter, more reflective, and begin to question the meaning of your existence? Illness can be a way of making you pay more attention to your life. When we get sick we might have been ignoring signs for weeks, months, or years. The eruption of disease is the final stage of an accumulation of physical, mental, emotional, and spiritual signs, designed to make you notice and make course corrections. The general societal and social hypnosis that affects all of us makes us unaware of these signs. We're busy with the day-to-day, caught up in the rat race, and take little time for silence.

Yet the signs are always there. They may come in the form of a friend's urging to eat healthier foods. They may come as a relative who ends up in the hospital from a heart attack, or perhaps your

184 | ENLIGHTENED MEDICINE

spouse telling you to get a better job where you're treated more fairly. Or sometimes, it's your body giving you a message. You may have trouble sleeping or have increased anxiety or depression. The inclination in modern society is to want to "fix" these signals with drugs: alcohol, street drugs, prescriptions, or over-the-counter pills. But masking the symptoms is a way of ignoring the signs.

Then there are general consequences to our actions. My wonderful godmother smoked a pack of cigarettes a day since her teens. In her early fifties, she was diagnosed with brain cancer. Within two months she had passed away. My mother was beside herself with shock, but I wasn't shocked at all. Most of the time, you can't get away with destructive behaviors for a long duration and live to tell the tale.

Obviously there are times when illness arrives and we can't explain it. It *is* tragic when a baby or child becomes deathly ill or when someone, who seems to live a stellar healthful life, suddenly becomes sick and dies. Instances such as those seem unfair and cruel. But that is where faith comes in. Loss of a loved one is hurtful and heartbreaking but it's also a time when we can turn to our Divine Source for comfort and solace in knowing that we can't necessarily see the grander picture.

ASKING YOURSELF THE BIGGER QUESTIONS AND SEEING THE BIGGER PICTURE

In life we're often focused on the little things and forget about the bigger picture our entire life and our role in it. Start to question things about your life purpose and why you're here before illness has a chance to develop. Take time daily to ask yourself, "Why am I here? What is my purpose?" Figure out what makes you passionate and propels you forward. It often has nothing to do with what you spend your days doing. Most of the time we live in the chaos of our day-to-day routines. The conversations we have with ourselves include: *What bills do I have to pay? What housework needs to get done?*

What do the kids need for school or lunches? What can I make for dinner? It's so easy to get caught up in the small things, that we forget the bigger things. And that's what it is: forgetting. Have you ever taken a road trip, seen something new, or even been exposed momentarily to large open fields and asked yourself, *What am I missing?*

In order to see the bigger picture, you must allow yourself to grow spiritually daily. It's nice to go to church, temple, or wherever you attend your religious practice once a week. But it's not enough. For consistent spiritual healing you need to constantly immerse yourself into spiritual awakening. As esoteric as that may sound, it all boils down to one word: silence.

Spiritual Practice One: Silence

Receiving messages from the Divine requires silence, including the silence of your body, mind, intellect, and emotions. But living in the modern world is not exactly a silent space. Even when you can catch a moment of silence, you can still hear the hum of an overhead fluorescent light or the whir of a computer fan. You may have to go to great lengths to experience silence, but by following a few of the suggestions below, you'll be able to get closer than before.

I know a lot of people aren't comfortable with silence. They've become so accustomed to constant external noise that silence creates a lot of anxiety. If silence bothers you, perhaps you can start with exploring why it bothers you. Are you afraid to sit with your own thoughts? Has it been a long time since you experienced silence, and it just feels different? Whatever the reasons, leaning into them rather than running away from them can open you up to a whole new level of healing.

When I teach meditation, many of my students are worried about staying silent for thirty minutes. I encourage them to build up to it by starting with ten or fifteen minutes and adding a minute or two every few days. To obtain silence, turn everything off in your home, car, or office. Having a silent space may be disconcerting at first, but if you add a few minutes of silence a day you'll crave it more. And you'll begin to turn off your radio in your car while driving or keep the TV off most of the time when at home. Then when you can't get your silence, you'll get cranky. It's rather funny how quickly it happens.

When you experience extended periods of silence, your mind starts to get noisier. This is completely normal and perhaps the reason why many people complain about having difficulty getting to sleep. Your body, including your mind, intellect, ego, past impressions, and experiences of the day are all striving to get your attention like a horde of small toddlers. When you're absorbed in daily activities, you tend to ignore these aspects of you. Yet as you sit in silence for the first time, all these parts of you say, "Hey, now it's my turn to get the attention." In the beginning you can feel as if you're going out of your mind. But you're not. I like to equate it to an emotional detox. Things happen in life that you don't like or even that you hate. They may make you feel extremely uncomfortable. It's human nature to want to stuff those feelings down to deal with later. If you've never taken the time to deal with emotional baggage, silence is when they tend to come up.

But try not to take it with fear. It's a good thing to detox your emotional body. Learning to observe yourself, to appreciate your surroundings, and to listen to the mind's chatter in silence are all healthy for you. When you're patient with this process, your mind will quiet down and you can redirect the energy in a more positive way.

Have you ever noticed that great ideas come to you when you're in the shower? It's because the shower is a place where we're not usually distracted with outside noise. Usually when we're trying to come up with creative solutions to problems or generate new ideas for projects we have to try really hard. But when you experience silence, these ideas come more naturally. As a result you can use silence to your benefit by putting those great ideas to work for you and save a lot of time and effort.

Taking an Electronic Device Detox

Never before in history have we had such a problem with constant distractions. Prior to the 1990s, it was common to have moments of silence. If you grew up in the 20th century, you probably remember a time when you would drive long distances and lose radio signal. You could be in the car for hours with no form of entertainment except the silence of your own mind to entertain you. My youngest child has no appreciation for car games, like finding license plates from other states, because he never had to. He's always had some form of entertainment in the car. Remember when you could go somewhere, even for an hour, where no one could contact you? Today we are so conditioned to take our cell phones "just in case" that we've become afraid to go without. Before cell phones, smart phones, and email you could actually take a vacation from work and no one from work could bother you.

Electronic devices have made boundaries confusing. They've made us stay "on" all the time. Downtime, quiet time, or alone time are no longer respected. While electronic devices have allowed us certain freedoms and advances, as well as saved us a whole lot of time, they have also robbed us of our spiritual awareness. For example, something as simple as waiting in line used to be an act of patience that allowed you to notice things. It allowed you to connect with others, commiserate, and maybe make a friend or two. It allowed you to observe your environment and think about your life. I remember camping out all night with friends to buy concert tickets at the crack of dawn. In those experiences we created create bonds with perfect strangers as we shared the excitement of getting the first tickets to the awaited show. Now if you observe people in line, most are on their phones, either talking, texting, or checking their email. It's as if each person is in their individual bubble, not in calm silence but in a jittery "what's next" bubble. Don't get me wrong: I'm just as much a slave to my smartphone as the next person. I have to consciously tell myself to put my phone down or to stop checking my email every five minutes. The reality is that it is a constant struggle to let the device go and opt to live in the here and now.

Since we are now conditioned to have devices on and around us all the time, we must make a conscious and planned effort to turn them off and put them down. I know people who have gone to extremes such as swearing off Facebook or other forms of social media for anywhere from a month to six months. That's okay, but not necessary. In order to gain silence, it's better to do it on a daily basis, and if you can, for most of the day one or two days per week.

You can do this very simply: plan to not turn on any devices for two hours after you wake up in the morning or after 7 P.M. You can take a nine to five break on weekends. Turn your phone on airplane mode and only keep it with you for emergencies. Some people I know will not turn on a device in the morning until they've taken time for a spiritual practice such as meditation, prayer, or reading spiritual literature.

If you're raising children, you can teach them how to have self-control and implement these electronic device detoxes. They're the adults of our future and they need to understand limitations surrounding electronic devices or they'll wind up as stressed out and sick as we have become as a result of not knowing when to shut it off.

Connecting with Mother Nature

If you live in a city or take a car everywhere, chances are you're disconnected with nature. The rhythms of nature operate at a much slower pace than we normally operate. Living indoors is a relatively new human concept. Yet our souls crave for the connection with nature. You don't have to be an outdoorsy type to appreciate and observe nature. But you *do* have to get outside.

We live in these artificial time warps with human-imposed expectations. We always are driven to do something by a specific time or expect that it will happen within a given time. And when it doesn't, we get frustrated. Personally, I know I suffer from constant impatience. Things must happen according to my timetable, and when they don't, I can get upset or discouraged. I can only imagine you've experienced something like this. Nature, however, isn't bound by such time restraints. Everything occurs naturally without pushing and squeezing things into the little box of time. Most often, nothing bad happens when events don't meet our time expectations – or any other expectations, for that matter. When you watch squirrels play in the forest, listen to birds sing, or observe flowers bloom throughout the spring, you're reminded that nature doesn't rush, yet it all works out in perfect timing.

Since humans have always been connected to nature, immersing yourself in it has a calming and healing effect. It helps regulate your Circadian rhythm and seasonal rhythms. In our modern times, we've created machines and sounds that mimic the sounds of nature. But all we need to do is get outside and appreciate it.

You might wonder what connecting with nature has to do with spirituality. When you feel, touch, see, smell, hear, and appreciate nature, you become one with it. That sense of oneness heals the chronic human disease, which is that of separation. We live in constant worry that we are separate, alone, and left to fend for ourselves. Nothing could be further from the truth. You're no more separate than the birds, trees, insects, vegetation, and other animals are from one another. You're never alone. And you fit in perfectly with the orchestration of the whole universe whether you realize it or not.

SPIRITUAL PRACTICE TWO: MEDITATION & VISUALIZATION

In modern times, many books have popularized meditation. Relatively new – or rather, recently re-introduced – to the Western world, most people still have no clue what meditation is or what its function is. When used for health and healing, my experience has taught me and studies have shown that meditation is by far one of the most powerful tools that exists. [176]

How Meditation Heals

The practice of meditation works to counter the body's most primitive response, fight-or-flight. Hard-wired in our limbic system in the part of the brain referred to as the reptilian brain, the fight-or-flight response was designed for survival and to keep our bodies safe. Activation of the fight-or-flight response was reserved for fighting off predators or running away from them. This reaction was essential for the survival of the human species. And it worked. However, in modern times most of us are not living in constant fear of having our lives threatened. But instead, our bodies go into the fight-or-flight response when we're upset or just plain stressed. Maybe you're late for work and your body responds with fight-or-flight . Your boyfriend forgets to text you and you respond with fight-or-flight... you understand the drill.

The problem is not necessarily the trigger that leads us to fight-or-flight; it's the effects of the primitive response. In your physical body, your blood pressure rises, your heart beats faster, your levels of cortisol, adrenaline and noradrenaline go up, your blood platelets get sticky, your blood sugar rises, your muscles tense up, blood is shunted away from your digestive organs and go to your limbs, your immune system becomes suppressed, and your growth hormones levels are reduced. All of this happens instantaneously. It's important that your physical body goes through these changes if you are in real and imminent danger or a loved one's life is at risk. But it's harmful to your body if you're not in danger. Your health won't be at risk if you go into fight-or-flight once in a while, but your health will be at risk if you're constantly responding this way.

You may have heard that "stress kills". That is only partially true. An unhealthy response to stress is what can kill people through lifestyle diseases. Stress will always be in your life. Stress can be good, unfavorable, or neutral. But the way you respond to stress is the one determining factor as to whether or not you will develop stress-related diseases.

The practice of meditation reverses the fight-or-flight response. In meditation, your blood pressure normalizes and even lowers, your heart rate returns to regular, your muscles relax, your immune function increases, your growth hormones increase, and every other negative effect of fight-or-flight reverses. And when you continue to meditate on a regular basis, your set point for going into fight-or-flight gets higher. That means it will take many more stress factors to make you respond with fight-or-flight than before. In time, you will become calmer, more relaxed, and healthier.

Meditation Reverses Aging

There is an enzyme in your body called telomerase. Telomerase is responsible for repairing telomeres, which are the structures located at the end of chromosomes.[177] They protect the ends of chromosomes (like a cap or the end of a shoelace) so that they don't stick to one another. By not sticking, no data from the DNA is lost and the DNA is not damaged with cell replication. Normally with each DNA replication, the chromosomes shorten. As we age, with each cell replication, we lose some of the ends of the telomeres on each chromosome. Telomeres are also lost from "end replication" during DNA replication (when the telomeres are eaten away from many division cycles)[178] and from oxidative stress accumulated through our own lifestyle choices, such as poor diet, smoking, and stress. When the telomere becomes too short, the chromosome cannot be replicated and the cell dies.

When our body is able to use telomerase properly, however, it can reverse aging. Telomerase is also found in cancer cells and is responsible for making cancer cells immortal. One way to fight cancer cells would be to find a way to turn off the telomerase in the renegade cells so they experience cell death.

A study led by Tonya Jacobs at the University of California-Davis showed that participants who meditated for six hours per day for three months during a long-term meditation retreat had 30% more telomerase activity than the control group who didn't meditate.[179] While researchers are not certain of the exact cause, they believe that meditation reduces stress hormones and therefore helps create healthier telomeres.[180] Since healthy telomeres can delay or reverse aging, regular meditation can contribute to reducing the effects of aging.

Meditation is a Skill

As powerful as it is, meditation must be learned. If you've ever seen anyone meditating, you might think that it looks easy. And yes, meditation is easy to do – but not easy to learn. Once you've mastered the skill of meditation, sitting down to meditate doesn't require Herculean strength or cardiovascular endurance. What is does require is mind control and discipline, two things that have been diminishing in our modern times.

If you live in the West, chances are you've rarely sat with your eyes closed in total silence for more than a few minutes. We simply don't foster a culture where this is a valued trait. And even if we wish that our children would just sit in silence for a good ten to fifteen minutes without moving, most of us don't even do it ourselves. In order to learn properly, it's important to get a good teacher to teach you meditation. Guided meditations are great, but they do create dependency on someone else's voice to get you to silence. Ideally, a good teacher will teach you how to meditate on your own, without guidance, and at best with a mantra.

You'll need a disciplined practice to reap the benefits of meditation to reverse the fight-or-flight response. Meditate daily and for maximal benefits, twice daily.

Meditation is Not Like Sleep

While you might feel well rested after meditating, it's not the same rest as sleep. Studies of meditating brains show that theta and alpha waves are activated during meditation, while delta and theta waves are activated in deep sleep.[181] In normal brain activity, delta waves are active during sleep, beta waves are active during goal-oriented tasks, alpha waves are active when you're awake but resting, and theta waves are active when you're daydreaming or doing a monotonous activity such as driving home from work.[182] However, alpha waves are the most prominent in mindfulness and meditation. And this is a good thing for your mental health since activation of alpha waves seems to decrease anxiety and depression.[183] So even if you feel like you're about to go to sleep when meditating, you can now rest easy knowing that your brain is wrapped up in a whole different –and beneficial– type of activity.

Meditation Changes Your Brain

Neuroscience has proven that meditation creates physical changes in the brain. Think about that for a moment: a practice that is non-physical in nature produces changes that are physical in nature, and science has hard evidence to prove it. That's pretty amazing – and even more reason to employ spiritual practices as a method for healing.

Here's the truth about your brain: Even though your average lifespan will be around 76 years in the Western world, after your mid-twenties your brain starts to decrease in volume and weight.[184] As a consequence your shrinking brain is more susceptible to functional impairments including increased risk of mental illness and neurodegenerative disease.[185] In order to appreciate longevity in health and vitality, it's important to understand ways in which we can slow down the brain's degenerative process. Meditation is a viable option for a positive approach to maintaining cognitive abilities. Evidence-based studies conclude its benefits in: increased attention, memory, verbal fluency, executive function, processing speed, cognitive flexibility, conflict resolution, and creativity.[186]

Dr. Sara Lazar, a neuroscientist at Massachusetts General Hospital and Harvard Medical School, was one of the first scientists to discover the benefits of meditation on brain scans. Lazar took a group of people who had never meditated before and put them through an eight-week mindfulness-based stress reduction program. After only eight weeks of meditation, she observed that five areas of the brain had physically changed: four areas had thickened and the area responsible for the fight-or-flight response, the amygdala, had shrunk.[187] In the same study, Lazar found that 50-year-old meditators had the same amount of grey matter in the prefrontal cortex as 25-year olds.[188]

> To help you better understand the importance of the prefrontal cortex let's explore it a little. The prefrontal cortex is the cerebral cortex, which covers the front part of the frontal lobe (located behind your forehead) and is the last portion of the brain to fully develop. Most neurologists agree that the prefrontal cortex is not fully mature until the age of twenty-five.[189] This region of the brain helps you with complex cognitive behavior, personality expression, complex decision-making, and moderating social behavior, such as impulse control.[190] It's most responsible for executive function, such as making sure your thoughts come out as actions that reflect those thoughts or goal setting. The prefrontal cortex helps you determine which actions are good, bad, or neutral and helps you see the consequences of a potential action, in other words, good judgment. For example, a person with a suppressed prefrontal cortex might not have appropriate social behavior. The prefrontal cortex is also responsible for focused attention, such as shutting out distractions

so you can concentrate. While children and adolescents have less mature prefrontal cortices, various stimuli and challenges can help with a more rapid development of the prefrontal cortex.

A 2005 study from Yale University also discovered an increase in gray matter and thickening of the frontal cortex in long-term meditators.[191] In this study, twenty participants were selected from local meditation groups. All of the participants practiced a form of meditation called Insight, a form of mindfulness meditation. The most promising finding in this study for the aging brain was that the differences in prefrontal cortical thickness were most pronounced in the older participants, suggesting that meditation might offset age-related cortical thinning.[192] And in a study by the Beth Israel Deaconess Medical Center in 2013, researchers found that Alzheimer's patients in the early stages of the disease showed less atrophy in the hippocampus region of the brain when they learned and practiced Mindfulness-Based Stress Reduction (MBSR) using meditation and yoga for eight weeks.[193]

All in all you can almost guarantee that if you start a daily meditation practice, in a short amount of time your brain will change for the better.

Disease Reducing Benefits of Meditation

Nevertheless, if increased brain mass doesn't quite convince you to add meditation as a daily practice, here is a brief list of what other diseases meditation can help to reduce risk or effect of...

- Meditation reduces anxiety and depression and in some cases works as well as medication.[194]
- Meditation helps to improve concentration, cognitive control, delayed gratification and impulse control in children and adults with Attention Deficit Disorder and Attention Deficit and Hyperactivity Disorder.[195]
- Meditation helps to reduce alcohol and drug abuse.[196]

- Meditation reduces the perception of pain and helps your brain manage pain better than morphine.[197]
- Meditation lowers your risk of heart disease and stroke.[198]

VISUALIZATION

If you can imagine it, you can achieve it. If you can dream it, you can become it. – William A. Ward

The power we have to imagine and visualize can be one of our greatest assets or one of our worst enemies. Have you ever had a host of symptoms and looked them up on WebMD only to learn that you had some sort of rare disease or terminal illness? At 3 A.M., in the darkness of your own home, you're planning your funeral and writing letters to say good-bye to your loved ones. Your body, defeated, slumps over the chair as you review the symptoms in your mind and your heart races. Then the next day, you find out that the dizziness, headaches, and blurred vision were not due to a stage four cancerous brain tumor, but an error in your corrective lenses.

Do you see where your mind can go for better and for worse? Just as you can visualize your death sentence, you can use your imagination to visualize perfect health and healing. And in general, it's probably best to stay away from WebMD.

Visualization is the act of getting a clear picture of what you really, really want. Often when we fear something, we go over this fear in our minds and that's what becomes prevalent. The vision of your fears manifesting becomes clearer in your mind than any other picture. But just as you envision something you fear, with the same amount of energy, you can envision something great. Do you want your health to get better? Do you want to lose weight? Hold those images in your mind. Get a clear mental picture of what it would be like to have optimal health each and every day.

If you suffer from arthritis and your hip hurts today, don't envision yourself being crippled or having a hard time walking. Envision yourself walking freely without a cane or walker. Hold the image of yourself doing yoga, tai chi, or biking. Imagine yourself moving freely without pain. If you've been diagnosed with a lump or tumor, envision the tumor as being benign. Imagine it going away. Hold the image of the mass shrinking in size with each minute. Your body will tend obey the images you consistently hold.

Have you or anyone you love ever suffered from a panic attack? A panic attack is nothing other than your brain obeying the images you give it. This severe form of anxiety starts with fear. It may appear that your fear is rational, but it's likely that it is actually irrational and unfounded. The person experiencing the panic attack has a fearful thought and then that fearful thought compounds into other fearful thoughts. They feel that their life is in danger. At that point, the thoughts create fearful images that manifest into bodily reactions. The heart beats faster, blood pressure goes up, muscles get tense, the mind races, the body starts to perspire, and so on. The person thinks they are dying or having a heart attack. And all of this began with a fearful thought or visualization that something bad was going to happen – and it did. The body obeyed the mental image.

Now, if this is true, then the opposite must also be true. If you hold the mental image that you are well and healthy, your body will follow suit. When I was going through my thyroid hormone issues, I experienced tons of panic attacks. I tried a lot of different things to overcome them but what ultimately helped was visualization. A nurse practitioner helped me with guided meditation and she taught me that if I was having a scary or disturbing thought to surround that thought with a mental image of beautiful flowers and send it on its way. And after several tries, it worked. While I haven't had a panic attack in years, I still use that mental imagery when I start to feel afraid or upset and it still works. Spontaneous healing is possible and happens all the time. If you send constant messages to your body that all is well, it can find the means to heal. Your positive mental imagery may also result in a behavioral change. For example, if you're a smoker and you're holding the mental imagery that your lungs are clean, but you're still smoking, your body may give you a sudden repulsion for cigarettes.

Focus on what you want for your health. Create a vision board, if you'd like! For years, I've kept the cover of a *National Geographic* from November 2006 on the study of centenarians and the secrets of living longer. On this cover, there is an 84-year old man doing a perfect yoga headstand on the beach. It spoke to me because that is how I want to be at 80, 90, or even 100 years old. That is a vision of the health I always intend to have. As a result of that visual, I became a yoga teacher in 2008 and plan to do yoga for the rest of my life. That is the absolute power of visualization.

Spiritual Practice Three: The Healing Power of Prayer

People across all ages and cultures have used prayer as a tool for healing. The most common approach to healing prayer has been "laying of hands," otherwise known as proximal intercessory prayer. In this method, the person praying lays their hands on the sick person and prays directly with them. The next most common method is intercessory prayer in a family, church, or organization, where the person or family members asks for healing prayer. And the last method is distant intercessory prayer, where someone prays for a person they do not know. In this method, the person receiving the prayer may also have no idea they are being prayed for. All forms of prayer can and do work, and while it's a complicated and mystical topic, let's try to unfold it.

For years, scientists have been studying prayer hoping to either validate or nullify its effects. And they've had a hard time doing either. Most scientific studies using prayer are double blind, meaning that they use the distant intercessory prayer method where the person praying doesn't know the sick person, and the sick person doesn't know the person who is praying – or even that they are being prayed for. In 2006, Harvard University did an extensive longitudinal study funded by the John Templeton Foundation on intercessory prayer, and the results were disappointing for supporters of prayer. The subjects, 1,802 patients receiving coronary artery bypass graft surgery, were divided into three groups: those who were told they were being prayed for and were, those who were prayed for but told that they may or may not receive prayers, and those who were not prayed for but told they may or may receive prayers. The group who knew they were being prayed for suffered worse post-operative complications than the other groups. These results left scientists wondering why prayer seemed to harm rather than help.[199]

Unfortunately for believers in prayer the results got a lot of attention in the media. One thing the authors of the study and doctors of behavioral medicine looked at after the study, were the conditions under which the study was done. One theory was that the group being prayed for had a form of performance anxiety, or a worry that they were so sick that the hospital had to call in the "experts" to pray for them. A hospital chaplain shared his theory that God is not subject to scientific investigation. My theory, however, is that in matters of faith, where there is doubt, miracles can't occur. The very fact that a study was being conducted indicates that there was doubt present. And doubt is the opposite of faith.

Faith is based on belief. If you believe you will be healed, there is a greater chance that you will be. In the Bible, there are many stories of people being healed based on faith and belief. In the New Testament, there is a story of a woman with a severe hemorrhaging disorder. She knew that if she could somehow get to Jesus and just touch his cloak, that she would be healed. And indeed, she worked to get through the crowd and barely touched Jesus' cloak, and at once she was healed.[200]

Doubt closes you off to receiving. God gives you free will to make your own choices. When He created you, He also gave you the free will to have a relationship with Him. You can make the choice to receive Him or not. You can make the choice to engage in a relationship with Him and ask for His gifts and blessings. But God will not force Himself on you. That is the nature of His unconditional love. As humans, we don't have the right to test God unless we are in a close relationship with Him (I base this on the fact that the Bible is also filled with stories of people who tested God, and those with favorable outcomes already had a close relationship with Him). For example in the Book of Genesis, Jacob, the son of Issac and the younger of twin brothers, stole his father's blessing by disguising himself as his twin Esau. (In the Jewish faith, the father's blessing of the eldest son is extremely important.) He said he would honor God through this blessing but he was just pretending in order to get his own way. Years later after losing a lot of his wealth and family, Jacob is still trying to make a selfish bargain with God instead of surrendering his life to Him. As a result, God appears to Jacob as a man in the darkness of the night and wrestles with him until Jacob surrenders, with a broken hip, might I add. Finally Jacob says to God, "I won't let you go until you give me your blessing." God does and changes Jacob's name to "Israel", which means, "he who fights with God."[201]

If healing miracles do come from heaven and God is the performer of those miracles, then who are we to question His judgment as to who gets healed and who doesn't? The very act of studying "God performance" puts us at a higher place than God, and makes God out to be a circus clown while we are the circus directors. The whole thing simply takes away the awesome power of miracles.

The truth is that miracles do occur. Spontaneous healing is something that happens regularly. Just because we cannot prove it doesn't mean that it isn't so. And that is the power of faith.

DETACHMENT AND SURRENDER

Whenever a baby is born we say, "Oh, how miraculous!" or "You're such a miracle, little one." And after that moment, we forget what a miracle it is to have human life. I love what Dr. Dyer used to say about it. He explained that we come to earth and say, "Thank you God. I'll take it from here." Our egos take over. Dr. Dyer taught that the word ego means, "To Edge God Out (E.G.O.)."[202] We tend to become total control freaks over our own lives.

Detachment is a concept that not many understand. If you take the word at face value, you could interpret it as "aloof" or "unattached." Yet the word "detachment," in the spiritual sense, means to surrender control. It means to let go of the need to micromanage. With attachment to outcome, we worry and get frustrated when things don't seem to go our way. We hold onto the notion that we must do everything ourselves. Unfortunately, in the Western world, we are also pretty good at executing this. We're taught to be independent go-getters. We try not to rely on anyone. But the truth is we all need each other to achieve our goals. We need our higher power to help us along the way. And most of all, we're not big enough to see the grander picture. We're but a speck in the entire universe, and if we're under the illusion that we've got it all figured out, we're in for major disappointment. Detaching from outcome means letting your ego quiet down.

So what does this mean in health? It means having faith and trusting that a power greater than yourself has got this for you. I know all too well what it means to be sick. You're scared, fearful, and you feel out of control. When you're attached to outcome, you do things like research the Internet endlessly for descriptions of your disease and possible remedies. You yell at doctors and demand things from nurses. You become the victim in your family looking for sympathy for your pitiful situation. All of those are examples of having a lack of faith. And what is the antidote? Surrender.

When you surrender, you do your due diligence, make your choices as far as treatment goes, and give it to God to do the rest. Honestly, there is much more to healing than medicine and modern science – even physicians will tell you this. They can give the exact same treatment to two patients, with the same condition, and one will heal and one will die. How do you explain this? The answer lies in the fact that we're not just mechanical organisms. There's an integrative interaction between our physical body, our mind, our soul, our emotions, our relationships, our occupations, and our environment. You can't separate parts of you and say, for example, "I will heal my soul today and my body tomorrow." It's all integrated.

Surrender is beautiful and magical. It takes the weight off your shoulders. It whisks away worry and anxiety. Worry says, "I'm alone." Surrender says, "I'm taken care of and loved." It embodies the expression, "Let go, and let God."

Allowing Yourself to Receive

Once you surrender, it's important that you know how to receive. Many of us are good at giving. We can easily give to others, but when it comes to receiving, we recoil. We say things like, "Oh, you shouldn't have." Or "I've got this." If your body is to heal, you have to become an expert at receiving. You must open yourself up and get ready for it.

When your Creator and your body are ready to heal you, and your reaction is "I don't deserve this" or "I'm not worthy," rest assured you won't receive it. Have you ever been at a wedding where the bride throws her bouquet into a crowd of single ladies? Who catches the bouquet? The one who has her arms wide open and is ready to jump as high as she can to catch it. And maybe you're not a single lady, but regardless of your gender, that's the way you need to be when the universe is handing you gifts.

Will & Desire

Finally, in this chapter on spirituality and health, I'd like to address will and desire. We've already pointed out that healing can't be limited to any one thing. And all medicals advancements aside, the one aspect of healing that stands above the crowd is the will and desire for healing.

My father, to whom I dedicated this book, is lucky to be alive. He has gone through many instances of cancer (bladder, kidney, colon), heart attacks, angioplasties, a quadruple bypass surgery, stroke, a lost kidney, a kidney replacement, and the list goes on. He is literally a medical miracle. Even he's astonished that he's still alive. But my father has always had one thing above all else: a desire to live and to combat any illness that comes his way. You might ask, "How can something invisible, like will, overcome something that's real and visible like cancer and heart disease?" The answer is that it just does.

Ask any hospital physician. When a patient has decided that it's over and they have no will to live, they usually die soon thereafter. We all need a purpose or reason to live. Whatever it may be, we must have a compelling reason to keep going. Will and inner drive are not something we can actually measure scientifically because the reason can change drastically. I've studied alcoholics from the most severe, to the young college student discovering a drinking problem early on. All of them had different reasons for getting sober. In the most severe cases, many of them wanted to die for years, but something kept them alive. What was that something? For some, it was a loving mother. For others, it was a knowing that God exists and that maybe He could help. Whatever it was, they had a will to live.

In *The Wheel of Healing with Ayurveda*, I share the story of my friend's mother who was diagnosed with and overcame stage four cancer two times. The first time, she was given a thirty-five percent chance of survival, and the second time, a twenty-five percent chance. When I asked her what made her recover, she simply said, "I chose to." With all the odds against her, she made a decision to live and her body obeyed. As Jesus said in Matthew 17:20, "Truly I tell you, if you have faith as small as a mustard seed, you can say to this mountain, 'Move from here to there' and it will move. Nothing will be impossible for you."[203] Healing begins with will and desire. Then it transforms to belief, faith, and surrender.

Even if you don't have a spiritual belief, search for something greater than yourself. You could embrace love for a family member, Mother Nature and planet earth, or a passion for something you've yet to accomplish. Find something apart from your physical being to live for, and have faith in it beyond all reasoning and you will have a greater chance at healing.

DELVING INTO THE SPIRITUAL

Considering spirituality for healing can be a daunting task for some. Often, skeptics will consider it only as a last resort as in the instance of a person, who in the midst of a car crash becomes instantly spiritual. Or, if you've ever experienced a hardship, never before considering God, you might start making bargains with Him if He gets you out of the snafu.

Try instead to incorporate some spirituality into your life on a daily basis. Download an app with guided meditations and listen daily. Or read some inspirational literature before going to bed at night. That way, when you most need it, you'll find it easier to integrate into your life and healing.

CHAPTER 10

EMOTIONAL LIFE

People find meaning and redemption in the most unusual human connections.
-Khaled Hosseini

I'VE READ A LOT of books on emotions and emotional healing. Starting with Daniel Goleman's book *Emotional Intelligence* in 1995, from an early age, I've been fascinated by the connection emotions have to physical health. In *The Wheel of Healing with Ayurveda* I dedicated an entire chapter to emotional healing. In this book, I'm focusing on two of the biggest problems in our emotional lives today: the problem of loneliness and isolation, and the problem of drugging ourselves into not feeling rather than working through our emotions. Finally, I'll give you some suggestions as to how you can start healing your emotional life.

YOU WERE MADE TO CONNECT WITH OTHERS

Depending on your beliefs, you were either a blank slate emotionally when you were born, or you had some inborn personality traits that determined how you acted and reacted to others and your environment. This is the big debate of nature versus nurture that psychologists have been studying for years. With mental illnesses like anxiety and depression being at an all-time high, it's a topic definitely worth studying.

Never in history have we been more connected and yet more disconnected at the same time. If you are a Gen X-er or older, you know of a time when communication had to happen in person, via the one household telephone, or through what we now call snail mail. But most of our communication happened real time and face-to-face with other people. Interpersonal skills were monumental to your survival in society. As a kid, you had to learn how to communicate face-to-face, have a solid handshake, and know how to speak properly to adults. For better and for worse, you had to get in front of people. And if someone wanted to ignore you, they could really ignore you and vice versa.

In today's world, much of our communication happens remotely. The ease of texting, emails, and social media communication makes it preferable to get the point across quickly and plug in to some social interaction without ever having to come face-to-face with others. Before the invention of TV, families listened to the radio, did chores, played games, took walks, and had picnics together. When families began to have one TV in the household, they used to watch the limited numbers of shows together. As TV sets got more affordable, families had two or more in the house and family members began to divide up and watch TV in separate rooms. While that was troublesome for the health of, not only the family, but also for the individual, we have now taken separateness to a whole other level. It seems that every family member is in his or her own separate media bubble.

One recent Christmas, my family took a picture on the couch after opening presents. Every single member, myself included, was lined up on the couch, with a laptop, staring at individual screens. This is no joke. We didn't plan it that way. It happened naturally. We took the picture only once we noticed it. Does this sound familiar to what you experience in your family?

This behavior doesn't only present itself on special family occasions, it's frequent and repeated behavior everywhere and in every circumstance. I used to have great conversations with my kids, especially as they were becoming teenagers, in the car while carting them around. Now they want to be on their phones. Instead of paying attention or goofing off at school concerts or sporting events, I now see young kids on tablets or phones. I've even noticed young couples on dates, more often than not staring at their phones instead of each other.

Cyberpsychologists explain that there is a perfectly good reason for this behavior. Electronic devices, and the things we use them for, have an addictive quality that stimulates the brain reward process. Whether you play a game, use instant messaging, see how many "likes" you have on your social media post, or all of the above at the same time, it triggers a response in the brain that makes you crave more. Human interaction in itself doesn't have the instantaneous reward factor of electronic devices. For rewarding human interaction, you need to work harder for it. That's one of the reasons it's so easy for a parent to put his or her child in front of the TV. The child is instantly calm and satisfied, and the parent doesn't need to think of creative ideas to entertain him or her.

Studies of Internet behavior show that people can and are just as addicted to their devices as they can be to alcohol, drugs, or tobacco. And the behavior can be just as unhealthy. The problem with addiction is that it interrupts the pattern of normal and healthy relationships and therefore social and mental health. As author Mary Aiken of *The Cyber Effect* argues, abstinence is simply not an option when it comes to email and Internet use as it might be in other addictions. So we must learn to adapt and create healthy habits in our usage of devices so that we can foster healthier and more connected relationships.

Creating Community: Person-to-Person Contact

While it's harder than ever to connect with people on a genuine level, it's important for your health that you make these connections a priority. Social isolation is not only a growing epidemic – up from 20% in the 1980s to 40% in 2016 – but it also affects your health more than you might think.[205]

In a 2010 study for the AARP magazine, researchers found that loneliness was "a significant predictor of poor health, as measured by the number of diagnosed medical conditions. Drug use was also positively associated with loneliness."[206] The full list of factors used to predict loneliness were:

- Younger age
- Poor health
- Less frequent sexual intercourse
- Being unmarried
- Getting little sleep
- Less frequent in-person contact with friends
- Fewer supportive people in their life
- Met more friends and acquaintances online than those who were not lonely

The results of the study showed that the older respondents were less lonely than the younger ones. And those who were married were the least lonely.[207]

As far as our health is concerned, social isolation affects us physically, mentally, and spiritually. Lonely people have interrupted sleep patterns, impaired immune function, and more inflammation. They have a 29% increased risk of heart disease and a 32% increased risk of stroke.[208] Loneliness can speed up cognitive decline and those who are lonely are twice as likely to die prematurely than those who aren't.[209]

Recent research suggests that loneliness is not necessarily due to poor social skills or the lack of social support but can be due, in part, to unusual sensitivity to social cues.[210] Lonely people are more likely to perceive social cues negatively and enter into self-preservation mode, thus exacerbating the problem. Then it has a ripple effect. If I pull away from you because I'm afraid you'll reject me, then you'll pull away from me because you think I don't love you. Do you understand how this can further isolate those who are already lonely?

If you see this as a problem for you or a loved one, behavioral psychologists can help them with this condition called "maladaptive social cognition." Through behavioral therapy, patients learn different ways of perceiving social interaction and social cues.

Older adults can become lonely due to the death of a spouse or loved one. In this case of social isolation, it's important that families and friends build a support network to make sure that the senior adult is still participating in activities to build community. In Palo Alto, California, Dr. Paul Tang of the Palo Alto Medical Foundation created a program called Link Ages, which ties together people across generations for acts of service. For example, a senior member can post a need for grocery shopping or gardening, and a college student might give two hours of their time to help. The service banks hours volunteered, and young folks can use these hours when they have a need. Perhaps the same college student needs help with their taxes, and can then receive two hours of time from a retired accountant.

One thing is for certain: connection to others via person-to-person contact increases our sense of wellbeing. Human love and connection is not only a nice thing to have, it's a necessity for survival. It's a well-known fact that human infants will fail to thrive if they're not given affection by their caregivers. As a human species, we survived because we knew how to form bonds.

While loneliness has been a problem throughout the ages, it appears that in our modern age, we need to relearn how to connect with others. Communication has modified our behavior in such a way that we need to readapt and learn new behaviors. But it's not only our responsibility to change our own behavior to ensure that we connect socially – it's also the responsibility of our family and friends to make sure we connect.

According to John Cacioppo, author of *Loneliness: Human Nature and the Need for Social Connection*, when we feel excluded from a group or feel socially isolated, our brain goes into self-preservation mode. Initially, we crave connection just as much as the physiological need for food and water. But as time goes on, the area in the brain responsible for empathy becomes less active. Because social isolation was a tribal response for members who didn't perform according to socially acceptable standards, our brain is hardwired to not seek out reentry back into a group after long periods of isolation. Since depression is a symptom of social isolation, it can make it even more difficult for a person to be self-motivated to get back into social connection.[211] That's when we need to look out for one another. Take an elderly neighbor out for dinner once in a while or call a friend who's recently gotten divorced.

Creating community and social connection are an ongoing part of healthy living rather than a one-time end goal. Keeping yourself healthy socially is hard work. While most of us are born into families and have automatic connections and social circles growing up, in today's world, we're usually required to work at maintaining friendships and family relationships. Through conscious effort, we must go outside of ourselves and reach out toward others. But many of us don't want to do that. Many of us feel others should come toward us. While that thought process might serve you in the short term, in the long term, it might result in your own loneliness.

Try the following social connection ideas to help foster healthy relationships:

- Volunteer for a cause or organization.
- Attend a church or spiritual center and other church-based functions.
- Create rules for online dating where you limit communication to three to four communications before you meet in person.
- Make your in-person time with friends weigh more heavily than your communication via email, text, or phone.
- Join local interest groups that match your interests on sites like Meetup.com.
- Limit your time watching TV or playing computer games each day. As a replacement, take a family member or friend out for coffee or ice cream.
- Keep at least one date night with your spouse or significant other every week.
- Hang out in places where people socialize, such as your local coffee shop. Strike up a conversation with a perfect stranger like we all used to do in the "good old days."
- Take group lessons and meet new people. Learn to act, study a new language, or take a cooking class.
- Host a dinner at your home for neighbors you haven't met yet.

Choosing Emotions Over Pills

Americans have a lot of anxiety. Anxiety disorders affect one in five American adults, or 40 million adults total.[212] Yet anti-anxiety medications are not the most prescribed in the United States. Instead, anti-depressants top the list for pills prescribed, followed by sedatives, hypnotics, anti-anxiety, and anti-psychotic medications.[213] A 2013 study, by the Medical Expenditure Panel Survey (MEPS) in the

United States, showed that one in six American adults takes at least one psychiatric drug. While many people need psychiatric drugs to function, many others choose to take them rather than working out mental health issues in therapy or by learning healthy ways to deal with emotions.

According to the CDC, patients often receive psychotropic medications without being evaluated by a mental health professional. Many Americans get the prescription for an anti-depressant or anti-anxiety drug from their primary care physician without being educated about other evidence-based treatments like cognitive behavioral therapy. Yet studies show that in mild to moderate levels of depression, cognitive behavioral therapy works better and with longer-term success than medication. In addition, patients who get the prescription from a primary care physician might also not be aware of the dangerous side effects of psychotropic drugs and the increased risk of misdiagnosis. To further this point, four out of five prescriptions for psychotropic drugs are written by physicians who aren't psychiatrists.[214]

Just as physical symptoms in your body exist to send you a message, feelings or emotional symptoms signal something, too. Intimately linked to the body, emotions fill our every cell. Whether you feel queasy with worry or heartbroken with sorrow, patching up the feelings with pills almost never helps. Sure, they might take away your feelings temporarily or suppress them, but as you've noticed, they always come back stronger and longer until you deal with them. Unfortunately, many of us have become experts at pushing our feelings aside and inevitably they come out as a more exacerbated emotion, such as rage or depression, or they resurface as a physical symptom.

The temporary pain of dealing with an emotion is much less painful than dealing with the consequences later. Yet how can we be expected to deal with emotional pain when most of us aren't taught? In fact, most of us are taught the exact opposite. When you were a kid your parents might have told you to "Stop crying or I'll give you something to cry about!" Or "Stiffen that upper lip and be a man." With phrases such as those, they taught us to not listen to how we were feeling. Then you grew up and had no idea how to handle yourself when things got tough. You might even feel embarrassed because in every other area of your life you hold it together, but when it comes to your emotions you feel less than competent. Don't blame yourself. Sometimes it comes from a lack of education. We aren't taught emotional education in school. So you might need to brush up on skills in emotional intelligence.

In *The Wheel of Healing with Ayurveda*, I talk about how to release painful emotions and manage your feelings. Psychotherapy is certainly a way to help learn how to cope with emotions. If seeing a therapist is cost prohibitive for you, you can read books, take a workshop or course, or join a support group. There are many ways you can learn how to deal with your emotions and all of them are valid if they have a positive impact on your life.

Develop Empowering Beliefs

Our minds are hard-wired to think negatively. Remembering negative events is a way the survival part of our brain keeps us safe. It's true that some of us are hardwired to be more optimistic and others more pessimistic. But much of the time we need to fight hard to keep our thoughts positive.

We can look at every situation from at least two different perspectives. And we have the power to choose which perspective to take. At times, it might seem that you don't have the choice, but you do. In the chapter on spiritual growth, I talked about faith and the practice of meditation. Both of those things will help you choose a more positive stance regardless of the circumstances.

With positive affirmations and empowering beliefs, you can retrain your brain to think more positively. In the beginning, it will seem like you're forcing yourself to embrace something you don't really believe. But after a while, your empowering beliefs become an internal mantra that brightens your day. Your brain expends energy on thought either way. Why not direct your thoughts in a way that will empower rather than drain you?

Think about how much time you spend on worry. Even Jesus, in Matthew 6:27, asks rhetorically "Can all your worries add a single moment to your life?" Medical studies show that worry does the exact opposite. It takes years off your life. But even though you might not know it, you have the power to control your thoughts. Thoughts are powerful things. When the mind is in constant chatter mode, thoughts are scattered. But as you harness a thought, rein it in, and decide to change it, you have the power to direct it in a way you want it to go. That is powerful. I'm sure you've heard the phrase, "Where your attention goes, energy flows." You move toward whatever you think about and repeat to yourself day after day.

As you're adopting this new way of thinking, it's helpful to write down your improved empowering beliefs. You might want to try:

I have perfect health and extraordinary energy.
I can afford healthy organic food all the time.
My relationships are strong and supportive.
I love myself because I know I'm loved.
My body is a temple and I love taking care of it.

Add some affirmations of your own and repeat them daily to yourself. Another helpful tool is to record yourself saying your empowering beliefs and listen to them every day. I know it can be difficult to listen to your own voice initially, but after a while you'll get used to it. It's very powerful.

Adopting this simple practice is free and easy. You'll notice it makes a big difference in your health and your life.

LEAVING YOUR PAST BEHIND YOU

What happens if you're driving a car while staring through the rearview mirror? Well, if you stare long enough, you'll crash into whatever is ahead of you. Many people are so absorbed with living in the past that they have a hard time being in the present. They're stuck rehashing old memories, grievances, and grudges from the past. Yet there's not a thing you can do to change your past. You can, however, change your perception of the events or conversations. You can ask yourself, "What lessons can I learn from that experience?" It's useless to think only about how things could have been.

I've had clients who tell me, "It's difficult to let go. There was so much pain and sorrow." Yes, that might be true, but pain and sorrow are just as much a part of life as joy and bliss. You can't have highs without lows. But you can try and look at the bigger picture. Think back to all of the things in your life that you considered bad or difficult at that time. Then think about where you are now. Are you different or are you living an opportunity as a direct result of that difficulty? I know I was devastated when I had cancer and the years I suffered after the diagnosis. But now, I write books about health and wellness as a result of that experience. Because of that horrifying experience, I hope to help millions of people with their health. That's a pretty awesome outcome!

When exploring your past, try to ponder the following questions if you have a hard time letting go:

1. What if I'm wrong?

You know you've been there. You encountered a situation where you thought a friend lied to you or left you out. Certain that you were right, you conjured up a story in your head about your friend betraying you. But when you confronted them, they told you a different version of the story. Yet you still felt they were lying. But in the end, you found out they had actually been telling the truth.

When it comes to relationships, we don't always see all the variables. Entertain the idea that even though something hurt you in the past, it might be possible that you were wrong about others' intent. You may even have been wrong about the details. When we do this, we open up to greater love and compassion for others and ourselves.

2. Is it possible that something else was going on?

Detectives searching for clues of a crime often have to dig deep to find the truth. Sometimes, what appeared to be true on the surface is something totally different underneath. For example, your mother who constantly praised your brother's talents, might never have told you that she did this out of fear of losing him because of a serious childhood illness that occurred before you were born. Parents may have hidden drug addictions or financial strife in an effort to protect you. Perhaps you grew up thinking they were mean and irrational when they were suffering themselves.

3. What if what happened wasn't about me?

We all, at some time or another, have a tendency to be ego-centered. It's human nature. I know I was extremely self-conscious as a young child. If a classmate looked at me wrong, I was sure they didn't like me. I felt I was always wearing the wrong clothes, saying the wrong thing, or just unlikable. A lot of these insecurities stemmed from low self-esteem due to many troubles at home. But as I got older, I realized that even the most popular girls in school had those exact same insecurities. Much of the time people are self-absorbed – not in a bad way, necessarily – but they are worried about how they appear to others. When you analyze your past, it might be a good idea to take the perspective that maybe the hurt or wrongful interaction was about the other person and their insecurities, and not about you.

As you examine your past with these three questions in mind, you can uncover a lot more information that can help you put things into perspective and move on. And if you have a hard time remembering, try asking others who were there. Also keep in mind that your memories might be skewed slightly, since you saw them through the eyes of a child. When we create memories we often focus on a feeling rather than the hard details of an event. Finding the feeling of the situation can help you unravel why you felt that way. However you see and feel those memories, painful or pleasurable, you can extract the lessons and move forward.

THE POWER OF FORGIVENESS

Part of letting go of your past is embracing the power of forgiveness. Even though it can be difficult, it's a powerful tool in moving on.

FORGIVING OTHERS

Forgiveness is mentioned in every major religion. As a Christian, I know that Jesus commands us to forgive. It's not an option; it's a command. Jesus states that as he has forgiven us our sins, we are to forgive others.

Whatever your religious or spiritual beliefs, try to comprehend this notion. When you forgive, it's not for the other person; it's for you. It reflects the state of your heart. In the process of forgiving, you lift the burden from yourself. It means you're no longer holding onto the poison that infiltrates your body. You're releasing it and giving it away to the stars, God, or the universe.

Forgiving others also helps you admit that you're not perfect. There's no such thing as a perfect human. When you hold a grudge against another person, it shows that you consider yourself superior.

Your ego might think you are indeed superior, but inside your heart you know you have as many flaws, if not more, than the other person.

Extending forgiveness doesn't mean you're condoning the other person's behavior. It doesn't even mean you're accepting it. Forgiving doesn't even imply that you must see the person face to face or let them know. In fact, there are certain circumstances in which it's totally inappropriate or dangerous to get into contact with the other person, as in the case of physical or emotional abuse. It's also possible to forgive a person who has passed away. Dr. Dyer used to tell the story of forgiving his father whom he had never met. He went to his father's gravesite and forgave him even though his father had died several years prior. He would recount that at that time he felt completely liberated and it was at that moment that he began his writing career.

FORGIVING YOURSELF

In recognition that you're not perfect, you can open up to a world of compassion toward yourself. Often at the root of deep sadness, anger, and depression lies a person's inability to forgive him or herself. As you begin to explore improved emotional health, entertain the idea that self-forgiveness is as important as forgiving others.

Regardless of your upbringing, educational background, or even personality, the need to be perfect is an illusion. It's an unattainable goal. Yet all of us at one time or another fall prey to guilt and to the idea that perhaps we could have done things differently and had better results. Self-reflection and self-improvement are traits of an enlightened person. You are correct in striving to improve. But cut yourself some slack. Most people are doing the best they can with the set of circumstances they're given at any moment. Most people are not out there plotting to do bad things to other human beings. Of course, if you did do something wrong or immoral, asking others for forgiveness and making amends will be part of the process of self-forgiveness.

A few days ago, I was walking with my son and reminiscing about the cats we had recently lost. One cat died of diabetes and the other died shortly thereafter of grief. I was expressing to him that I still felt extremely guilty about the cats' death. While I wasn't directly responsible, I had to make a judgment call I didn't feel good about. In 2012, my cat Éclair was diagnosed with diabetes. The only medicine the vet would prescribe was extremely expensive. For several years, we got the expensive insulin, which worked fine, but the cat never really regained full health. Finally in 2016, I got fed up and asked a vet to prescribe a less expensive pet insulin. It didn't work as well, but it was better than nothing. Then, when it came time for a prescription refill, the vet asked me to come in for a $200 blood test for the cat to renew the prescription. We didn't have the funds and I couldn't find a vet who would give me the prescription. So I switched the cat to an herbal diabetic medication. Unfortunately, he started to decline in health. Even though my decision at the time down came to feeding my kids or medicating my cat, I still felt extreme guilt. And imagine my further guilt when the second cat, older but seemingly healthy, died a few weeks after the first cat died from the grief of losing her friend. It was all too much for me to handle.

You might be thinking, "Michelle, that's silly. It's a cat." You're right. But guilt is guilt. And lack of forgiveness toward yourself is all the same. I can't change the past. But I can forgive myself in knowing that I did the best I could do given the circumstances.

THE HEALTH BENEFITS OF FORGIVENESS

Finally, practicing forgiveness is essential to your emotional and physical health. Studies show that those who refuse to forgive others tend to withdraw socially and feel deep loneliness. Holding onto resentments causes stress-related responses in the body including not only anxiety and depression, but also increased heart rate and elevated blood pressure when the event is recalled. But with each act of forgiveness, you increase empathy and compassion, which in turn brings you to better health.

EMOTIONAL GROWTH

When you change your diet or start a workout program, it's easy to see immediate results. But changing your emotional response or clearing out negative emotions takes more time. As we uncover one layer of emotions, there always seem to be others underneath. Rather than looking at emotional growth as a short-term exercise, try to embrace it as a lifelong journey. There are certain aspects of your personality that will be a constant challenge for you because of how you're hardwired.

For me, it's impatience. No matter how many books I've read or seminars I've taken, I still struggle with patience. I used to get upset with myself. But now I've learned to laugh at myself when impatience creeps up on me. Since I've learned to lighten up a little, I tend to catch it sooner. If your emotional struggle comes wrapped as anger, depression, anxiety, or any other negative emotion, learn how to evolve it the best you can, then be playful with it. Try not to let it become a monster of an issue in your life anymore.

Finally, be open to receiving professional help when you need it. I'm a firm believer in therapy. It has helped me in different stages in my life. Emotional struggles aren't meant to be dealt with alone and not all of us have an emotionally safe person to confide in. Fortunately seeing a therapist doesn't carry the stigma that it once did and finding the right one can often help you get over your emotional hurdles so you can regain emotional strength.

CHAPTER 11

HEALING MODALITIES

IN LIGHT OF ALL the evidence that allopathic medicine falls short when it comes to treating chronic lifestyle illness, it's becoming increasingly important for physicians and other healthcare workers to learn more about different healing modalities to help treat these diseases. You, too, can help yourself and your healthcare provider when you learn how to enhance your health by opening up the possibilities for health and healing through these same modalities.

When we consider healing, we must take into account the end goal: a healthy, happy, and vibrant human being. It matters not how we get there; the important thing is accomplishing that goal. When it comes to chronic illness, the cases of illness are rising so rapidly that we don't have time to consider lengthy scientific-based studies that may not have conclusive evidence for another five, ten, or twenty years. The time is now. Many of the healing modalities and therapies below have been used for thousands of years and work, both alone and in combination with other treatments.

Since cost is often an issue, I'm urging physicians and those who work directly with patients to learn a few of these healing modalities and to implement them into their medical practices so they can be covered by insurance. If you're a patient, try one or two of these healing modalities to increase your chances of healing in conjunction with the treatments your physician has already prescribed.

Many people remain skeptical of alternative medical practices or healing modalities until something happens in their personal lives and opens their minds to these other methods. Perhaps a family member's newly found meditation practice helped them get off of blood pressure medication, or maybe a friend was able to manage chronic pain through weekly acupuncture sessions. Whatever the reason, most people come to these practices either through direct experience or desperation.

In this chapter, I'm going give you a brief introduction to the different types of healing modalities available today. While this list won't be exhaustive, it should give you some direction as to which ones to try as you consider integrating Western medicine with other healing practices. Remember, like with all the other suggestions in this book, use your common sense. If something doesn't feel right for you, it probably isn't. And if a healing practice you'd like to try raises some questions in your mind, do more research and consult with your healthcare practitioners before you begin.

MY FATHER'S HEALING MIRACLE WITH REIKI

Seven years ago my father had quadruple bypass surgery at Cleveland Clinic. My sister and I knew our father remained in a coma several days after the surgery, but we didn't understand why.

"We have to leave him intubated, because every time we try to remove the tube, he moves into a panic." The doctor explained. "If we try to remove the tube while he's moving, it could puncture his lungs."

Every day after that, the medical team in the ICU attempted to bring our father out of the coma and remove the tubing but with no success. Seven days later, we were nervous that it might never happen.

Cleveland Clinic, being a progressive and cutting edge hospital, has practitioners of many different healing modalities integrated with traditional practices. Some of the services provided by the clinic include reflexology, massage therapy, Reiki, healing touch, Code Lavender Holistic Care, aromatherapy, guided imagery, and spiritual support. Fortunately, all of these integrative services are offered for free.[216]

While we waited for something to happen to bring our dad out of the induced coma, we had different healing practitioners come to try and help. The first man who arrived was a chaplain who asked if he could pray over our dad. We agreed, hoping it would help. Next, a Reiki practitioner came. My sister and I had no idea what Reiki was at the time, but with nothing to lose, we allowed her to conduct a Reiki session on our dad. After she finished, the medical team came by once again to try and remove the tube. Within five minutes, it was out with absolutely no problem and our dad didn't even budge through the whole process.

Was it a coincidence? We don't believe it was. My sister and I are still thoroughly convinced that the Reiki session and prayers helped the medical team remove the tube effortlessly and easily after trying for eight days. Our father was a passive recipient of these services. He couldn't have succumbed to the placebo effect while unconscious. As a family member in a dire situation with a loved one, you don't care how your loved one gets better. In the Cleveland Clinic, we experienced options and choices far beyond anything that had ever been offered in our father's dozens of hospital stays. The gift of those choices is something I believe must be available to every patient and loved one experiencing an illness.

PHYSICAL BODY-BASED HEALING

Most people are familiar with body-based therapies and are therefore more accepting of them. Body-based healing deals with the physical body either by touch or manual manipulation. Even though these therapies are administered on the surface, healing can occur on deeper levels. If you've ever gotten a massage, for example, a good massage therapist will encourage you to drink plenty of water afterward. The massage not only stimulates the skin and relaxes muscles, but it also releases toxins from the lymphatic system. Increased hydration will allow those toxins to be released through your pores, urine, and feces.

Let's look at three body-based healing modalities: massage, reflexology, and chiropractic.

1. Massage

Getting a massage feels great and relaxing. Most people who get massages today go to release stress. But massage has been used for thousands of years for other therapeutic reasons. The first written records of massage date back to ancient Egypt and China between 2700 BCE and 2500 BCE. In India, Ayurvedic texts show massage from 1500 BCE, but the therapeutic practice may date back as far as 3000 BCE.[217]

There exists many different types of massage, including Swedish, deep-tissue, sports, acupressure, Thai massage, and Ayurvedic massage. Each one has a slightly different method or focus but all deal with touch and manipulation of skin, muscles, tendons, and ligaments. Massages are helpful for lymphatic drainage, anxiety, digestive disorders, fibromyalgia, headaches, insomnia, myofascial pain syndrome, soft tissue strains or injuries, and overall health and wellbeing.

Your Massage Session

Many people are apprehensive about getting a massage because they're uncomfortable with being naked, especially with a therapist of another gender. Put your fears to rest. Depending on the type of massage, many places have a "dress down to your comfort level" policy. If you opt to stay dressed, it's best to wear a layer of tight form fitting clothes so it's easier for the therapist to get to your body without massaging too much through the clothes, which won't be to your benefit. Additionally, you can always ask for whatever gender massage therapist you want. When in doubt, call ahead and ask. Your massage session will typically last between thirty and ninety minutes.

Precautions for Massage

Massage therapy has very few risks. However, people with bleeding disorders, low blood platelet counts, and on blood thinners should avoid vigorous massage. By the same token, massage should not be done on parts of the body with blood clots, fractures, open or healing wounds, weakened bones, or where there has been recent surgery. In addition, cancer patients should consult with their oncologist before getting a massage. Massage should also be avoided if you have a recent flare up due to rheumatoid arthritis, deep vein thrombosis, and if you've had a recent burn or surgery.[218] Finally, use your commonsense and avoid massage if you have an infectious disease, even a cold or flu virus.

2. REFLEXOLOGY

Also originating in ancient Egypt, reflexology heals by stimulating pressure points on the feet and hands. It's based on the principle that there are reflex areas on the feet and hands corresponding to glands, organs, and other parts of the body. Reflexology involves apply pressure to the areas corresponding to the body parts that need healing and to increase blood flow, release stress, and normalize function. Author and physician Dr. Andrew Weil states that while scientific research hasn't shown hardcore evidence of reflexology's medical use, he supports the use of reflexology as a therapy for stress release.[219]

Your Reflexology Session

You can expect a reflexology session to last anywhere from thirty to sixty minutes. During the session, you will be barefoot but no lotions or oils will be used. Some reflexologists will offer a foot bath before the therapy session begins. For some, a reflexology massage can be quite intense, so make sure you're feeling healthy on the day of the massage.

Precautions for Reflexology

Reflexology shouldn't be used as therapy for those with a gout attack, active blood clots, burns, wounds, and active infections on the hands and feet. In addition, if you've recently had the removal of a cancerous tumor, wart, or lesion, refrain from getting a reflexology treatment until the wound is healed. Pregnant women should refrain from reflexology sessions since intense pressure on the feet may stimulate premature contractions.

3. CHIROPRACTIC

In the United States, chiropractic has been around since 1895, when developer D.D. Palmer performed his first chiropractic manipulation and helped heal a deaf man.[220] Palmer noticed that even though manipulations of the body had been performed for thousands of years, no one had actually developed a philosophical or scientific rationale as to why it worked. As a result, he developed his philosophy and created the first chiropractic school in 1897 called the Palmer College of Chiropractic in Davenport, Iowa, where the original school still stands today.[221]

Chiropractic focuses on disorders of the musculoskeletal and nervous systems. Doctors of chiropractic practice a drug-free, hands-on approach to healthcare through spinal manipulation and adjustment, as well as nutritional, dietary, and lifestyle counseling. Chiropractic can help with back pain, headaches, bowel irregularity, neck pain, ear infections, and joint pain. All 50 states recognize and regulate chiropractic as a healthcare profession, and many health insurance companies cover chiropractic sessions.

Your Chiropractic Session

Your first chiropractic visit will include a medical intake, much like the one your primary care physician does, including your health history. Next, the chiropractor will do a physical exam following with an exam of your spine and neck. During your spinal examination, they will mainly focus on the areas where you're experiencing pain or discomfort. Afterward you will receive your first adjustment. An adjustment is the chiropractic term for therapeutic manipulation of the spine and other joints to help realign the body. After your adjustment the chiropractor will often apply other non-manual treatments such as ice packs, heat, electrical stimulation or orthodic supports for your shoes. Finally your chiropractor will discuss the follow up plan with you for further treatment. Your initial visit will take about one hour, and follow-up visits are anywhere between five to twenty minutes.

Precautions for Chiropractic

While chiropractic sessions are typically considered safe, there are a few contraindications to treatment including: a ruptured disc, untreated cardiovascular problems, bone weakness such as osteoporosis, congenital abnormalities of the spine, congenital scoliosis, and surgical hardware that fuses the spine. The chiropractor is trained to first and foremost do no harm. So if you're uncertain about whether or not one of these conditions might impede treatment, it's best to consult with a chiropractor and they will be able to give you a clearer answer.

Body-based therapies are a great start and an easy bridge to alternative therapies. Let's explore some mind-body therapies that can help you reduce the effects of stress, lower anxiety, and help you sleep better.

MIND BODY THERAPIES

While many healing modalities overlap between the physical, mental, emotional, and spiritual, the following three therpies have been popularized as mind-body in particular. Yoga has grown in popularity over the past ten years, and you've likely been familiarized with yoga as an exercise program by seeing it offered at your gym or community center. Meditation and mindfulness have also gained increased awareness over the past few years, and hypnotherapy has recently resurfaced. Hypnotherapy's therapeutic uses range from addiction treatment to pain-free childbirth. Let's now take a deeper look at these three mind-body therapies.

1. YOGA

Having practiced yoga since age eighteen and having been a yoga teacher since 2008, I'm not completely objective when it comes to yoga as a practice. However, it's no mistake that yoga has become popular in recent years in the West. It helps lower stress, anxiety, increases flexibility and strength, and makes you feel good overall. But in this section, I'm going to present a side of yoga and its therapeutic use that most people are not aware of.

First of all, yoga is not simply an exercise program. It's an integrative philosophy encompassing whole health and whole life. The yoga poses you practice in a class are but one aspect. The various breathing exercises called *pranayama* are also of great therapeutic value. Each breathing exercise is designed to stimulate and improve functions in the body, whether lowering blood pressure, increasing metabolism, stimulating brain activity, or lowering heart rate. Proper breathing alone will heal many ailments.

My greatest success story with breath work comes from a client who began with me at age 89. Her name is Lucy [4], and when she started, she had just come out of the hospital with pneumonia and was sent home with a respirator and oxygen tank. Out of desperation, her daughter hired me to teach her mom how to properly breathe. When Lucy started, she was frail and had a hard time taking a deep breath. During our 55-minute lesson, she would panic often and we had to take frequent breaks. But despite the struggle Lucy persevered, and I worked with her twice weekly for three months before moving down to once per week. After six months, she had decreased her need for oxygen by 1.5 liters. Now, two years later, at age 91, I see Lucy twice per month. While she still has the oxygen machine, she has never had to increase the amounts again. What's more, she has spunk, vitality, and does chair yoga with me, moving like a pro. She has so much energy, I have to tell *her* to slow down so I can keep up.

The best part is by teaching her how to breathe properly she received the gift of life with her practice of yoga.

The second therapeutic use commonly overlooked in yoga classes is the mind-body connection and the power of focus. The word *yoga* in Sanskrit translates to "yoke" or "union," and celebrates the union between your body, mind, soul, and spirit. The practice of yoga is about bringing together the parts of you that are often separate. For example, you might feel a pain in your lower abdomen but not make the connection that this pain is due to an argument you had with your spouse earlier in the day. Yoga helps you make that connection faster so you can quickly heal, versus fall into negative patterns.

Finally, you might be hesitant to practice yoga because you believe it's affiliated with a religion. Please know that yoga is a philosophy, not a religion. It's a lifestyle, just like eating vegetarian or being sober. Those lifestyle choices stem from a set of beliefs and

---

4 Name is changed to protect client identity.

lead followers to perform in a particular way. But that doesn't make vegetarianism or sobriety a religion.

If you're a beginner, find a yoga teacher who is certified to teach hatha yoga or Iyengar yoga, both of which are designed to guide you to learn the poses gently and safely.

2. MEDITATION

In the chapter on spiritual health, I went extensively into the benefits of practicing meditation. I gave you information on how meditation works in the body and mind and outlined the benefits of meditation. In this section, I will explain how to do a simple meditation.

Many people are confused about meditation. Because they aren't sure what it is, they get nervous when they think about the prospect of meditating. Another thing I often hear as a meditation teacher is, "I can't meditate. I'm too agitated. There is no way I can sit still." Most everyone who begins meditation feels the same way. In modern society, we're not used to sitting still. We're used be being entertained.

Meditation is a skill, and it takes practice just like any other skill. There is no big mystery to it. You don't need any special equipment for practicing meditation. All you need is you and a quiet place to sit. Try the following meditation if you're a beginner, or if you need a break throughout the day. You can read it into your phone's voice memo, or have a friend do it for you so you can play it back whenever you need it. You can try to stay in this meditation for at least five minutes, or you can increase the length up to twenty minutes with practice.

Simple Breathing Meditation

Find a comfortable and quiet place to sit and close your eyes. Make sure your back is straight so you can breathe fully. With your eyes closed, begin to place your awareness on your breath. Notice how your body moves in rhythm to the breath. Observe the gentle rise and fall of your chest with each breath. Now take that breath a little deeper into the lower part of your belly. Relax all of the muscles in your lower abdomen now. As you relax the muscles, you'll notice that the breath moves deeper into your lower abdomen naturally. You will now feel your belly expand fully as you inhale and relax inward as you exhale. Try not to force or control it, just let the breath move there naturally. As you continue to watch the breath in your mind's eye, you will notice your muscles relax. You might even notice that you need to take fewer breaths as you feel more and more relaxed. As your whole body begins to relax, you'll notice that your mind will start its chatter. It may be quiet at first but then it will get louder and ask for your attention. When this happens, gently bring your awareness back to your breath and body. Go back to the slight movement of your lower abdomen with your now relaxed breathing. Each time your mind wanders to thoughts or sensations in the body, gently bring your mind back to the breath. If a thought is persistent, surround it with a mental image of flowers and send it along on its way. Then move your awareness back to your breath. Stay in your meditation as long as you'd like. When you're ready to end your meditation, wiggle your fingers and toes, touch the chair or place where you're sitting and slowly open your eyes. Take a minute or two before returning to activity.

3. HYPNOTHERAPY

When I think of hypnosis, I tend to equate it to old television shows where a performer brings an audience member on stage and makes them bark like a dog or do some other silly trick. In fact, hypnotherapy or hypnosis by a licensed therapist is a wonderful tool for helping you with certain psychological and behavioral disorders. To name a few, hypnotherapy can be used to treat phobias, anxiety, substance abuse disorders, sexual dysfunction, and bad habits. Hypnotherapy can also help with pain management and gastrointestinal issues related to chemotherapy and pregnancy.[222] Hypnosis is not a therapy in itself, but rather a method to help therapists achieve greater breakthroughs with patients.

Hypnosis has been used for centuries for pain control, even during the Civil War when physicians had to amputate limbs.[223] The validity of hypnosis in pain management has been proven in numerous studies, including a study at Mount Sinai School of Medicine where a 15-minute hypnosis session was administered to 200 breast cancer patients in a clinical trial. The hypnosis resulted in shorter surgeries, less post-operative pain relief medication, and less sedative during surgery.[224] As a prenatal yoga teacher, I've had students in recent years claim to have had a "pain-free" childbirth by using the techniques taught in the Hypnobirthing or HypnoBabies childbirth courses.

The goal of hypnotherapy is to create change in a patient while they are in the hypnotic state. A hypnotherapist will bring you into a relaxed hypnotic state through guided suggestion similar to a guided meditation. Once the patient is in the hypnotic state, they're open to suggestion and discussion if they trust the hypnotherapist.

To demystify the state of hypnosis, know that the hypnotic state is like that of daydreaming or relaxation, like in those moments before you drift off to sleep or when you're in a deep meditative state. You're in control, and you can accept or reject any suggestions. Think about the last time you got into your car and routinely made your way home – and when you arrived, you had no idea how you got there because you were daydreaming. Has that ever happened to you? You were in a self-induced hypnotic state, but your body and mind somehow knew how to get you home.

If you're interested in finding a hypnotherapist, look for one certified by either The American Society of Clinical Hypnosis (ASCH) or the Society for Clinical and Experimental Hypnosis.

ENERGY MEDICINE

In the Western world, it's not typical to talk about the energy body. Our focus is mostly on the physical body, and in some cases on the mental state. Yet as humans, we are multi-layered. Invisible forces affect us on a physical and emotional level. Our Western mind wants to see physical proof of something before we believe it. But we tend to believe in things we don't see all of the time. For example, you believe that your cell phone works to make calls, send texts, and receive data from the Internet, yet there's nothing physical connecting your phone to get this information. And some forces of nature, though invisible, can also affect us. Although it's been difficult to prove this scientifically, hospital emergency workers and police officers are among those who see increased activity of crime and accidents during a full moon phase.[225]

Another invisible force that affects your health is the transfer of energy and information of our cells. Even though our cells may appear solid and stagnant, they are vibrating at great frequency.

In the West, when we think about energy, we think about calories or perceivable energy levels (being tired, et cetera). In the East, energy refers to a layer surrounding you (also known as your energy body) and how fast or slow energy and information are transferred from one cell to the next.

Even though it may sound esoteric, you have already experienced invisible energy in one way or another. Have you ever turned a corner on a city street at night and all of the sudden felt the hairs on your arms raise as you sensed imminent danger? Then, as you looked ahead, you saw two men about to get into fight or pull out a gun. How did your body know? Your energy field collided with the negative and hostile energy field of the two men in question. Or have you ever walked into room where two people had been arguing? The room felt cold and the air stiff. What was that? Your energy field picked up the lingering energy of that argument.

The purpose of energy healing is twofold: it's designed to help unblock energy blockages that might cause disease in your body and mind, and also to clear away negative energy you may have picked up from experiences, situations, and people throughout your life. Some people carry more negative energy than others. Caretakers, or those who are empathetic, compassionate, and overly sensitive tend to absorb others' negative energy and carry it with them. If you're in this category, you might unknowingly and unwillingly be carrying other peoples' baggage. Carrying this energy can make you feel heavy and lethargic. Have you ever had a lengthy conversation with a person who made you feel absolutely drained? That is the effect of carrying another person's energy.

An experienced energy healer can help you pinpoint areas in your body where you have blockages or are holding onto to negative energy. Consider it as adjunct therapy to other forms of healing, even psychotherapy. For example, let's suppose you experienced heartbreak from a relationship in your recent past. You processed that heartbreak with anger and sadness, but haven't completely let it go. Therapy might help you process the strengths and weaknesses in your relationship, or patterns of behavior that led to the ending of it, but an energy healer will tell you where you're holding onto those feelings in your body. The healer will also make suggestions as to how you can release that negative energy. Oftentimes, we process feelings intellectually and think we've done all we can to get over a relationship or experience. But if we're holding onto negative emotions energetically, they can still be harmful to our health.

In several Eastern countries, there are several names for this energetic life force. The East Indian word for energetic life force in Sanskrit is *prana*. In Chinese medicine this same concept is *chi* as in tai chi, and in Japanese, *qi* like in the practice of qi gong. All of these words describe the exact same thing: the energetic body that surrounds us and lives within us. The following two healing modalities give an example of how you can heal your energetic body and open your physical body up to greater healing.

1. Reiki

Modern Reiki energy medicine was first developed by Japanese Buddhist monk Mikao Usui in 1922. The word Reiki comes from two Japanese words: *rei*, which means "universal," and *ki*, which is "life force energy". Reiki, which is energy transfer by laying of hands, is simple, natural, and safe. It's also easy to learn. Once you're trained by a Reiki master, you can even apply Reiki techniques on yourself for self-healing. Sixty hospitals in the United States, including the Cleveland Clinic, include Reiki in their alternative healing offerings.[226]

In a Reiki session, the person receiving treatment either sits or lies down fully clothed. The practitioner lays hands over or on different parts of the body for anywhere between three and ten minutes. The practitioner also uses different hand positions. Each Reiki session lasts between 45 to 90 minutes. When you receive Reiki, you might feel a transfer of heat from the practitioner's hands or light pulses to your body. Since you only receive the Reiki energy that you need, it's safe for everyone, including children and pregnant women.

As with most energy healing, proving healing through Reiki is difficult. However, studies comparing healing methods have shown that Reiki is often just as effective as other therapies. For example, the results of a 2013 study published in the Journal for Evidence-Based Complementary and Alternative medicine showed that a 10-minute Reiki therapy session demonstrated results just as beneficial as a 10-minute physical therapy session for patients with restricted shoulder mobility.[227] Another study from the same journal published in 2010 showed an improvement in mood in college students previously diagnosed with depression or anxiety after six 30-minute Reiki sessions over a two to eight week period.[228] Yet skeptics, even in the realm of alternative medicine, say that Reiki has more of a placebo effect. But in cases like my father's, I would propose that it was a little more than a placebo effect or mere coincidence.

Let your personal experience be your guide. Many who come to energy healing do so out of desperation, and when they experience positive results, they're convinced of its therapeutic benefits.

2. ACUPUNCTURE

Acupuncture is an ancient healing practice from China that predates recorded history. The philosophy goes back to Taoist tradition from 8,000 years ago. One of the most famous texts on the practice, *Systemic Classics of Acupuncture and Moxibustion*, was compiled between 260 and 265 CE by famous Chinese physician Huang Fu Mi. This text outlined 349 acupuncture points that are still used today.[229]

Traditional Chinese medicine teaches that health is achieved by a balance of the complementary forces, *yin* and *yang*, and the life force, *qi* (or *chi*). In an acupuncture session, the practitioner inserts needles along certain meridians (or pathways) in the human body to allow greater energy to flow. The needles are sometimes heated or stimulated with electricity after insertion and remain in the meridians for 5 to 30 minutes. Acupuncture is relatively safe with few to no side effects. According to the NIH National Center for Complementary and Integrative Health, acupuncture is most effective with pain management, especially lower back pain, neck pain, migraines, and osteoarthritis knee pain.[230] However, in 2003, the World Health Organization listed even more conditions that can potentially benefit from acupuncture, including high and low blood pressure, chemotherapy-induced nausea and vomiting, peptic ulcers, painful periods, dysentery, morning sickness, dental pain, and labor induction.[231]

Acupuncture is not recommended for those with bleeding disorders or those who take blood thinners. Patients might experience light bruising or a little bleeding at the site of needle insertion, but this is rare. In a worst-case scenario, a needle would break or puncture an organ, but again, this is extremely rare.

Your best bet is to go with an acupuncturist with a certification from the National Certification Commission for Acupuncture and Oriental Medicine (NCCAOM). Depending on state licensing requirements, acupuncturists who aren't physicians usually need this certification.

ALTERNATIVE AND COMPLEMENTARY MEDICAL SYSTEMS

While many alternative therapies come from ancient medical systems, understanding complete medical systems and how you can benefit from them is important to your integrative medicine strategy. In this section, I'll introduce you to the basics of four healing systems: Naturopathic Medicine, Traditional Chinese Medicine (TCM), Ayurvedic Medicine, and homeopathy. While many of these alternative medical systems are similar, they all have their unique approaches to health.

1. NATUROPATHIC MEDICINE

Naturopathic medicine, or Naturopathy, is based on holistic health. It seeks to treat the whole person. The focus is on natural and preventive care first. A Naturopathic Doctor of Medicine is trained in allopathic medicine alongside other alternative forms of healing, such as homeopathy, acupuncture, massage, chiropractic, and herbal cures. Doctors of Naturopathy are also educated in nutrition and relaxation techniques like meditation.

While the foundation for Naturopathy goes back for thousands of years, the first school of Naturopathy was founded in New York City and graduated its first class in 1902.[232] In 2017, there were seven accredited Naturopathic programs across North America, according to the Association of Accredited Naturopathic Medical Colleges (AANMC). Education to become a naturopathic physician is quite extensive. Candidates pursuing an ND degree must complete three years of pre-med education and have a Bachelor's degree. Once accepted into a program, they undergo four years of professional medical curriculum that results in a Doctor of Naturopathic Medicine degree. But in addition to the medical curriculum, a naturopathic doctor is required to complete four years of training in clinical nutrition, acupuncture, homeopathic medicine, botanical medicine, physical medicine, and counseling.

The goal of treatment is to completely resolve the patient's symptoms as well as pinpointing the underlying cause of illness. Naturopathic treatment is based on seven philosophical principles...

1. Establish the foundation for optimal health.
Identify and remove obstacles to cure. Examples of obstacles to health include poor diet, lack of exercise, sleep disturbances, or chronic stress levels.

2. Stimulate the self-healing mechanisms.
Stimulate the healing power of nature using therapies like botanical medicines, clinical nutrition, hydrotherapy, homeopathy, and acupuncture.

3. Support and restore weakened systems.
Aid regeneration of damaged organs through of lifestyle changes, clinical nutrition, homeopathy, and orthomolecular therapy.

4. Address physical alignment.
Restore structure integrity to the body through spinal manipulation, massage, and craniosacral therapy.

5. Control natural symptoms to restore and regenerate.
Use natural substances to palliate when a specific pathology must be addressed.

6. Use pharmacologic substances to stop disease.
Naturopathic doctors are trained in pharmacology, and if their state license allows for it, they can prescribe these themselves or refer out to a conventional medical doctor.

7. Determine necessity for high force interventions, such as surgery, chemotherapy, or radiation.
When life must be preserved, NDs refer patients out to MDs in the proper field. However, they support their patients with complementary and supportive therapies to minimize symptoms and side effects.

Your first visit to a naturopath will last anywhere between 60 to 90 minutes and will likely cost around $200. Though the price might seem high, you're likely to spend a lot less on regular doctor visits and prescriptions in the long run, since your naturopath's focus will be on preventive health. Some insurance providers may cover the cost of your naturopathic doctor's visit but since insurance plans change coverage often, it's best to check before you pay out-of-pocket. To find a naturopathic doctor in your area, go to naturopathic.org.

2. Traditional Chinese Medicine (TCM)

Traditional Chinese Medicine originates from China and is rooted in the ancient philosophy of Taoism. TCM encompasses many different practices, including acupuncture, Chinese herbal medicine, Chinese therapeutic massage, dietary therapy, moxibustion (burning of mugwort near the skin), tai chi, and qi gong.[233] The goal of TCM is to help the patient achieve balance, wellness, and harmony. The ancient Chinese people believed that illness and disease indicated that a person was in disharmony with their environment. As such, TCM embodies the belief that your body is actually an integrated body, mind, and spirit, and that you are completely connected to nature.

Another fundamental principle of TCM is that you were born with a natural self-healing ability, and that prevention is the best cure. But when you are sick, sages taught that healing came first through diet, then acupuncture, and then through Chinese herbs.

In addition, TCM uses the principles of The Yin and Yang Theory and The Five Element Theory. The Yin and Yang theory is the most fundamental concept in TCM. It centers around the concept that all things in the universe are either yin or yang. However, there are no absolutes. Nothing is ever 100% yin or 100% yang, but rather a balance of the two forces. The forces are opposite but complementary.

The Five Element theory, on the other hand, is based on the five elements: wood, fire, earth, metal, and water. This theory has been used for thousands of years to diagnose and treat illness. That said, not every Traditional Chinese Medical practitioner uses The Five Element theory, since it's complicated and can take decades to learn.

You can expect your initial consultation with a TCM practitioner to last anywhere between 30 to 60 minutes. Your first treatment will be scheduled at the same visit. The practitioner will take an extensive medical history, do a thorough pulse and tongue examination, and a brief physical exam at the site of the problem. Follow up appointments and treatments generally last around 20 minutes. The number of sessions will depend on the nature of the complaint as well as the duration of the symptoms. To find a certified TCM practitioner, you can go to the National Certification Commission for Acupuncture and Oriental Medicine (NCCAOM), or NCCAOM.org.

3. Ayurvedic Medicine

Similar to TCM, Ayurvedic medicine, originating in India, has been around for thousands of years. Ayurveda is a holistic medical system that treats the whole person and seeks to tackle the root cause of illness. Ayurveda also works in concert with the laws of nature and teaches healing through gentle means. The idea is to coax the body gently back into health by looking at symptoms and illness simplistically. If an Ayurvedic practitioner can take a simple approach and the body responds, it's much better to let the body heal itself.

The basis for Ayurvedic healing starts with the Five Great Elements: space, air, fire, water, and earth. Out of the five elements form three mind-body types, or *doshas* in Sanskrit, called *Vata*, *Pitta*, and *Kapha*. Each person has all three mind-body types, and therefore all five elements. However, each person has a unique proportion of each dosha, with one or two that are most predominant. Symptoms and illness occur when the doshas are out of balance. Healing occurs by rebalancing the doshas. An Ayurvedic practitioner will help a client by making recommendations for changes in diet and lifestyle, as well as meditation, yoga, yoga breathing, Ayurvedic massage, Ayurvedic herbal medicine, and detoxification of the body.

Since Ayurveda is a newly accepted practice in the United States, there are no standardized governing bodies regulating practitioner certification. A couple of Ayurvedic medical and physician groups, like the Association of Ayurvedic Professionals of North America (AAPNA) and the National Ayurvedic Medical Association (NAMA), have united Ayurvedic professionals across the U.S. and Canada with a common goal to self-regulate. Still, Ayurveda is effective and useful at getting a patient back to health quickly and easily provided the patient is willing to follow a practitioner's guidelines. My own background is in Ayurveda, and as a practicing Ayurvedic consultant I've seen my clients turn many medical conditions around in just a few weeks when they follow Ayurvedic recommendations. You can learn more in my book, *The Wheel of Healing with Ayurveda*. To find an Ayurvedic practitioner near you, go to: AAPNA.org or AyurvedaNama.org.

4. HOMEOPATHY

Homeopathy has an interesting history in the United States. It was the number one rival of allopathic medicine as it was developing in the mid to late nineteenth century. In fact, many allopathic physicians who had spent years in medical school became threatened by homeopathy for fear that their businesses would fail if too many patients sought cures from what medicine deemed a practice of quackery.

Samuel Hahnemann, the founder of homeopathy, discovered the principles by accident. He struggled to make a living as a physician for fifteen years and after translating a medical book by William Cullen[5], he decided to experiment on himself by taking daily doses of *Peruvian bark* (or *cinchona*). Cullen had recommended Peruvian bark to help cure malaria because of its bitter and astringent properties, but Hahnemann wasn't convinced. After taking the bark for several days, his body responded with fever, chills, and other symptoms similar to malaria. As a result, he concluded that the reason Peruvian bark worked to cure malaria was because it caused similar symptoms.[234]

Hahnemann developed a system to treat symptoms through plant-based remedies that mimic the symptoms of the illness, administered in small doses. A homeopathic remedy increases the symptoms briefly so that your body can react to heal the disease on its own.

While it might be challenging to find a homeopath in your area, homeopathic remedies are readily available in health food stores and online. I've even seen homeopathic remedies for children in mainstream grocery stores. If you've ever bought arnica or calendula gel or cream, you've bought a homeopathic remedy. Even though they're derived from natural substances, homeopathic remedies are considered drugs by the Food and Drug Administration in the U.S. They're regulated by the Homeopathic Pharmacopoea of the United States (HPUS), thus assuring the consistency in the production and safety of the remedies. You can easily treat mild illness with homeopathic remedies by observing the symptoms and matching them to the remedy. The National Center for Homeopathy has a great website with

---

5 William Cullen (1710-1790), famous Scottish physician and medical professor who taught many of the pioneers of modern medicine including Benjamin Rush.

guidelines to self-treat and has a directory of providers. Go to Home-opathyCenter.org.

OTHER HEALING MODALITIES

There are a lot of other ways you can accelerate your healing process, too. For example, putting an aromatherapy diffuser in your office with stimulating essentials oils, such as peppermint or eucalyptus, can improve alertness and mental clarity while working. In fact, it's sometimes the totality of many little things that can make a huge difference in the rapidness of healing. Even if some of these healing arts seem insignificant, they might be worth trying to create a supportive healing environment.

1. FENG SHUI

A 3,000-year-old practice from China, feng shui is the art of object placement designed to create balance and bring about good fortune. The word *feng* means "wind" and *shui* means "water." In Chinese culture, wind and water combined bring about good health and therefore good fortune. Proper feng shui practices increase the flow of chi in any space.

A good way to start practicing feng shui is to remove any clutter. Clearing your spaces is the first step. Get rid of things that no longer serve you, or things that don't fit in your home. Next, get a good book on feng shui for your home or office and start with the basics. It'll be hard to heal your body when your spaces are blocked. Once you start making your spaces more harmonious, you'll begin to feel better.

2. CHAKRA HEALING

The word *chakra* is a Sanskrit word that translates to "wheel" or "disc." Think of a chakra as a concentration of energy in different areas of the body. In the body, there are seven main chakras that start at the base of the spine and move up to the crown of the head. For example, the area of your heart is the fourth chakra. The space where your heart is situated in your body encompasses, not only your heart but also your lungs, bronchial passages, thymus gland, and major arteries and lymphatic vessels. Keeping your heart chakra open and aligned energetically heals your heart and the entire area surrounding it. With this in mind, to heal your heart chakra you can focus on physical health such as eating properly and exercising but your heart also absorbs emotional energy from your love relationships and you must heal that too.

Healing your chakras is a type of energy healing, but you can find specific massage therapists who will pinpoint blockages in your chakras and help release them. I talk extensively about chakra healing in my book *Chakra Healing for Vibrant Energy: Exploring Your 7 Energy Centers with Mindfulness, Yoga, and Ayurveda*.

3. CRYSTALS AND GEMS

Ask a woman wanting to get married and she'll tell you: a diamond is very therapeutic. But all joking aside, many crystals and gems emit healing energy. Many spas have sauna rooms with different crystals and gems. For example, a rock salt room can improve cardiovascular health and relieve stress, and oak charcoal can help improve overall health. Even something as simple as putting a genuine Himalayan rock salt lamp in your home can help boost your respiratory health.

4. ANIMAL THERAPY

If you own a pet, you already know the therapeutic benefits of playing with or petting an animal. One of the first studies on pet therapy published in the 1980s found that heart attack patients who had pets at home lived longer than those who didn't.[235] Animal-Assisted Therapy (AAT) can facilitate psychotherapy for kids or assist with those in addiction recovery. According to scientist Andrea Beetz in Frontiers in Psychology, interaction with animals increases our levels of oxytocin, the chemical that makes us feel happy and connected.[236] While cat and dog therapy are beneficial, a lot of research has also been done on the benefits of Equine-Assisted Therapy (EAT) or horse therapy, which started as a type of therapy for those with physical disabilities and extended to patients with mental illness and behavioral problems. For example, horses are known to respond in direct relation to human behavior. So if a patient mistreats the horse or therapist in front of the horse, the horse will mirror the attitude by being unwilling to move, by nudging the patient, or by nipping at them. In turn the patient is less likely to repeat the undesirable behavior in the future.[237] It's an interesting form of modeling that might be more effective than if a human were to use mirroring in the same way.

Animal therapy can also be beneficial for:

- Those with cardiovascular diseases
- People undergoing chemotherapy
- Those in long-term care facilities
- Veterans with post-traumatic stress disorder
- Stroke victims and those undergoing physical therapy
- People with mental disorders
- Children who are sick or who have disabilities

Many hospitals provide pet therapy. You can find pet therapy through different organizations such as PawsforPeople.org or EquestrianTherapy.com.

You can also explore many other healing modalities, such as music therapy, art therapy, or even color therapy. Different types of therapies will appeal to different people. Have fun exploring which methods of healing resonate most with your personality!

Things to Keep in Mind

As you explore complementary healing modalities, try to keep a few things in mind...

1. You're not going to like all of them – nor should you.

Certain types of healing modalities will speak to you more than others. If you're completely skeptical of a method once you start, sticking with it probably won't help. At the very least, do not waste your time and money. Use your intuition when choosing rather than listening to outside opinions.

2. Stick with a healing modality long enough to see results.

If you're on the fence as to whether or not a therapy is working, try sticking with it for at least a few sessions, or even a few months to see if you experience healing benefits. In general gentler and more natural practices take more time than allopathic medicine. Allow your body the time to heal.

3. Do your homework and find a good expert in the field.

Just as you might do if you were to hire a plumber or mechanic, get references and talk to former clients. The downside to some alternative practices is that they're not covered by health insurance, which means you'll be paying out of pocket. Finding someone good the first time can save you money in the long run and help you get better sooner.

4. Refrain from trying too many therapies at once.

If you try too many things at once, it'll be difficult for you to know what's working and what's not. I know a horrible diagnosis can send you into a tailspin and you'll want to do as many things as possible to get better. But more is not necessarily better. Quality will be better than quantity. Remember, when you're sick, you also need to let your body rest. If you're busy going to 50 appointments weekly, you're not resting. Instead, pick one or two alternative therapies, alter your diet, drink lots of water, and get plenty of quality sleep.

CHAPTER 12

CREATING A BALANCED LIFE

WHEN YOU'RE DIAGNOSED WITH or healing from an illness, thinking about how to deal with life afterward is daunting. You might be thinking, *where's the freedom and ability to be carefree?* You feel limited and worried. Without the proper perspective, you can be frozen from taking action toward getting yourself healthy and balanced. In an ideal world, we would be living balanced lives all the time with a focus on preventive health. But that's not often our reality. Whether you've been diagnosed with cancer, diabetes, high blood pressure, obesity, or have suffered a stroke or other illness, your balanced life can start today.

STEP ONE: ADOPT A BASIC WHOLE FOODS DIET

Recently, I was at a seminar where the focus was on lifting limitations and living a life full of fantastic health on all levels. Toward the end of the seminar, various speakers were promoting their own works and philosophies, all mostly about diet. Among them, two of the speakers presented material that was not only in direct conflict with what we had been taught earlier in the day, but also in direct conflict with each other. That's when it hit me: I realized that most Americans are perpetually confused about what to eat.

Let me explain. If you go anywhere else in the world, people are not conflicted about what to eat. Generally speaking, each country has cultural dishes and foods they've been eating for generations. Many cultures don't question what to eat or how to eat. But Americans seem to change their eating habits as quickly as the wind changes. In recent years, people have gone from fat-free, to carb-free, then to gluten-free, then to Paleo. Now more than ever, most Americans are completely confused about what's good for you and what isn't. And the confusion doesn't seem to stop at food. At the same seminar, many speakers were talking about the best water to drink or the best physical activity to perform. It seems that the more we know, the less we know. Sometimes the answers lie in what's simple.

I'd like to offer you a solution that takes you back to the basics.

Regardless of what you read in the latest blog, magazine, or diet book, you can't go wrong with adopting a whole food diet and eating in moderation. What are whole foods, you might ask? Whole foods come from the earth and are minimally processed. Understandably, some food needs to be preserved for transportation or presentation and might have a wax coating or be wrapped in packaging. But I encourage you to try and eat a diet of fresh whole foods.

In this type of diet, you'll be eating organic fresh fruit, and vegetables, organic nuts, seeds, beans, and lentils, fresh organic oils, whole grains, fresh organic meats and fish (if you're not a vegetarian or vegan), and natural sweeteners like organic honey and maple syrup. You can also include grass-fed organic dairy. In addition, try drinking either reverse osmosis water or ionized alkaline water. You'll forgo all processed food, microwaved food, leftovers (only eat leftovers within 24 hours of cooking), and most canned and frozen food.

If you stick to the basics in diet, you won't have to constantly wonder, "Am I eating the right foods?" Your body will know. You'll be retraining your body to find its natural intelligence.

You can eat a mostly vegetarian or vegan diet, and if you desire, eat organic chicken, red meat, or fish once a week. Keep variety in your diet. Try not to eat the same things every day or at every meal throughout the week. Add colors to your diet through colorful vegetables and fruits. You will ensure that you're getting the most phytonutrients and antioxidants throughout the week.

Remember the 90-10 rule: make sure that 90% of the time, you're eating organic whole foods, and 10% of the time, you can let loose and eat other foods. Have a piece of cake or chocolate. Enjoy a pizza with your family. To calculate your 10%, figure out how many meals you eat per week. For example, if you eat three meals per day, seven days per week, you would be disciplined with your whole foods diet for nineteen meals weekly and let yourself have a little fun with the other two.

Finally, let's explore moderation. In the West most of us don't know how to be moderate when it comes to food and drink. In recent decades, portion sizes have gotten larger, more sugars have been added to food, and we've become more sedentary. As a result, it's very difficult to gauge how much we need to maintain weight. According to the Department of Agriculture in 1970, the average American consumed around 2,169 calories per day, but by 2008 that number climbed to 2,674 – or an increase of 23%.[238] That's shocking, but even more shocking is a recent statistic published by *Business Insider* on June 13, 2017, which states that Americans today consume more than 3,600 calories daily.

So how many calories should you consume? The answer to this question depends largely on your age, body structure, and activity level. According to the USDA Food Patterns, an American man should consume anywhere between 2,000 and 3,000 calories daily depending on age and activity level, and an American woman should consume anywhere between 1,600 and 2,400 calories daily.[239] With such wide ranges, it can be tricky to know the right fit for you. To figure it out, you might need to become a bit of a detective. If you find you're gaining weight each year, start tracking your total daily calorie intake plus any activity on an app like My Fitness Pal. It's free and easy to use. Once you've averaged your total calorie intake daily for one week, you can set a daily calorie goal and lower it until you find you're either maintaining your weight or losing it – whatever your preference.

At age 47, I've learned that the only way to make sure that I don't gain weight is to track my food intake daily. Even though I'm fairly active, I've noticed that my metabolism has slowed down after forty. Tracking keeps me accountable to myself and alerts me if I'm consuming too much.

Now that you've learned to balance your diet and your food intake, let's explore how to minimize pollutants in your body and environment.

STEP TWO: GET RID OF POLLUTANTS

As we learned in the chapter on eating clean, most of our food and water contains pollutants. Recently, one of my favorite teachers, Tony Robbins, revealed that he had mercury poisoning from eating too much fish. Because we live in such a polluted world, mixing up what you eat from day to day will help your body more easily rid itself of metals and toxins.

Many people feel depressed, feel anxious, or experience chronic fatigue because of the toxins in their food and environment. As part of living a balanced life, it's best to rule out these things as a cause, and the best way to do that is to detoxify your environment.

CLEANING AND PURIFYING

Try to get rid of (but don't dump or pour) all cleaning products in your home that aren't earth-friendly. (To discard them you can wrap tops on the bottles in a strong adhesive tape, such as duct tape, and put them in your trash. You can do the same thing with unused prescription medications that you need to throw out.) Instead of bug repellent, use essential oils. Look up ways to clean with simple and natural products such as baking soda, vinegar, and Borax. Then check your hair and skin care products. Try to find those with the most natural ingredients. Finally, add houseplants to your home to purify the air. I'm a big fan of houseplants that are easy to care for, as I don't have the time or patience to tend to finicky plants. One word of caution, however: if you have a cat or dog, many household plants can be toxic if they nibble on them. Trying hanging baskets or high shelves for your houseplants.

The best air purifiers that are easy to care for are...

- **Spider Plant:** Likes sunlight and hanging baskets.
- **Dracaena:** Toxic to cats and dogs if eaten. Low-maintenance plant that likes indirect sunlight and slightly moist soil.
- **Ficus/Weeping Fig:** Likes bright indirect or filtered light. Poisonous to animals.
- **Peace Lily:** Likes low light. Poisonous to animals.
- **Lady Palm:** Tolerates low-light and can hang out in a dark corner of your home.
- **Boston Fern:** Good in hanging baskets but needs a lot of moisture and humidity.
- **Snake Plant:** Thrives in low light. May be harmful to pets if ingested.
- **Bamboo palm:** Helps keep the air moist.
- **Aloe Vera:** If you burn yourself in the kitchen, you can snip off a leaf and squeeze the aloe vera juice onto your skin. Poisonous to animals.

Removing Allergens

If you experience a lot of allergies, try an ionic air purifier. In addition to plants, many find that an air purifier helps them sleep better at night and reduces sinus congestion. Make sure you're changing your air filters monthly, install carbon monoxide detectors in your home, and check for sources of mold. Most importantly, open your windows and use old-fashioned fresh air at least once weekly to circulate the air in your home.

Step Three: Balance Your Exercise Program

First of all, I'm assuming you already have an exercise program. And if you don't, it's best to start and maybe revisit chapter eight. Many Westerners take an all-or-nothing approach to exercise. You don't need to overindulge – just start simple. The best exercise program will include cardiovascular activity 3-5 days per week for at least 30 minutes each time, weight resistance activity 1-2 days per week, and stretching 1-2 days per week.

Cross-training is the easiest way to minimize injury. For example, you could pick two of your cardio days and go walking. On the other two, you could ride a stationary bike. And on an optional day, you could take a cardio dance class. When doing weight resistance training, you could focus one day on arms and upper body, and then the next day on abs and lower body. Mixing up your routine will also help you from getting bored from it.

Step Four: Balance Your Daily Routine

Modern Western living is not conducive to a balanced life. Many people I see in my practice come to me because of stress, anxiety, and sheer exhaustion. Much of that comes from a schedule that is already disjointed and chaotic. Consistency in daily routine – which include healthy practices – is the antidote to much of the stress you experience throughout your week. It's easy to fall into the trap of claiming,

"I'm too busy to integrate healthy practices into my day. Have you seen the demands of my job and family?" But the truth is if you don't schedule in the practices that will keep you healthy, you won't ever do them. Think about getting up an hour earlier to meditate, do some yoga, tai chi, or qi gong, and make a healthy breakfast and lunch to take to work. You can use your lunch hour to walk, work out at the gym, or do some yoga breathing and meditation. Plan your meals in advance. Take time to rest.

If you find that your schedule is completely crazy and you're feeling simply overwhelmed, write down your day in advance and allocate time for each activity. Make sure to include driving or commuting times. When I'm feeling overwhelmed with my projects and teaching, I just do this, and I separate each activity into chunks. For example: for writing I might need to do research, actual writing, and editing, and that goes into one chunk. For video production, I need to prepare, set up, film, edit, and upload to YouTube, etc. When I do this, I feel less stressed, as my "to do" list seems smaller.

STEP FIVE: CREATE BALANCE BETWEEN BODY, MIND, EMOTIONS, & SOUL

When creating optimal health, it's important to explore all aspects of yourself. I recently had a client who has spent the last several years working hard to build up her career. She was always conscientious about exercising and eating a healthy diet. But because of her steadfast dedication to her career and her exercise regimen, she hadn't nourished her relationships or her spiritual health. She became extremely anxious and nervous and was losing sleep. Even though on the outside it appeared that all was well in her life, inside she felt something was missing.

We all fall into the trap of focusing on one aspect of our life and ignoring others. If you're feeling out of sorts, examine your life and see what you might be forgetting to nurture. Has it been a long time since you explored your feelings about a relationship or situation? Have you been intellectualizing too much and left out the more intuitive or spiritual side to you? Have you forgotten to take a vacation, play, and have fun? Life is a constant changing dynamic and we are never finished products. Try to look at your life as an adventure, or as a fun challenge to figure out!

Holistic healing comes from recognizing that whatever ails you could be "something else." What appears on the surface is usually a sign of something much deeper. If you've ever had the good fortune of watching over a preschooler, you know that as the day goes on, they can sometimes get more argumentative, push your buttons, and be generally unpleasant. When you look on the surface, you might think, *Wow! This kid is a brat. Look how poorly they're behaving!* But when you consider the situation more deeply, you deduct, *Oh wow! This kid has been playing for five hours straight with no break. It's 5 P.M., and they're probably hungry – plus, they missed their nap. I need to get them something to eat.*

Or if you've ever had an argument with your significant other over something silly like dirty socks in the bathroom, dishes left in the sink, or a wrongly-purchased food item, stop to ponder the knee-jerk reaction. You know in your gut that those arguments are probably about something more significant.

The same goes for holistic healing. Instead of running to the doctor's office for a small panic attack or a bad case of heartburn, think about a bigger picture of your life over the past week. Is the panic attack due to the fact that you've been running yourself ragged with 16-hour days for the past week? Or have you been completely ignoring a relationship that you know needs attention? Are you perhaps experiencing heartburn because you know you should stop eating fried food and drinking alcohol, but for the past five days, you've been doing nothing but that?

Holistic healing means complete honesty with yourself about your life and lifestyle. Self-honesty is one of the most difficult things to espouse as a habit. For example, I log in my food on an app, and sometimes it gets tempting to fudge my food intake or my weight. Doesn't that sound a little silly? I'm the only one seeing it. And yet it's easy to fall into the trap of self-deception.

The seven deadly chronic lifestyle diseases and other chronic lifestyle illnesses are tragic. The only way we're really going to combat them is independently, with hard work, dedication, and self-honesty.

STEP SIX: CREATE BALANCE BETWEEN WESTERN MEDICINE AND ALTERNATIVE PRACTICES

As you begin to listen to your body and sharpen your intuition, you'll know when it's time to go see an allopathic doctor or head to the emergency room. Please don't be stubborn. Listen to that intuition.

When my middle son was two years old, we traveled to France to see his grandparents. On the plane, he contracted a nasty gastrointestinal virus. He had diarrhea and was vomiting everything he ingested. We started giving him little sips of water every hour, then when he was vomiting that, we gave him soda. After a couple of days, my mother-in-law brought us to see her homeopath. I believe wholeheartedly in homeopathy and because of my belief, I listened to the homeopath and started giving my son the remedies. But in my heart, something didn't feel quite right.

The next day, he was listless and ashen. The only thing he could mutter was "mama" in a very weak voice. So I insisted that my mother-in-law drive us to the emergency room. She argued that the homeopathy was working and that the stomach virus was just taking its normal course. But my own mother's intuition was screaming at me to do something. We got my son to the hospital just in time. He was severely dehydrated and had to stay in the hospital for several days.

Your Western mindset might think that was negligent of me to have waited, but I believe we went at just the right time. With viruses, it's difficult to know whether the fever will break or the symptoms will clear up within a day or two. That's why it's important to become aware of the red flags and inner voice that tells you it's time to check with a doctor.

But that said, many people ignore their body's symptoms and wait way too long to get help. It's my hope that by practicing integrative medicine and embracing your power to get well now, you'll become more aware of your body's signals and choose to get a check up before an illness becomes more serious.

FINAL THOUGHTS ABOUT YOUR POWER TO GET WELL NOW

This is the beginning of your journey to becoming empowered in your capacity to self-heal and to awaken the innate intelligence of your body. With that, I'd like to offer you a few last words of wisdom.

First of all, belief is everything. Your beliefs form your habits, and your habits form who you are. As you consider working with your body, mind, emotions, and soul on healing, you might get some pushback – not just from your own mind, but from others, too. Until you're feeling strong again, try to keep others and their opinions out of it. And by others, I'm not referring to your physicians, but rather your family, friends, colleagues, and acquaintances. Many of them will try to infuse doubt in your ability to heal.

It's important to remember that we haven't been raised in a society that celebrates self-healing. We were raised in a society that taught you not to trust your body. The doctor knows best. Trusting your body is a foreign concept to most people. Let me reiterate: there is a time and place for doctor visits, tests, medical procedures, prescription medications, and surgery. But if you employ the healing methods outlined in this book and begin to tell others about them, their doubts may seep into your own mind and make you question yourself.

After I had my thyroid removed it took a while to find the correct medication and dosage and during that time I felt horrible. I was experiencing panic attacks, depression, mood swings, and extreme fatigue. After telling one endocrinologist about my symptoms, he tested and then told me my thyroid levels were normal. But at age 29 and with all of those symptoms, I certainly wasn't feeling normal. I went for a second opinion with another endocrinologist and he told me the exact same thing. After a few months of feeling the same, I went back and asked him to retest. The blood test results came back the same as before, and he told me it wasn't a physical problem, but a psychological one, instructing me then to go see a psychiatrist. I did indeed go to see a psychiatrist – one who didn't do any extensive testing or questioning, but instead, simply gave me a prescription for Xanax. I knew it was wrong, but for my first few panic attacks after seeing the psychiatrist, I took a Xanax. And I didn't feel any better; it just made me tired.

One day, I was sitting on the front steps of my townhome and crying because I couldn't believe that I had all of these terrible symptoms and that not a single doctor believed that they were related to the thyroid medication. After some prayer and meditation, I made the decision to believe in myself and my intuition. I took the Xanax prescription and threw it in the dumpster. Even though no one believed in me, I needed to believe in myself and get to the bottom of my symptoms.

The story has a happy ending: I found an integrative medical practitioner who understood that my body wasn't responding to the thyroid medication I was taking, even though my blood tests were showing normal levels. But if I hadn't trusted my body and my intuition, I might be on a whole host of medications to this day, much worse off than I am as I write this.

Secondly, experiment with what works and what doesn't. When I was going through the thyroid medication debacle, I kept a spreadsheet of my daily symptoms and the different things I was trying to be able to get better. I logged all of the vitamins and herbs I was taking, my exercise regimen, my overall mood for the day, my diet, and my interactions with others. I wanted to know what variables made a difference. That daily log helped me figure out which practices to keep and which ones to discard. If you're experiencing a chronic lifestyle illness, a daily log will be extremely beneficial to you, especially if you have to modify your diet or take new medications.

Thirdly, all of this will seem like a lot of work in the beginning, but it will get easier. At first, you'll need to think about absolutely everything. You're retraining your brain to adopt new and perhaps foreign daily habits. I remember the first time I learned to drive a stick shift car. There were so many variables that it seemed impossible to think of anything else. The first thirty times I drove it, I was convinced that I would never get the hang of it. But after the first month, it became second nature. You'll experience the same thing with your integrative practices. For example, maybe for the first 30, 40, or even 50 years of your life, you have never considered getting up a half an hour early to meditate – or even considered meditation at all. But now, you find yourself getting up an hour early to meditate and do a few yoga poses. And on top of that, you find you need less sleep.

Fourth, you'll need to mourn your old habits, otherwise you'll go back to them. You can mourn anything you know in your heart you must give up to live a healthier life. It could be an object, or it could be a principle. When I learned that I'd have to take thyroid medication for the rest of my life, I was bitter for a long time. I always had the notion that I would live such a healthy life that I would never have to take a prescription drug other than the occasional antibiotic. It took me years to accept it, but eventually, I had to make peace with it. So instead I let it be my anchor. I now say, "This is the only prescription medication I will ever have to take." For diabetics, it could be about sugar. You might have to give up sugar, but you can gain a lot of energy or weight loss in return.

Finally, remain consistent in action and try not to get complacent. The feeling of wellness inside always precedes physical healing. For example, if you've had a bad cold for a week, you wake up one morning feeling rested and energetic even though your nose is still running. That's because the subtle changes that allow you to feel healthy take place subconsciously before your body is symptom-free. At that point, it can be easy to give up and go back to old habits. Be aware of the urge to get lazy about your new healthy habits and instead double down. Big changes happen as a result of an accumulation of little changes.

Creating new healthy habits take time. Be patient with yourself, but be disciplined about practicing them. Realize that there are many things you can control about your health and wellbeing, and a few things that remain out of your control. Use faith or focus on a positive outcome, and you'll find you'll have a much better prognosis overall.

In closing, please share this knowledge with others. I'm but one author with one voice. But think about all of the people you have in your life. Giving even a small piece of ancient healing wisdom to just a few people can have a ripple effect. With your help, we can raise consciousness about health and reverse the trend of chronic lifestyle illness not only for the United States, but also across the globe.

God bless you, healing warrior! Peace and healing to you always.

GLOSSARY of MEDICAL TERMS

adaptogen: A plant extract that increases the body's ability to resist the damaging effects of stress and promote or restore normal physiological functioning.

adjuvant therapy: Treatment given to a patient, usually after surgical removal of their primary tumor when there is known to be a high risk of future tumor recurrence. Adjuvent therapy is aimed at destroying these microscopic cells.

allopathy: The orthodox system of medicine, in which the use of drugs is directed to producing effects in the body that will directly oppose and so alleviate the symptoms of disease.

Alzheimer's disease: A progressive form of dementia occurring in middle age or later, characterized by loss of short-term memory, deterioration of behavior and intellectual performance, and slowness of thought.

analgesic: A drug that relieves pain.

angioplasty: Repair or replacement of a narrowed or completely obstructed blood vessel.

antimicrobial: Destroying or inhibiting the growth of microorganisms and especially pathogenic microorganisms.

antioxidant: A substance capable of neutralizing oxygen free radicals, the highly reactive and damaging atoms and chemical groups produced by various disease processes and by poisons, radiation, smoking and other agencies.

antigens: Any substance that may be specifically bound by an antibody molecule.

aphrodisiac: An agent (such as a food or drug) that arouses or is held to arouse sexual desire.

antirheumatic: Alleviating or preventing rheumatism.

antiparasitic: Acting against parasites.

antispasmodic: A drug that relieves spasm of smooth muscle in the gut.

anthelmintic: Any drug or chemical agent used to destroy parasitic worms.

astringent: A drug that causes cells to shrink by precipitating proteins from their surfaces. Astringents are used in lotions to harden and protect the skin and to reduce bleeding from minor abrasions.

Attention-Deficit Disorder (ADD)/ Attention- Deficit/Hyperactivity Disorder (ADHD): A mental disorder, usually of children, characterized by a grossly excessive level of activity and a marked impairment of the ability to attend. Learning is impaired and behavior may be disruptive.

autonomic nervous system: The part of the peripheral nervous system responsible for the control of involuntary muscles (e.g. heart, bladder, bowels) and hence those bodily functions that are not consciously directed, including regular beating of the heart, intestinal movements, sweating, and salivation. Consists of the sympathetic and the parasympathetic nervous systems.

benzodiazepine: A group of pharmacologically active compounds used as anxiolytics (minor tranquilizers) and hypnotics. Common side effects of these drugs are drowsiness and dizziness, and prolonged use may result in dependence. Examples of benzodiazepines: diazepam and chlordiazepoxide.

biopsy: The removal of a small piece of living tissue, cells, or fluid from an organ or part of the body for microscopic examination. Biopsy is an important means of diagnosing cancer from examination of a fragment of the tumor.

bloodletting (phlebotomy): The surgical removal of some of a patient's blood for therapeutic purposes.

bypass surgery: A surgical procedure to divert the flow of blood or other fluid from one anatomical structure to another; a shunt. A bypass can be temporary or permanent and is commonly performed in the treatment of cardiac and gastrointestinal disorders.

candida: A genus of yeasts that inhabit the vagina and alimentary tract and can–under certain conditions–cause candidosis (yeast infection).

carminative: A drug that relieves flatulence, used to treat gastric colic and discomfort.

chemotherapy: The prevention or treatment of disease by the use of chemical substances. The term is increasingly restricted to the treatment of cancer but is also still sometimes used for antibiotic and other treatment of infectious diseases.

cirrhosis of the liver: A condition in which the liver responds to injury to some of its cells by producing interlacing strands of fibrous tissue between which are nodules of regenerating cells. Cirrhosis is caused by chronic progressive conditions such as alcoholism or hepatitis.

cystitis: Inflammation of the urinary bladder, often caused by infection. It is usually accompanied by the desire to pass urine frequently, with a degree of burning.

dermis: The thick layer of skin that lies beneath the epidermis. It consists mainly of loose connective tissue within which are blood capillaries, lymph vessels, sensory nerve endings, sweat glands, and their ducts, hair follicles, sebaceous glands, and smooth muscle fibers.

diaphoretic: An agent that promotes sweating.

diuretic: A drug that increases the volume of urine produced by promoting the excretion of salts and water from the kidney.

dopamine: A chemical found in the brain that acts as a neurotransmitter and an intermediate in the biosynthesis of epinephrine.

emollient: Making soft or supple especially to the skin or mucous membrane.

endocrine system: The glands and parts of glands that produce endocrine secretions, help to integrate and control bodily metabolic activity and include especially the pituitary, thyroid, parathyroids, adrenals, islets of Langerhans, ovaries, and testes.

endorphin: One of a group of chemical compounds, similar to the encephalins, that occur naturally in the brain and have pain-relieving properties similar to those of the opiates. They are also responsible for sensations of pleasure.

epidermis: The outer layer of the skin which is divided into four layers.

expectorant: A drug that enhances the expulsion of mucus from the respiratory tract.

free radicals: An atom or molecule that bears an unpaired electron and is extremely reactive, capable of engaging in rapid chain reactions that destabilize other molecules and generate many more free radicals.

fibromyalgia: Pain and stiffness in the muscles and joints that is either diffuse or has multiple trigger points.

gene mutation: A permanent alteration in the DNA sequence that makes up a gene, such that the sequence differs from that which is found in most people.

hemostasis: The arrest of bleeding.

hepatitis: Inflammation of the liver usually caused by a virus classified as hepatitis A, B, C, D, or E. Can also be caused by toxic substances or immunological abnormalities.

homeostasis: The physiological process by which the internal systems of the body (e.g. blood pressure, body temperature) are maintained at equilibrium, despite variations in the external conditions.

hydrogenated oil: An oil with trans-fatty acids that has been chemically changed from a room-temperature liquid state into a solid by adding hydrogen. Hydrogenated oils can affect heart health because they increase "bad" (LDL) cholesterol and lower "good" HDL cholesterol.

hyperglycemia: Abnormally increased glucose in the blood, such as in diabetes mellitus.

hypertension: High arterial blood pressure.

islets of Langerhans: Small groups of endocrine cells scattered through the material of the pancreas. There are three main histological types: alpha cells, which secrete glucagon; beta cells, which produce insulin; and D cells which, release somatostatin and pancreatic polypeptide.

lignans: Group of chemical compounds found in plant-based foods including flaxseeds, sesame seeds, pumpkin sees, and rye.

lymph: A transparent, slightly yellow liquid of alkaline reaction, found in the lymphatic vessels and derived from the tissue fluids. Lymph is collected from all parts of the body and returned to the blood via the lymphatic system.

lymphatic system: A network of vessels that conveys electrolytes, water, proteins, etc.– in the form of lymph– from the tissue fluids in the blood stream.

lymphocyte: A variety of white blood cell, present also in the lymph nodes, spleen, thymus gland, gut wall, and bone marrow.

macrobiotic diet: Rooted in a traditional Japanese diet and popularized in the 1960s, this diet includes a daily regime of whole grains, notably brown rice, seaweed or other leafy green vegetables, and beans.

mastectomy: Surgical removal of the breast.

neuropathy: A functional disturbance or pathological change in the peripheral nervous system causing weakness or numbness.

neurotransmitters: A chemical substance released from nerve endings to transmit impulses across synapses to other nerves and across the minute gaps between the nerves and the muscles or glands that they supply.

omega-3 fatty acids: A class of essential fatty acids in fish oils primarily, especially from salmon and other cold water fish, that acts to lower the levels of cholesterol and LDL (low-density lipoproteins) in the blood. Omega-3 fatty acids are also found in flaxseed oil, canola oil, and walnuts.

oxidation: A process in which a chemical substance changes because of the addition of oxygen.

Parkinson's disease: A chronic progressive neurological disease chiefly later in life that is linked to decreased dopamine production in the substantia nigra (a deeply pigmented gray matter in the midbrain), is of unknown cause, and is marked especially by tremor of resting muscles, rigidity, slowness of movement, impaired balance, and a shuffling gait.

pathogen: A microorganism, such as a bacterium, that parasitizes an animal (or plant) or a human and produces a disease.

pathology: the structural and functional deviations from the normal that constitute disease or characterize a particular disease.

pesticide: Chemicals that farmers put on their crops to kill harmful insects.

perineum: The region of the body between the anus and the urethral opening, including both skin and underlying muscle.

phytoestrogen: A compound naturally occurring in plants. The estrogen present in plants may function like animal estrogen found in humans. When phytoestrogens are consumed, the human body may respond as if real estrogen were present.

Therefore, they could serve as a type of natural hormone replacement, especially in menopausal women.

placebo: A medicine that is ineffective but may help to relieve a condition because the patient has faith in its powers.

Proliferation: The reproduction or multiplication of similar forms especially of cells and morbid cysts.

purgative: laxative

quinine: A drug used to treat malaria. Large doses can cause severe poisoning. Small doses are used to treat nocturnal leg cramps.

rejuvenative: A substance that keeps cells young.

rheumatism: Any disorder in which aches and pains affect the muscles and joints. (i.e. rheumatoid arthritis, rheumatic fever, osteoarthritis, gout)

serotonin: A compound widely distributed in the tissues, particularly in the blood platelets, intestinal wall, and central nervous system. It also acts as a neurotransmitter, and its levels in the brain are believed to have an important influence on mood.

stroke (apoplexy): A sudden attack of weakness affecting one side of the body as a consequence of an interruption of blood flow to the brain.

synapse: The minute gap across which nerve impulses pass from one neuron to the next, at the end of the nerve fiber.

thyroid gland: A large endocrine gland in the base of the neck. It consists of two lobes, one on either side of the trachea, joined by an isthmus. The thyroid gland is concerned with regulation of the metabolic rate by the secretion of thyroid hormone, which is stimulated by thyroid-stimulating hormone from the pituitary gland and requires trace amounts of iodine.

toxin: A poison produced by a living organism, especially by a bacterium. In the body toxins act as antigens, and special antibodies are formed to neutralize their effects.

ulcer: A break in the skin extending to all its layers, or a break in the mucous membrane lining the alimentary tract, that fails to heal and is often accompanied by inflammation.

urethritis: Inflammation of the urethra. This may be due to gonorrhea, another sexually transmitted disease, or the presence of a catheter in the urethra.

venesection (phlebotomy): The surgical opening or puncture of a vein in order to remove blood or to infuse fluids, blood, or drugs in the treatment of many conditions.

NOTES

1. See glossary for definition.

2. *Centers for Disease Control and Prevention,* "Chronic Disease Overview, http://www.cdc.gov/chronicdisease/overview/.

3. "The Chronic Care Model," *Improving Chronic Illness Care,* Accessed January 9, 2018, http://www.improvingchroniccare.org/index. php?p=The_Chronic_Care_Model&s=2.

4. Doug Irving, "Chronic Conditions in America: Price and Prevalence," *Rand Review,* July 12, 2017, https://www.rand.org/blog/rand-review/2017/07/ chronic-conditions-in-america-price-and-prevalence.html.   Accessed: January 3, 2018.

5. *Centers for Disease Control and Prevention,* "Long-Term Trends in Diabetes," CDC's Division of Diabetes Translation, April 2017, https://www. cdc.gov/diabetes/statistics/slides/long_term_trends.pdf.

6. "National Diabetes Statistics Report: 2017," *Diabetes.org,* http://www. diabetes.org/assets/pdfs/basics/cdc-statistics-report-2017.pdf.

7. *Harvard T.H. Chan School of Public Health,* "Child Obesity," Obesity Prevention Source, http://www.hsph. harvard.edu/obesity-prevention-source/obesity-trends/ global-obesity-trends-in-children/.

8. Adrienne Santos-Longhurst and George T. Krucik, MD, MBA, "Type 2 Diabetes Statistics and Data," *Healthline,* September 8, 2014, http://www. healthline.com/health/type-2-diabetes/statistics.

9. Doug Irving, "Chronic Conditions in America: Price and Prevalence," *Rand Review,* July 12, 2017, https://www.rand.org/blog/rand-review/2017/07/ chronic-conditions-in-america-price-and-prevalence.html.

10. *American Society of Addiction Medicine,* Adopted by the ASAM Board of Directors, April 19, 2011, http://www.asam.org/quality-practice/ definition-of-addiction.

11. *Centers for Disease Control and Prevention,* "Chronic Disease Prevention and Health Promotion," Accessed April 14, 2016, http://www.cdc.gov/ chronicdisease/.

12. *Centers for Disease Control and Prevention,* "Chronic Disease Prevention and Health Promotion," Accessed April 14, 2016, http://www.cdc.gov/ chronicdisease/.

13. Frank W. Booth Ph.D., Christian K. Roberts Ph.D., and Matthew J. Laye Ph.D., "Lack of Exercise is a Major Cause of Chronic Diseases," *Comprehensive Physiology,* April 1, 2012, http://www.ncbi.nlm.nih.gov/pmc/

articles/PMC4241367/ and *The World Health Organization*, "Chronic Diseases and Their Common Risk Factors," http://www.who.int/chp/chronic_disease_report/media/Factsheet1.pdf.

14. "National Diabetes Statistics Report: 2017," *Diabetes.org*, http://www.diabetes.org/assets/pdfs/basics/cdc-statistics-report-2017.pdf.

15. Ross DeVol and Armen Bedroussian, "An Unhealthy America: The Economic Burden of Chronic Disease," *The Milken Institute*, October 2007, http://assets1b.milkeninstitute.org/assets/Publication/ResearchReport/PDF/chronic_disease_report.pdf.

16. Morgan Lewis Jr., "Medical Malpractice Costs Continue to Climb," *Medical Economics*, January 11, 2012, http://medicaleconomics.modernmedicine.com/medical-economics/news/clinical/practice-management/medical-malpractice-costs-continue-climb.

17. Tara Weiss, "Reasons to Not Become a Doctor," *Forbes*, May 5, 2008, https://www.forbes.com/2008/05/05/physicians-training-prospects-lead-careers-cx_tw_0505doctors.html.

18. Bruce Horovitz and Julie Appleby, with Kaiser Health News. "Prescription Drug Costs Are Up; So Are TV Ads Promoting Them," USA Today, March 16, 2017, https://www.usatoday.com/story/money/2017/03/16/prescription-drug-costs-up-tv-ads/99203878/.

19. Pam Belluck, "Children's Life Expectancy Being Cut Short by Obesity," March 17, 2005, *The New York Times*, http://www.nytimes.com/2005/03/17/health/childrens-life-expectancy-being-cut-short-by-obesity.html?_r=0.

20. *World Health Organization,*"Health Statistics," http://www.who.int/topics/statistics/en/.

21. "Life Expectancy In U.S. Drops For First Time in Decades Report Finds," Rob Stein on *Morning Edition, NPR News*, December 8, 2016, http://www.npr.org/sections/health-shots/2016/12/08/504667607/life-expectancy-in-u-s-drops-for-first-time-in-decades-report-finds.

22. Lenny Berstein,"U.S. Life Expectancy Declines for the First Time Since 1993," *The Washington Post*, December 8, 2016, https://www.washingtonpost.com/national/health-science/us-life-expectancy-declines-for-the-first-time-since-1993/2016/12/07/7dcdc7b4-bc93-11e6-91ee-1adddfe36cbe_story.html?utm_term=.f1965c01a9f4.

23. Imre Zoltan,"Ignas Semmelweis," *Encyclopaedia Britannica*, https://www.britannica.com/biography/Ignaz-Semmelweis.

24. Rebecca David, "The Doctor Who Championed Hand-Washing

and Briefly Saved Lives," *NPR Morning Edition*, January 15, 2015, http://www.npr.org/sections/health-shots/2015/01/12/375663920/the-doctor-who-championed-hand-washing-and-saved-women-s-lives.

25. "Florence Nightingale Nurse," *Biography.com*, https://www.biography.com/people/florence-nightingale-9423539.

26. "Florence Nightingale Biography," *Bio*, http://www.biography.com/people/florence-nightingale-9423539.

27. Ira Dixon, "Civil War Medicine: Modern Medicine's Civil War Legacy," *CivilWar.org*, http://www.civilwar.org/education/history/civil-war-medicine/civil-war-medicine.html?referrer=https://www.google.com/

28. Stanley B. Burns M.D., "Nursing in the Civil War," *Behind the Lens: A History in Pictures*, PBS, http://www.pbs.org/mercy-street/uncover-history/behind-lens/nursing-civil-war/.

29. "Florence Nightingale," *HistoryBits.com*, http://www.historybits.com/florence-nightingale.htm.

30. "Jonathan Letterman," *Civil War Trust*, https://www.civilwar.org/learn/biographies/jonathan-letterman.

31. "William A. Hammond," *U.S. Army Medical Department Office of Medical History*, http://history.amedd.army.mil/surgeongenerals/W_Hammond.html.

32. Ina Dixon, "Civil War Medicine: Modern Medicine's Civil War Legacy," *The Civil War Trust*, http://www.civilwar.org/education/history/civil-war-medicine/civil-war-medicine.html?referrer=https://www.google.com/.

33. Ina Dixon, "Overview Civil War Medicine: Modern Medicine's Civil War Legacy," *The Civil War Trust*, https://www.civilwar.org/learn/articles/civil-war-medicine.

34. "Louis Pasteur Biography: Chemist, Scientist, Inventor (1822-1895)," *Bio.*, http://www.biography.com/people/louis-pasteur-9434402.

35. Charles Singer M.D., "Medical Progress from 1850 to 1900," *British Medical Journal*, Jan. 7, 1950. https://www.ncbi.nlm.nih.gov/pmc/articles/PMC2036402/pdf/brmedj03580-0098.pdf.

36. Albert Lyons, "The Nineteenth Century: The Beginnings of Modern Medicine (Part 1)," *HealthGuidance.org*, http://www.healthguidance.org/entry/6352/1/The-Nineteenth-Century--The-Beginnings-of-Modern-Medicine-Part-1.html.

37. Chandrasekhar Krishnamurti and Chakra Rao SSC, "The Isolation of

Morphine by Serturner," *Indian Journal of Anaesthesia*, November 2016, 861-862, https://www.ncbi.nlm.nih.gov/pmc/articles/PMC5125194/.

38. "Pharmacology," *Encyclopedia Brittanica*, https://www.britannica.com/science/pharmacology.

39. William T. Jarvis PhD., "Misuse of the Term Allopathy," *National Council Against Health Fraud*, http://www.ncahf.org.

40. "Scientific Medicine," *University of Toledo Libraries*, http://www.utoledo.edu/library/canaday/exhibits/quackery/quack2.html.

41. Erika Janic, "What's So Heroic About "Heroic Medicine?" December 2, 2010, https://erikajanik.com/2010/12/02/whats-so-heroic-about-heroic-medicine/.

42. "Scientific Medicine," *University of Toledo Libraries*, http://www.utoledo.edu/library/canaday/exhibits/quackery/quack2.html.

43. William G. Rothstein, *American Physicians in the Nineteenth Century: From Sects to Science*. 1972, Johns Hopkins University Press, pages 156-169.

44. James Whorton M.D., "Counterculteral Healing: A Brief History of Alternative Medicine in America," *Frontline PBS*, http://www.pbs.org/wgbh/pages/frontline/shows/altmed/clash/history.html.

45. Thomas Paine, *Exploring American History: Medicine, Disease and Epidemics*, Marshall Cavendish Corporation, 2008, page 679.

46 . "The History of Medicine 1800-1850," *International Wellness Directory*, http://www.mnwelldir.org/docs/history/history03.htm,

47. P. Stavrakis, "Heroic Medicine, Bloodletting and The Sad Fate of George Washington," *Maryland Medical Journal* (Baltimore, MD: 1985) 46:10 page 539-40, http://www.healthguidance.org/entry/6352/1/The-Nineteenth-Century--The-Beginnings-of-Modern-Medicine-Part-1.html.

48. "General History of the Practice of Dentistry: Outline of Its Evolution," Pages 23-28. *American Dental Education Association*.

49. Damon Isherwood, "6-World Changing Ideas That Were Originally Rejected," *Lifehack*, Accessed January 10, 2018, http://www.lifehack.org/articles/lifestyle/6-world-changing-ideas-that-were-originally-rejected.html.

50. Sneha Mantri, "Holistic Medicine and the Western Medical Tradition," *AMA Journal of Ethics: Illuminating the Art of Medicine*, March 2008, Volume 10, Number 3;177-180. http://journalofethics.ama-assn.org/2008/03/mhst1-0803.html.

51. "Greek Medicine: Hippocrates and the Rise of Rational Medicine,

History of Medicine Division National Library of Medicine National Institutes of Health, https://www.nlm.nih.gov/hmd/greek/greek_rationality.html.

52. Wang Jin-Huai, "Timeline of Chinese Medicine: Understanding the Past," *Association for Traditional Studies,* http://www.traditionalstudies.org/historical-timeline-of-chinese-medicine/.

53. Martyn Shuttleworth, "Islamic Medicine: History of Medicine," *Explorable,* https://explorable.com/islamic-medicine.

54. Martyn Shuttleworth, "Islamic Medicine: History of Medicine," *Explorable,* https://explorable.com/islamic-medicine.

55. "Legends of America: Native American Medicine," *Legends of America,* http://www.legendsofamerica.com/na-medicine.html.

56. Harris Coulter, *Divided Legacy: The Conflict Between Homoeopathy and the American Medical Association,* Page 5, Berkeley, California: North Atlantic Books, 1973.

57. Diana Zuckerman Ph.D. and Anna E. Mazzucco Ph.D., "2016 Update: When Should Women Start Regular Mammograms?" *StopCancerFund.org,* http://www.stopcancerfund.org/p-breast-cancer/update-when-should-women-start-regular-mammograms-40-50-and-how-often-is-regular/.

58. "Statistics Adapted from the American Cancer Society's Publication, Cancer Facts & Figures 2016 and The National Cancer Institute Surveillance Epidemiology and End Results (SEER) Database," http://www.cancer.net/cancer-types/breast-cancer/statistics.

59. "Breast Cancer: Treatment Options," *Cancer.net* Editorial Board, February 2016, http://www.cancer.net/cancer-types/breast-cancer/treatment-options.

60. *Mayo Clinic,* "Ductal Carcinoma In Situ (DCIS)," The Mayo Clinic Staff, https://www.mayoclinic.org/diseases-conditions/dcis/basics/definition/con-20031842.

61. Diana Zuckerman Ph.D. and Anna E. Mazzucco Ph.D., "2016 Update: When Should Women Start Regular Mammograms?" *StopCancerFund.org,* http://www.stopcancerfund.org/p-breast-cancer/update-when-should-women-start-regular-mammograms-40-50-and-how-often-is-regular/.

62. "ACOG Revises Breast Cancer Screening Guidance: Ob-Gyns Promote Shared Decision Making," *ACOG,* June 22, 2017, https://www.acog.org/About-ACOG/News-Room/News-Releases/2017/ACOG-Revises-Breast-Cancer-Screening-Guidance--ObGyns-Promote-Shared-Decision-Making.

63. Cat Alford, "The Ultimate Student Loan Repayment Guide for

Doctors," *Student Loan Hero*, April 6, 2016, https://studentloanhero.com/featured/ultimate-student-loan-repayment-guide-for-doctors/#.

64. Edward W. Campion M.D. and Stephan Morrissey, Ph.D., "A Different Model-Medical Care in Cuba," *The New England Journal of Medicine*, January 24, 2013; 368: 297-299. http://www.nejm.org/doi/full/10.1056/NEJMp1215226#t=article.

65. Edward W. Campion M.D. and Stephan Morrissey, Ph.D., "A Different Model-Medical Care in Cuba," *The New England Journal of Medicine*, January 24, 2013, http://www.nejm.org/doi/full/10.1056/NEJMp1215226#t=article.

66. "Cuban Medicine," *NPR Latino USA*, May 15, 2015, 4:10 p.m. ET.

67. "Cuban Medicine," *NPR Latino USA*, May 15, 2015, 4:10 p.m. ET.

68. Elizabeth D. Kantor PhD, MPH and al., "Trends in Prescription Drug Use Among Adults in the United States from 1999-2012," JAMA, 2015;314 (17): 1818-1830, November 3, 2015, http://jama.jamanetwork.com/article.aspx?articleid=2467552&resultClick=3.

69. Beth Han MD, PhD, MPH and al, "Nonmedical Prescription Opioid Use and Use Disorders Among Adults Aged 18 Through 64 Years in the United States 2003-2013," JAMA, 2015;314 (14) October 13, 2015, http://jama.jamanetwork.com/article.aspx?articleid=2456166&resultClick=3.

70. "Prescription Drug Side Effects," *Drug Watch*, https://www.drugwatch.com/side-effects/.

71. Jason Millman, "It's true: Drug companies are bombarding your TV with more ads than ever," *The Washington Post*, March 23, 2015, https://www.washingtonpost.com/news/wonk/wp/2015/03/23/yes-drug-companies-are-bombarding-your-tv-with-more-ads-than-ever/?tid=a_inl.

72. Bruce Horovitz and Julie Appleby. "Prescription Drug Costs Are Up: So Are TV Ads Promoting Them," *Kaiser Health News*, March 16, 2017, https://www.usatoday.com/story/m$3.5 billiononey/2017/03/16/prescription-drug-costs-up-tv-ads/99203878/.

73. "2016 Edition Marketing Fact Pack," *Advertising Age*, http://gaia.adage.com/images/bin/pdf/20151211marketingfactpackweb.pdf.

74. Megan Thielking, "Sky-High C-Section Rates in the U.S. Don't Translate to Better Birth Outcomes," *STAT*, December 1, 2015, https://www.statnews.com/2015/12/01/cesarean-section-childbirth/.

75. Tara Parker-Pope, "Overtreatment is Taking a Harmful Toll," *NY Times Well Column*, August 27, 2012, http://well.blogs.nytimes.com/2012/08/27/overtreatment-is-taking-a-harmful-toll/?_r=0.

76. Charles Ornstein et al., "Drug-Company Payments Mirror Doctors' Brand-Name Prescribing," *NPR Morning Edition*, March 17, 2016, 5:00 AM ET, http://www.npr.org/sections/health-shots/2016/03/17/470679452/drug-company-payments-mirror-doctors-brand-name-prescribing.

77. L.J. Devon, "Homeopathy Officially Recognized by Swiss Government as Legitimate Medicine to Coexist with Conventional Medicine," Natural News, Friday, April 22, 2016, http://www.naturalnews.com/053765_homeopathy_Swiss_government_alternative_medicine.html.

78. Bismah Malik, "World's 'First' Ayurvedic Surgery Conducted in Meerut, India," May 2, 2016, *International Business Times*, http://www.ibtimes.co.in/worlds-first-ayurvedic-surgery-conducted-meerut-india-676981.

79. "Did the Catholic Church Forbid Bible Reading?" CatholicBridge. com, http://catholicbridge.com/catholic/did_the_catholic_church_forbid_bible_reading.php.

80. Bernard Starr, "Why Catholics Were Denied Their Bibles for 1,000 Years," *Huff Post*, July 20, 2013, https://www.huffingtonpost.com/bernard-starr/why-christians-were-denied-access-to-their-bible-for-1000-years_b_3303545.html.

81. Henry Cloud and John Townsend, *Boundaries: When to Say Yes, How to Say No to Take Control of Your Life*, Zondervan, 2017.

82. "Schools Moving to Merit Pay," *The Washington Post*, September 1, 1986. https://www.washingtonpost.com/archive/politics/1986/09/01/schools-moving-to-merit-pay/c1ca0c80-8f5a-4384-bc6c-ee88969376b1/?utm_term=.40cb2a54b951.

83 . "Body Systems and Homeostasis," McGraw Hill College Division, http://www.mhhe.com/biosci/genbio/maderbiology/supp/homeo.html.

84. Rachel Rettner, "The Human Body: Anatomy, Facts and Functions," *Live Science*, March 10, 2016, 01:45 p.m. ET, http://www.livescience.com/37009-human-body.html.

85. "The Power of the Placebo Effect," Harvard Men's Health Watch, May 2017, https://www.health.harvard.edu/mental-health/the-power-of-the-placebo-effect.

86. Cara Feinberg, "The Placebo Phenomenon," *Harvard Magazine*, January-February 2013, http://harvardmagazine.com/2013/01/the-placebo-phenomenon.

87. Raine Sihvonen M.D. et al., "Arthroscopic Partial Meniscectomy Versus Sham Surgery for a Degenerative Meniscal Tear," *The New England*

Journal of Medicine, December 26, 2013, 369:2515-2524, http://www.nejm.org/doi/full/10.1056/NEJMoa1305189#t=article.

88. Joseph Walker, "Fake Knee Surgery as Good as Real Procedure Study Finds," *The Wall Street Journal*, Dec. 25, 2013, http://www.wsj.com/articles/SB10001424052702304244904579278442014913458.

89. Wayne W. Dyer, *The Power of Intention: Learning to Co-Create the World Your Way*. 2005: Hay House.

90. "Food Allergy 101," *FARE Food Allergy Research and Education*, https://www.foodallergy.org/life-food-allergies/food-allergy-101/facts-and-statistics.

91. Stephanie Watson, "Organic Food No More Nutritious Than Conventionally Grown Food," *Harvard Health Publications*, Harvard Medical School, September 5, 2012.

92. WJ Crinnion, "Organic Foods Contain Higher Levels of Certain Nutrients, Lower Levels of Pesticides and Benefits for the Consumer," *Alternative Medicine Review*, April 15, 2010, http://www.ncbi.nlm.nih.gov/pubmed/20359265.

93. WJ Crinnion, "Organic Foods Contain Higher Levels of Certain Nutrients, Lower Levels of Pesticides and Benefits for the Consumer," *Alternative Medicine Review*, April 15, 2010, http://www.ncbi.nlm.nih.gov/pubmed/20359265.

94. Brian Palmer, "The Environmental Footprint of Organic vs. Conventional Food," *The Washington Post*, September 17, 2012.

95. Robert Mikkelsen and T.K. Hartz, "Nitrogen Sources for Organic Crop Production," *Better Crops*, Vol. 92 (2008, No. 4), http://ucanr.edu/sites/nm/files/76659.pdf.

96. John Reganold, "Can We Feed 10 Billion People on Organic Farming Alone?" *The Guardian*, August 14, 2016, https://www.theguardian.com/sustainable-business/2016/aug/14/organic-farming-agriculture-world-hunger.

97. Abbie Fentress Swanson, "What is Farm Runoff Doing to the Water? Scientists Wade In," *NPR All Things Considered*, July 5, 2013, https://www.npr.org/sections/thesalt/2013/07/09/199095108/Whats-In-The-Water-Searching-Midwest-Streams-For-Crop-Runoff.

98. "Ethanol: What Is It?" *University of Illinois Extension*, https://web.extension.illinois.edu/ethanol/.

99. Jonathan Foley, "It's Time to Rethink America's Corn System,"

Scientific American, March 5, 2013, https://www.scientificamerican.com/article/time-to-rethink-corn/.

100. "Omega-3 Fatty Acids: An Essential Contribution," *Harvard T.H. Chan School of Public Health,* https://www.hsph.harvard.edu/nutritionsource/omega-3-fats/.

101. "Eat the Peach, Not the Pesticide," *Consumer Reports Special Report: Pesticides in Produce,* March 19, 2015, https://www.consumerreports.org/cro/health/natural-health/pesticides/index.htm.

102. "Non-Organic Foods (Pesticides, Contaminated Sewage Sludge, Hormones)," *Holistic Med,* http://www.holisticmed.com/toxic/pesticides.html#pesticides.

103. "Organic Foods: All You Need to Know," *Help Guide.org,* http://www.helpguide.org/healthy-eating/organic-foods.htm.

104. "Living Near Agriculture Increases Rates of Serious Health Problems," *Chem-Tox.com,* January 2016, https://chem-tox.com/agriculture/index.htm.

105. Jörgen Magnér et al., "Human Exposure to Pesticides from Food: A Pilot Study," *Swedish Environmental Research Institute,* January 2015 Report, https://www.coop.se/contentassets/dc9bd9f95773402997e4aca0c11b8274/coop-ekoeffekten_rapport_eng.pdf.

106. Megan Boyle, "5 Essential Facts About Pesticides on Fruits and Vegetables," *Environmental Working Group,* May 12, 2016, https://www.ewg.org/enviroblog/2016/05/five-essential-facts-about-pesticides-fruits-and-vegetables#.WkQ16xM-cWp.

107. Pascale Mollier, "The Cocktail Effect of Pesticides," *INRA Science and Impact,* November 22, 2016, http://www.inra.fr/en/Scientists-Students/Food-and-nutrition/All-reports/Cocktail-effects-of-toxic-substances/The-cocktail-effect-of-pesticides.

108. "What Is Sewage Sludge?" *Center for Food Safety,* https://www.centerforfoodsafety.org/issues/1050/sewage-sludge/what-is-sewage-sludge.

109. Wendy Priesnitz, "The Real Dirt on Sewage Sludge," *Natural Life Magazine,* http://www.life.ca/naturallife/9712/sludge.htm.

110. Rebekah Wilce, "Under Pressure, Whole Foods Agrees to Stop Selling Produce Grown in Sewage Sludge," January 15, 2014, *The Center for Media and Democracy's PR Watch,* http://www.prwatch.org/news/2014/01/12359/whole-foods-agrees-stop-selling-produce-grown-sewage-sludge.

111. *United States Environmental Protection Agency,* "Frequent Questions About Biosolids," https://www.epa.gov/biosolids/frequent-questions-about-biosolids.

112. Kevin Ferguson, "'Biosolids' and Human Health," *The New York Times,* April 16, 2009, https://green.blogs.nytimes.com/2009/04/16/biosolids-and-human-health/.

113. Peter Hess, "Turns Out That Using Human Poop to Fertilize Crops Isn't Such a Great Idea," *Motherboard,* April 22, 2016, https://motherboard.vice.com/en_us/article/8q8xnk/turns-out-that-using-human-poop-to-fertilize-crops-might-not-be-such-a-great-ide.

114. "Pathogenic E. coli Binds to Fresh Vegetables," *Society for General Microbiology,* April 15, 2014, https://www.sciencedaily.com/releases/2014/04/140415203813.htm.

115. "Recombinant Bovine Growth Hormone," *Organic Consumers Association,* https://www.organicconsumers.org/categories/rbgh.

116. Timothy F. Landers RN, CNP, PhD et al., "A Review of Antibiotic Use in Food Animals: Perspective, Policy, and Potential," *Public Health Reports,* Jan-Feb. 2012; 127(1) 4-22, https://www.ncbi.nlm.nih.gov/pmc/articles/PMC3234384/.

117. Samuel S. Epstein M.D., "Monsanto's Hormonal Milk Poses Risk of Prostate Cancer, Besides Other Cancers," *Cancer Prevention Coalition,* Accessed December 29, 2017, http://www.holisticmed.com/bgh/prostate.html.

118. "Organic Foods: All You Need to Know," *Help Guide.org,* http://www.helpguide.org/articles/healthy-eating/organic-foods.htm.

119. Allison Aubrey, "Does Subsidizing Crops We're Told to Eat Less of Fatten Us Up?" *NPR,* July 18, 2016, https://www.npr.org/sections/thesalt/2016/07/18/486051480/we-subsidize-crops-we-should-eat-less-of-does-this-fatten-us-up.

120. Kristen Leigh Painter, "Americans Are Eating More Organic Food Than Ever, Survey Finds," *Star Tribune,* May 24, 2017, http://www.startribune.com/americans-are-eating-more-organic-food-than-ever-survey-finds/424061513/.

121. "Study: 82% of U.S. Households Buy Organic Food Regularly," *AG Web Powered by Farm Journal,* March 24, 2017, https://www.agweb.com/article/study-82-of-us-households-buy-organic-food-regularly-naa-nate-birt/.

122. Stepahanie Eckelkamp, "A New Investigation Suggests Imported

Organics Aren't Up to Snuff," *Rodale Organic Life*, September 27, 2017, https://www.rodalesorganiclife.com/food/trust-imported-organic-food.

123. "Dietary Guidelines for Americans 2015-2020," *USDA Dietary Guidelines.Gov*, https://health.gov/dietaryguidelines/2015/resources/2015-2020_Dietary_Guidelines.pdf.

124. Michael O Shroeder, "Death By Prescription," *U.S. News & World Report*, September 27, 2016, https://health.usnews.com/health-news/patient-advice/articles/2016-09-27/the-danger-in-taking-prescribed-medications.

125. "Overprescribed America," *Top Masters in Healthcare*, http://www.topmastersinhealthcare.com/drugged-america/.

126. J. Lazarou and Corey B.H. Pomeranz P.N., "Incidence of Adverse Drug Reactions in Hospitalized Patients: A Meta-Analysis of Prospective Studies, *Journal of the American Medical Association*, 1998;279(15):1200-1205, PM:9555760.

127. "Adverse Drug Reactions," *Worst Pills, Best Pills*, Accessed December 29, 2017, http://www.worstpills.org/public/page.cfm?op_id=4#fn1.

128. Jim Avila and Michael Murray, "Prescription Painkiller Use at Record High for Americans," *ABC News*, April 20, 2011, http://abcnews.go.com/US/prescription-painkillers-record-number-americans-pain-medication/story?id=13421828.

129. Brian Krans, "The Most Addictive Prescription Drugs on the Market," May 16, 2011, *Healthline.com*, http://www.healthline.com/health/addiction/addictive-prescription-drugs#Amphetamines8.

130. *Centers for Disease Control and Prevention*, "Prescription Opioid Overdose Data," Accessed December 29, 2017, https://www.cdc.gov/drugoverdose/data/overdose.html.

131. *Centers for Disease Control and Prevention*, "Understanding the Epidemic," https://www.cdc.gov/drugoverdose/epidemic/index.html.

132. Bruce Horovitz and Julie Appleby, "Prescription Drug Costs Are Up; So Are TV Ads Promoting Them," *Kaiser Health News*, March 16, 2017.

133. Peter Olson and Louise Sheiner, "The Hutchins Center Explains: Prescription Drug Spending," *Brookings*, April 26, 2017, https://www.brookings.edu/blog/up-front/2017/04/26/the-hutchins-center-explains-prescription-drug-spending/.

134. https://www.drugwatch.com/dangerous-drugs.php.

135. "Cinnamon," Accessed December 29, 2017, *Examine.com*, https://examine.com/supplements/cinnamon/.

136. Bharat B. Aggarwal and Ajaikumar B. Kunnumakkara, *Molecular Targets and Therapeutic Uses of Spices: Modern Uses for Ancient Medicine*, Singapore: World Scientific Publishing Company, 2009, Page 176.

137. Sanjay K. Banerjee and Subir K. Maulik, "Effect of Garlic on Cardiovascular Disorders: A Review," *Nutrition Journal*, November 19, 2002, https://www.ncbi.nlm.nih.gov/pmc/articles/PMC139960/.

138. A. Pérez-Sánchez et al., "Protective Effects of Citrus and Rosemary Extracts on UV-Induced Damage in Skin Cell Model and Human Volunteers," *Journal of Photochemistry and Photobiology B: Biology*, April 20, 2014, https://pdfs.semanticscholar.org/5c45/95238425711a5ee2e98cc1c82fd d0848ce90.pdf.

139. Gabriëlla Harriët Schmelzer and Ameenah Gurib-Fakim, Medicinal Plants, Wagningen: *PROTA Foundation*: Backhuys Publishers 2008.

140. S. Bissa and A. Bohra, "Antibacterial Potential of Pot Marigold," *Journal of Microbiology and Antimicrobals*, Vol. 3 (3), pp.51-54, March 2011, http://www.academicjournals.org/article/article1380019254_Bissa%20 and%20Bohra.pdf.

141. "Licorice," *University of Maryland Medical Center*, Accessed December 31, 2017, http://www.umm.edu/health/medical/altmed/herb/licorice.

142. "Licorice," *University of Maryland Medical Center*, Accessed December 31, 2017, http://www.umm.edu/health/medical/altmed/herb/licorice.

143. "Valerian," *National Institutes of Health Office of Dietary Supplements*, Accessed December 31, 2017, https://ods.od.nih.gov/factsheets/ Valerian-HealthProfessional/#en20.

144 Alyse Wexler, "Valerian Root for Insomnia and Anxiety: Does It Work?" *Medical News Today*, June 25, 2017, https://www.medicalnewstoday. com/articles/318088.php. Date accessed: December 31, 2017.

145. See glossary for definition of hydrogenated oil.

146. "Foods That Increase Dopamine: Think "Tyrosine," *Mental Health Daily*, Accessed December 31, 2017, http://mentalhealthdaily. com/2015/04/07/foods-that-increase-dopamine-think-tyrosine/.

147. Sarah Williams C.P., "Just a Spoonful of Castor Oil," *Science*, May 21, 2012, http://www.sciencemag.org/news/2012/05/just-spoonful-castor-oil.

148. "12 Great Health Benefits of Castor Oil," *E Times of India*, August 11, 2017, https://timesofindia.indiatimes.com/life-style/health-fitness/diet/ health-benefits-of-castor-oil/articleshow/40063531.cms.

149. "Eucalyptus," *RXList*, Accessed December 31, 2017, https://www.

rxlist.com/consumer_eucalyptus-page4/drugs-condition.htm.

150. "Lavender," University of Maryland Medical Center, http://www.umm.edu/health/medical/altmed/herb/lavender.

151. Robert Preidt, "Artificial Sweeteners Trick the Brain: Study, *WebMD*, August 11, 2017, https://www.webmd.com/diabetes/news/20170810/artificial-sweeteners-trick-the-brain-study.

152. *National Institute on Alcohol Abuse and Alcoholism*, "Alcohol Facts and Statistics," Accessed November 17, 2017, https://www.niaaa.nih.gov/alcohol-health/overview-alcohol-consumption/alcohol-facts-and-statistics.

153. *Centers for Disease Control and Prevention*, "National Diabetes Statistics Report 2017," https://www.cdc.gov/diabetes/pdfs/data/statistics/national-diabetes-statistics-report.pdf.

154. *Harvard T.H. Chan School of Public Health*, "Eating Fried Foods Tied to Increased Risk of Diabetes, Heart Disease," Accessed November 17, 2017, https://www.hsph.harvard.edu/news/hsph-in-the-news/eating-fried-foods-tied-to-increased-risk-of-diabetes-and-heart-disease/.

155. "What Is Reverse Osmosis?" *PureTec Industrial Water*, Accessed November 18, 2017, http://puretecwater.com/reverse-osmosis/what-is-reverse-osmosis.

156. Qun Wu, Di Jiang, and al., "Electronic Cigarette Liquid Increases Inflammation and Virus Infection in Primary Human airway Epithelial Cells," *PLOS One*, Sept. 22, 2014, https://www.ncbi.nlm.nih.gov/pmc/articles/PMC4171526/.

157. Lorraine Bracco, "30 Cleansing Foods to Naturally Detox Your Body," *Rodale Wellness*, January 5, 2017, https://www.rodalewellness.com/food/cleansing-detox-foods.

158. *American Institute for Cancer Reserch*, "Phytochemicals: The Cancer Fighters in Your Foods," Accessed January 2, 2018, http://www.aicr.org/reduce-your-cancer-risk/diet/elements_phytochemicals.html?referrer=https://www.google.com/.

159. Dylan Smith, "Shed Toxins with Hot Water: The Best Digestive Medicine," *Everyday Ayurveda*, March 4, 2017, http://everydayayurveda.org/hot-water-best-digestive-medicine/.

160. Cadegiani, Flavio A. and Claudio E. Kater. "Adrenal Fatigue Does Not Exist: A Systematic Review." *BMC Endocrine Disorders*. August 24, 2016. https://www.ncbi.nlm.nih.gov/pmc/articles/PMC4997656/.

161. Trisha McNary, "Exercise and Its Effects on Serotonin & Dopamine

Levels," *Livestrong*, September 11, 2017, https://www.livestrong.com/article/251785-exercise-and-its-effects-on-serotonin-dopamine-levels/.

162. "Exercise, Depression, and the Brain," *Healthline*, Accessed January 18, 2018, https://www.healthline.com/health/depression/exercise#1.

163. Michael Castleman M.A., "Want to Prevent Colds? Have Sex Weekly," *Psychology Today*, June 1, 2009.

164. "Is Sex Exercise? And Is It Hard on the Heart?" *Harvard Health Publications, Harvard Medical School*, June 2011, http://www.health.harvard.edu/newsletter_article/is-sex-exercise-and-is-it-hard-on-the-heart.

165. "The Surprising Health Benefits of Having More Sex," *The Telegraph*. June 27, 2017, http://www.telegraph.co.uk/health-fitness/body/surprising-health-benefits-having-sex/.

166. "Is Sex Good for Your Health?" *DiabetesHealth.com*, May 21, 2011, https://www.diabeteshealth.com/is-sex-good-for-your-heart-health/.

167. Cadegiani, Flavio A. and Claudio E. Kater. "Adrenal Fatigue Does Not Exist: A Systematic Review." *BMC Endocrine Disorders*. August 24, 2016. https://www.ncbi.nlm.nih.gov/pmc/articles/PMC4997656/.

168. Trisha McNary, "Exercise and Its Effects on Serotonin & Dopamine Levels," *Livestrong*, September 11, 2017, https://www.livestrong.com/article/251785-exercise-and-its-effects-on-serotonin-dopamine-levels/.

169. "Exercise, Depression, and the Brain," *Healthline*, Accessed January 18, 2018, https://www.healthline.com/health/depression/exercise#1.

170. Michael Castleman, M.A., "Want to Prevent Colds? Have Sex Weekly," *Psychology Today*, June 1, 2009.

171. "Is Sex Exercise? And Is It Hard on the Heart?" *Harvard Health Publications. Harvard Medical School*, June 2011, http://www.health.harvard.edu/newsletter_article/is-sex-exercise-and-is-it-hard-on-the-heart.

172. "The Surprising Health Benefits of Having More Sex. *The Telegraph*. June 27, 2017. http://www.telegraph.co.uk/health-fitness/body/surprising-health-benefits-having-sex/.

173. "Is Sex Good for Your Health?" *DiabetesHealth.com*, May 21, 2011, https://www.diabeteshealth.com/is-sex-good-for-your-heart-health/.

174. "Kissing Kids' Owies May Benefit Health," *Children's Health on NBCNews.com*, May 18, 2010, http://www.nbcnews.com/id/37215005/ns/health-childrens_health/t/kissing-kids-owies-may-benefit-health/#.WmEPF5M-cWp.

175. Evan L. Ardiel, MSc and Catherine H Rankin, PhD, "The Importance

of Touch in Development," *Paediatrics Child Health,* March 2010; 15 (3): 153-156, https://www.ncbi.nlm.nih.gov/pmc/articles/PMC2865952/.

176. Dr. Deepak Chopra, "Discover Meditation's Healing Power," *The Chopra Center,* https://chopra.com/articles/discover-meditation%E2%80%99s-healing-power.

177. Maia Szalavitz, "Explaining Why Meditators May Live Longer," *Time,* December 23, 2010,,http://healthland.time.com/2010/12/23/could-meditation-extend-life-intriguing-possibility-raised-by-new-study/.

178. "Telomeres and Telomerase," *Khan Academy,* https://www.khanacademy.org/science/biology/dna-as-the-genetic-material/dna-replication/a/telomeres-telomerase.

179. Maia Szalavitz, "Explaining Why Meditators May Live Longer," *Time,* December 23, 2010, http://healthland.time.com/2010/12/23/could-meditation-extend-life-intriguing-possibility-raised-by-new-study/.

180. Tina Kaczor, ND, FABNO, "Meditation Increases Telomerase Activity and Improves Mental Health," *Natural Medicine Journal,* June 2013 Vol. 5 Issue 6, https://www.naturalmedicinejournal.com/journal/2013-06/meditation-increases-telomerase-activity-and-improves-mental-health.

181. "Brain Waves and Meditation," *Science Daily,* March 31, 2010, https://www.sciencedaily.com/releases/2010/03/100319210631.htm.

182. "What Is the Function of Various Brainwaves?" *Scientific American,* https://www.scientificamerican.com/article/what-is-the-function-of-t-1997-12-22/.

183. Christopher Bergland, "Alpha Brain Waves Boost Creativity and Reduce Depression," April 17, 2015, *Psychology Today,* https://www.psychologytoday.com/blog/the-athletes-way/201504/alpha-brain-waves-boost-creativity-and-reduce-depression.

184. Fotenos, A.F., Snyder, A.Z., Girton, L.E., Morris, J.C., and Buckner, R.L., "Normative Estimates of Cross-Sectional and Longitudinal Brain Volume Decline in Aging and AD," *Neurology,* 2005, 64, 1032–1039. doi: 10.1212/01.WNL.0000154530.72969.11.

185. Kooistra, M., Geerlings, M.I., van der Graaf, Y., Mali, W. P., Vincken, K. L., Kappelle, L. J., et al., "Vascular Brain Lesions, Brain Atrophy, and Cognitive Decline. The Second Manifestations of Arterial Disease–Magnetic Resonance (SMART-MR) Study. *Neurobiol. Aging,* 2014, 35, 35–41. doi: 10.1016/j.neurobiolaging.2013.07.004.

186. Eileen Luders, Nicolas Cherbuin, and Florian Kurth, "Forever

Young(er): Potential Age-Defying Effects of Long-Term Meditation on Gray Matter Atrophy," *Frontiers in Psychology*, January 21, 2015, https://www.frontiersin.org/articles/10.3389/fpsyg.2014.01551/full#B13.

187. Brigid Shulte, "Harvard Neuroscientist: Meditation Not Only Reduces Stress, Here's How It Changes Your Brain," *Washington Post*, May 26, 2015, https://www.washingtonpost.com/news/inspired-life/wp/2015/05/26/harvard-neuroscientist-meditation-not-only-reduces-stress-it-literally-changes-your-brain/.

188. Brigid Shulte, "Harvard Neuroscientist: Meditation Not Only Reduces Stress, Here's How It Changes Your Brain," *Washington Post*, May 26, 2015, https://www.washingtonpost.com/news/inspired-life/wp/2015/05/26/harvard-neuroscientist-meditation-not-only-reduces-stress-it-literally-changes-your-brain/.

189. "Prefrontal Cortex," *Good Therapy.org*, https://www.goodtherapy.org/blog/psychpedia/prefrontal-cortex.

190. Matthew Dahlitz, "Prefrontal Cortex," *Neuropsychotherapist.com*, January 4, 2017, https://www.neuropsychotherapist.com/prefrontal-cortex/.

191. "Meditation Associated with Increased Grey Matter in the Brain," *Yale University*, November 11, 2005, https://www.sciencedaily.com/releases/2005/11/051110215950.htm.

192. Sara W. Lazar et al., "Meditation Experience Is Associated with Increased Cortical Thickness," *Neuroreport*, November 28, 2005; 16 (17): 1893-1897, https://www.ncbi.nlm.nih.gov/pmc/articles/PMC1361002/.

193. "Stress Reduction Through Meditation May Aid In Slowing the Progression of Alzheimer's Disease," *Beth Israel Deaconess Medical Center*, Nov. 18, 2013, *EurekAlert!.* http://www.eurekalert.org/pub_releases/2013-11/bidm-srt111813.php

194. Jonathan Greenburg, Benjamin G. Shapero, et al., "Mindfulness-Based Cognitive Therapy for Depressed Individuals Improves Suppression of Irrelevant Mental-Sets," *European Archives of Psychiatry and Clinical Neuroscience*, April 2017, Volume 267, Issue 3, pp. 227-282.

195. Daniel Goleman, "Exercising the Mind to Treat Attention Deficits," *The New York Times Well Blogs*, May 12, 2014, http://well.blogs.nytimes.com/2014/05/12/exercising-the-mind-to-treat-attention-deficits/?_r=0.

196. Alberto Chiesa. *The Journal of Alternative and Complementary Medicine*, January 2010, 16(1): 37-46. doi:10.1089/acm.2009.0362.

197. F. Zeiden et al., "Brain Mechanisms Supporting Modulation of Pain

by Mindfulness Meditation," *Journal of Neuroscience,* https://www.ncbi.nlm.nih.gov/pmc/articles/PMC3090218/

198. Laura Blue, "Strongest Study Yet Shows Meditation Can Lower Risk of Heart Attack and Stroke," *Time,* Nov. 14, 2012, http://healthland.time.com/2012/11/14/mind-over-matter-strongest-study-yet-shows-meditation-can-lower-risk-of-heart-attack-and-stroke/.

199. H. Benson et al., "Study of the Therapeutic Effects of Intercessory Prayer (STEP) in Cardiac Bypass Patients: A Multicenter Randomized Trial of Uncertainty and Certainty of Receiving Intercessory Prayer," *American Heart Journal,* April 15, 2006; 1 (4): 934-42, https://www.ncbi.nlm.nih.gov/pubmed/16569567.

200. *New American Standard Bible (NASB)* Mark 5:25-34.

201. *New Believer's Bible NLT.* Tyndale House Publishers: July 1, 2007.

202. "The Shift by Dr. Wayne Dyer," *The God Project: Self Discovery Through Books, Experiences, & Movies,* January 12, 2010, https://marthaspiva.wordpress.com/2010/01/12/the-shift-by-dr-wayne-dyer/.

203. *New Believer's Bible* NLT. Tyndale House Publishers: July 1, 2007.

Mary Aiken,*The Cyber Effect: An Expert in Cyberpsychology Explains How Technology Is Shaping Our Children, Our Behavior, and Our Values—and What We Can Do About It,* Spiegel & Grau, 2017.

204. Dhruv Khullar, "How Social Isolation Is Killing Us," *The New York Times,* December 22, 2016, https://www.nytimes.com/2016/12/22/upshot/how-social-isolation-is-killing-us.html.

205. "Loneliness Among Older Adults: A National Study of Adults 45+," Conducted for the *AARP Magazine,* September 2010, https://assets.aarp.org/rgcenter/general/loneliness_2010.pdf.

206. "Loneliness Among Older Adults: A National Study of Adults 45+," Conducted for the *AARP Magazine,* September 2010, https://assets.aarp.org/rgcenter/general/loneliness_2010.pdf.

207. Nicole K. Valtorta et al., "Loneliness and Social Isolation as Risk Factors for Coronary Heart Disease and Stroke: Systematic Review and Meta-Analysis of Longitudinal Observational Studies," *BMJ Journals,*Volume 102, Issue 13, http://heart.bmj.com/content/102/13/1009.

208. Dhruv Khullar, "How Social Isolation Is Killing Us," *The New York Times,* December 22, 2016, https://www.nytimes.com/2016/12/22/upshot/how-social-isolation-is-killing-us.html.

209. Christopher M. Masi et al., "A Meta-Analysis of Interventions to

Reduce Loneliness," *Personality and Social Psychology Review*, August 15, 2011, 15 (3): 10.1177, https://www.ncbi.nlm.nih.gov/pmc/articles/PMC3865701/.

210. John T. Cacioppo, *Loneliness: Human Nature and the Need for Social Connection*, W.W. Norton & Company, August 10, 2009.

211. "Facts and Statistics," *Anxiety and Depression Association of America*, Accessed December 10, 2017, https://adaa.org/about-adaa/press-room/facts-statistics.

212. Sara G. Miller, "1 in 6 Americans Takes a Psychiatric Drug," *Scientific American*, December 13, 2016, https://www.scientificamerican.com/article/1-in-6-americans-takes-a-psychiatric-drug/.

213. Brendan L. Smith, "Inappropriate Prescribing," *American Psychological Association*, June 2012, Vol. 43, No. 6, http://www.apa.org/monitor/2012/06/prescribing.aspx.

214. "Forgiveness: Your Health Depends on It," *John Hopkins Medicine*, Accessed December 10, 2017, https://www.hopkinsmedicine.org/health/healthy_aging/healthy_connections/forgiveness-your-health-depends-on-it.

215. "Forgiveness: Your Health Depends on It," *John Hopkins Medicine*, Accessed December 10, 2017, https://www.hopkinsmedicine.org/health/healthy_aging/healthy_connections/forgiveness-your-health-depends-on-it.

216. "Integrative and Lifestyle Medicine," *Cleveland Clinic Wellness Institute*, Accessed January 24, 2018, https://my.clevelandclinic.org/departments/wellness/integrative.

217. "History of Massage Therapy," *Natural Healers*, Accessed January 24, 2018, https://www.naturalhealers.com/massage-therapy/history/.

218. "Contraindications of Massage," *Pro's Choice Massage Support Services*, Accessed January 24, 2018, https://proschoicemassage.com/contraindications-of-massage/.

219. "Acupuncture," *WEIL Andrew Weil, M.D.*, https://www.drweil.com/health-wellness/balanced-living/wellness-therapies/acupuncture/.

220. "Origins and History of Chiropractic Care," *American Chiropractic Association*, Accessed January 24, 2018, https://www.acatoday.org/About/History-of-Chiropractic.

221. "The Palmer Family Heritage/ History of Palmer College of Chiropractic," *Palmer College of Chiropractic*, Accessed January 24, 2018, http://www.palmer.edu/about-us/history/palmer-family/.

222. "Hypnotherapy," *Psychology Today*, https://www.psychologytoday.com/therapy-types/hypnotherapy.

223. Brendan L. Smith, "Hypnosis Today," *American Psychological Association*, January 2011, Vol. 42, No. 1, http://www.apa.org/monitor/2011/01/hypnosis.aspx.

224. Brendan L. Smith, "Hypnosis Today," *American Psychological Association*, January 2011, Vol. 42, No. 1, http://www.apa.org/monitor/2011/01/hypnosis.aspx.

225. Hal Arkowitz and Scott O. Lilianfield, "Lunacy and the Full Moon," *Scientific American*, February 1, 2009, https://www.scientificamerican.com/article/lunacy-and-the-full-moon/.

226. Tim Newman, "Reiki: What Is It? And What Are the Benefits?" *Medical News Today*, September 6, 2007, https://www.medicalnewstoday.com/articles/308772.php.

227. Ann Linda Baldwin, Kirstin Fullmer, and Gary E. Schwartz, "Comparison of Physical Therapy with Energy Healing for Improving Range of Motion in Subjects with Restricted Shoulder Mobility," *Journal of Evidence-Based Complementary and Alternative Medicine*, November 14, 2013, https://www.ncbi.nlm.nih.gov/pmc/articles/PMC3847956/.

228. Deborah Bowden, Lorna Goddard, and John Gruzelier, "A Randomized Controlled Single-Blind Trial of the Efficacy of Reiki at Benefitting Mood and Well-Being," *Journal of Evidence-Based Complementary and Alternative Medicine*, March 27, 2011, https://www.ncbi.nlm.nih.gov/pmc/articles/PMC3092553/.

229. Scott Suvow, "The History of Acupuncture," *Kootney Columbia College of Integrative Health Sciences*, http://kootenaycolumbiacollege.com/articles/history-of-acupuncture/.

230. NIH, "Acupuncture in Depth," *NIH National Center for Complementary and Integrative Health*, https://nccih.nih.gov/health/acupuncture/introduction.

231. Bartosz Chmielnicki M.D., "WHO Official Position," *Evidence-Based Acupuncture*, https://www.evidencebasedacupuncture.org/who-official-position/.

232. "History of Naturopathic Medicine," *National University of Natural Medicine*, https://nunm.edu/history-of-naturopathic-medicine/.

233. "Moxibustion," *Acupuncture Today*, Accessed January 17, 2018, http://www.acupuncturetoday.com/abc/moxibustion.php.

234. Irvine Loudon, "A Brief History of Homeopathy," *Journal of the Royal Society of Medicine*, Dec. 2006; 99 (12) 607-610, https://www.ncbi.nlm.nih.gov/pmc/articles/PMC1676328/.

23. E. Friedmann et al., "Animal Companions and One-Year Survival of Patients After Discharge from a Coronary Care Unit," *Public Health Reports*, July-August 1980; 95 (4): 307-312, https://www.ncbi.nlm.nih.gov/pmc/articles/PMC1422527/.

236 Jeanene Swanson, "Animal Therapy in Addiction Recovery," *Addiction.com*. September 24, 2014, https://www.addiction.com/4308/animal-therapy-in-recovery/.

237. Erica Jex Gergely, "Equine-Assisted Psychotherapy: A Descriptive Study," December 2012, http://scholarworks.wmich.edu/cgi/viewcontent.cgi?article=1111&context=dissertations.

238. Diane Suchetka, "Americans Are Consuming More Calories Than Ever: Fighting Fat," *Cleveland.com*, April 5, 2010, http://www.cleveland.com/fightingfat/index.ssf/2010/04/americans_are_consuming_more_calories_than_ever.html.

239. USDA Food Patterns," *United States Department of Agriculture*, https://www.cnpp.usda.gov/USDAFoodPatterns.

Bibliography

PREFACE

"What Is Macrobiotics?" *Kushi Institute.* January 4, 2018. https://www.kushiinstitute.org/what-is-macrobiotics/.

INTRODUCTION

Centers for Disease Control and Prevention. "Chronic Disease: The Leading Causes of Death and Disability in the United States." https://www.cdc.gov/chronicdisease/overview/.

"Child Obesity." *Harvard T.H. Chan School of Public Health.* Accessed January 8, 2018. https://www.hsph.harvard.edu/obesity-prevention-source/obesity-trends/global-obesity-trends-in-children/.

The Henry J. Kaiser Family Foundation "How Much Does the U.S. Spend on Health and How Has It Changed?" *Health Costs.* May 1, 2012. https://www.kff.org/report-section/health-care-costs-a-primer-2012-report/.

Woolston, Chris M.S. "Type 2 Diabetes and Kids: The Growing Epidemic." *Health Day.* https://consumer.healthday.com/encyclopedia/diabetes-13/misc-diabetes-news-181/type-2-diabetes-and-kids-the-growing-epidemic-644152.html.

CHAPTER ONE: THE HEROIC DEVELOPMENT OF MODERN MEDICINE

"About ADAA Facts and Statistics." *Anxiety and Depression Association of America.* https://adaa.org/about-adaa/press-room/facts-statistics.

"Benjamin Rush." *Biography.com.* Accessed January 8, 2018. https://www.biography.com/people/benjamin-rush-9467074#synopsis.

"The Chronic Care Model." *Improving Chronic Illness Care.* Accessed January 8, 2018. http://www.improvingchroniccare.org/index.php?p=The_Chronic_CareModel&s=2.

Davis, Rebecca. "The Doctor Who Championed Hand-Washing and Briefly Saved Lives." *NPR Morning Edition.* January 12, 2015. https://www.npr.org/sections/health-shots/2015/01/12/375663920/the-doctor-who-championed-hand-washing-and-saved-women-s-lives.

Flannery, Michael A. "The Early Botanical Medical Movement as a Reflection of Life, Liberty, and Literacy in Jacksonian America." *Journal of the Medical Library Association.* October 2002; 90 (4): 442-454. https://www.ncbi.nlm.nih.gov/pmc/articles/PMC128961/.

"The History of Medicine in America." *International Wellness Directory. Minnesota Wellness Publications, Inc.,* 2013. http://www.mnwelldir.org/docs/history/history01.htm#underlying_.

"The History of Modern Medicine." *International Wellness Directory. Minnesota Wellness Publications, Inc.,* 2013. http://www.mnwelldir.org/docs/history/history03.htm.

"Islamic Medicine." *Encyclopedia.com. Originally published by Oxford University Press,* 2001. http://www.encyclopedia.com/medicine/anatomy-and-physiology/anatomy-and-physiology/islamic-medicine.

Jin-Huai, Wang. "Historical Timeline of Chinese Medicine." *Association for Traditional Studies,* 2013. http://www.traditionalstudies.org/historical-timeline-of-chinese-medicine/.

Lyons, Albert S. "The Nineteenth Century-The Beginnings of Modern Medicine (Part 1)." *Health Guidance for Better Health.* http://www.healthguidance.org/entry/6352/1/The-Nineteenth-Century--The-Beginnings-of-Modern-Medicine-Part-1.html.

"What Is Modern Medicine?" *Medical News Today.* MNT Editorial Team. January 5, 2016. https://www.medicalnewstoday.com/info/medicine/modern-medicine.php.

Whorton, James, M.D. "Countercultural Healing: A Brief History of Alternative Medicine in America." *PBS Frontline.* November 4, 2003. https://www.pbs.org/wgbh/pages/frontline/shows/altmed/clash/history.html.

"Preventing Chronic Diseases: A Vital Investment." *World Health Organization.* http://www.who.int/chp/chronic_disease_report/contents/part2.pdf.

CHAPTER TWO:

Angell, Marcia. "Why Do Drug Companies Charge So Much? Because They Can." *The Washington Post.* September 25, 2015. https://www.washingtonpost.com/opinions/why-do-drug-companies-charge-so-much-because-they-can/2015/09/25/967d3df4-6266-11e5-b38e-06883aacba64_story.html?tid=a_inl&utm_term=.ce33da2ebc75.

"Is the Cuban Healthcare System Really As Great As People Claim?" *The Conversation,* November 30, 2016. http://theconversation.com/is-the-cuban-healthcare-system-really-as-great-as-people-claim-69526.

Millman, Jason. "It's True: Drug Companies Are Bombarding Your TV with More Ads Than Ever." *The Washington Post.* March 23, 2015. https://www.washingtonpost.com/news/wonk/wp/2015/03/23/yes-drug-companies-are-bombarding-your-tv-with-more-ads-than-ever/?tid=a_inl&utm_term=.217e9c12d6a5.

Rothstein, William G. *American Physicians in the Nineteenth Century: From Sects to Science.* Johns Hopkins University Press, 1972.

Scott, Dylan. "The Untold Story of TV's First Prescription Drug Ad." *STAT.* December 11, 2015. https://www.statnews.com/2015/12/11/untold-story-tvs-first-prescription-drug-ad/.

CHAPTER THREE: POWER AND TRUST BETWEEN YOU AND YOUR DOCTOR

Dekker, Rebecca, PhD, RN. "State of Maternity Care." *ImprovingBirth. org.* November 28, 2012.

CHAPTER FIVE: EAT CLEAN

"About Sewage Sludge." *Center for Food Safety.* http://www.centerforfoodsafety.org/issues/1050/sewage-sludge/about-sewage-sludge#.

Barclay, Eliza. "Is It Safe to Use Compost Made from Treated Human Waste?" *NPR.* May 12, 2013. https://www.npr.org/sections/thesalt/2013/05/07/182010827/is-it-safe-to-use-compost-made-from-treated-human-waste.

Barron, Jess. "This Is How Eating Organic Food Affects Pesticide Levels in Your Body." *Livestrong.com.* April 21, 2016. https://www.livestrong.com/blog/exactly-eating-organic-food-affects-pesticide-levels-bodies/.

Barron, Jess. "21 Foods to Buy Organic (Even if You're on a Budget)." *Livestrong.com.* August 26, 2017. https://www.livestrong.com/slideshow/1004202-20-foods-always-buy-organic-even-youre-budget/#slide=2.

Best, Jason. "The Surprising Truth About Who's Really Buying Organic." *TakePart.* April 21, 2015. http://www.takepart.com/article/2015/04/21/who-is-buying-organic.

"Bt Corn: The Popular Food That Turns Your Gut into a Pesticide Factory." *Mercola.com.* June 14, 2011. https://articles.mercola.

com/sites/articles/archive/2011/06/14/why-are-there-so-many-food-allergies-now.aspx.

"Eating with a Conscience." *Beyond Pesticides.* Accessed January 8, 2018. https://www.beyondpesticides.org/programs/organic-agriculture/eating-with-a-conscience.

"Eat the Peach, Not the Pesticide." *Consumer Reports Special Report: Pesticides in Produce.* http://www.consumerreports.org/cro/health/natural-health/pesticides/index.htm.

Greenaway, Twilight and Adrien Schless-Meier. "Just Because Your Chicken is Organic Doesn't Mean It Was Raised Humanely." *Mother Jones,.* April 23, 2015. http://www.motherjones.com/environment/2015/04/organic-standards-animal-welfare.

"The Overuse of Antibiotics in Food Animals Threatens Public Health." *Consumers Union Policy & Action from Consumer Reports.* Accessed December 28, 2017. http://consumersunion.org/news/the-overuse-of-antibiotics-in-food-animals-threatens-public-health-2/.

PBS Frontline, "Modern Meat: An Interview with Michael Pollen." http://www.pbs.org/wgbh/pages/frontline/shows/meat/interviews/pollan.html.

Priesnitz, Wendy. "The Real Dirt on Sewage Sludge." *Natural Life Magazine.* http://www.life.ca/naturallife/9712/sludge.htm.

Robinson, Lawrence, Jeanne Segal, Ph.D., and Robert Segal. "Organic Foods: What You Need to Know." *HelpGuide.org.* Last updated: October 2017. https://www.helpguide.org/articles/healthy-eating/organic-foods.htm.

Rochman, Bonnie. "Not Just Your Imagination: Kids Really Are More Allergic." *Time.* Oct. 12, 2010, http://healthland.time.com/2010/10/12/not-just-your-imagination-kids-really-are-more-allergic/.

United States Department of Agriculture. "Organic Standards." Agricultural Marketing Service. https://www.ams.usda.gov/grades-standards/organic-standards.

"Whole Foods Market Announces Enhanced Standards for Fresh Produce and Flowers." *Whole Foods Market Newsroom.* September 26, 2013. http://media.wholefoodsmarket.com/news/produce-rating-release#sthash.HpGm4KBK.dpuf.

Wilce, Rebekah. "Under Pressure, Whole Foods Agrees to Stop Selling Produce Grown in Sewage Sludge." January 15, 2014. *The Center for Media and Democracy's PR Watch.* http://www.prwatch.org/news/2014/01/12359/whole-foods-agrees-stop-selling-produce-grown-sewage-sludge.

"17 Chicken Facts the Industry Doesn't Want You to Know." *Free From Harm.* August 28, 2014. http://freefromharm.org/animalagriculture/chicken-facts-industry-doesnt-want-know/.

CHAPTER SIX: HEAL WITH HERBS

"Adverse Drug Reactions." *Worst Pills, Best Pills.* Accessed December 29, 2017. http://www.worstpills.org/public/page.cfm?op_id=4#fn1.

Aggarwal, Bharat B. *Healing Spices: How to Use 50 Everyday and Exotic Spices to Boost Health and Beat Disease.* New York: Sterling Publishing, 2011.

Bellebuono, Holly. *The Essential Herbal for Natural Health.* Boston: Roost Books, 2012.

Bright, Sierra. "12 Remarkable Benefits of Sweet Almond Oil for Beautiful Skin and Hair." *Natural Living Ideas.* June 24, 2015. http://www.naturallivingideas.com/sweet-almond-oil-benefits/.

"Calendula: The Anti-Inflammatory, Antiviral Herb That Heals." *Dr. Axe Food Is Medicine.* https://draxe.com/calendula/.

"Castor Oil." *Gale Encyclopedia of Alternative Medicine.* The Gale Group, 2005. http://www.encyclopedia.com/science-and-technology/chemistry/organic-chemistry/castor-oil.

"Castor Oil Pack Detoxification." *The Healthy Home Economist.* http://www.thehealthyhomeeconomist.com/castor-oil-pack-detoxification/.

"Castor Oil May Help Relieve Arthritis, Sciatica, and Back Pain." *Mercola Take Control of Your Health.* http://articles.mercola.com/sites/articles/archive/2012/04/28/castor-oil-to-treat-health-conditions.aspx.

"Clove Oil Uses and Benefits." *Dr. Axe Food Is Medicine.* https://draxe.com/clove-oil-uses-benefits/.

Crampton, Linda. "Licorice Root for Tooth Decay, Gum Disease, and Oral Health." *Heal Dove.* January 27, 2016. https://healdove.com/oral-health/Licorice-Root-For-Tooth-Decay-and-Gum-Disease-Benefits-and-Dangers.

Dennis, Brady. "Nearly 60 Percent of Americans – The Highest Ever – Are Taking Prescription Drugs." *The Washington Post.* November 3, 2015. https://www.washingtonpost.com/news/to-your-health/wp/2015/11/03/more-americans-than-ever-are-taking-prescription-drugs/?utm_term=.44abd0c3d83e.

The Doctors Book of Herbal Home Remedies: Cure Yourself with Nature's Most Powerful Healing Agents. The Editors of Prevention Health Books. Rodale Books, 2000.

Faerman, Justin. "Gotu Kola: The Many Benefits of the Ancient Herb of Enlightenment and Longevity." *Conscious Lifestyle Magazine.* http://www.consciouslifestylemag.com/gotu-kola-benefits-of-the-herb-of-enlightenment/.

Gehrmann, Beatrice, Wolf-Gerald Koch, Clause O. Tschirch, Helmut Brinkmann. *Medicinal Herbs: A Compendium.* New York: The Haworth Herbal Press, 2005.

Hoffman, Matthew. "Picture of the Skin: Human Anatomy." *WebMD.* http://www.webmd.com/skin-problems-and-treatments/picture-of-the-skin#1.

"How to Use Almond Oil for Your Skin & Overall Health." *Dr. Axe Food Is Medicine.* https://draxe.com/almond-oil/.

"How to Use Witch Hazel to Clear Up Your Skin Fast." *Dr. Axe Food Is Medicine.* https://draxe.com/witch-hazel/.

"List of Amphetamines." http://amphetamines.com/list-of-amphetamines/. Accessed December 29, 2017.

"Properties of Coconut Oil." *Organic Facts.* https://www.organicfacts.net/health-benefits/oils/properties-of-coconut-oil.html.

Reidenberg, MD, FACP. "Adverse Effects of Suddenly Stopping a Medicine." *Weill Cornell Medical College.* May 23, 2011. http://weill.cornell.edu/cert/patients/suddenly_stopping_medicine.html.

Roemheld-Hamm, Beatrix, M.D., PH.D. "Chasteberry." *American Family Physician.* September 1, 2005. http://www.aafp.org/afp/2005/0901/p821.html.

Schutz, Sarah. "Is This Super Spice The Next Turmeric?" *Mind Body Green*, May 4, 2017.

"Sesame Oil Health Benefits and Uses." *Banyan Botanicals.* https://www.banyanbotanicals.com/info/ayurvedic-living/living-ayurveda/herbs/sesame-oil/.

Simon, David M.D. and Deepak Chopra, M.D. *The Chopra Center Herbal Handbook: Forty Natural Prescriptions for Perfect Health.* New York: Three Rivers Press, 2000.

Tapp, Melissa. "3 Homeopathic Must-Haves for Your Summer Vacation." *Wellness Today*, June 26, 2014. http://www.wellnesstoday.com/spirit/3-homeopathic-must-haves-for-your-summer-vacation.

Ternes, Tracy. "Your Skin, It Absorbs." *Down to Earth Organic & Natural.* https://www.downtoearth.org/health/general-health/your-skin-it-absorbs.

Tirtha, Swami Sadashiva. *The Ayurveda Encyclopedia: Natural Secrets to Healing, Prevention, & Longevity.* Unadilla, New York: Ayurveda Holistic Center Press, 2007.

"Top 25 Peppermint Oil Uses and Benefits." *Dr. Axe Food is Medicine.* https://draxe.com/peppermint-oil-uses-benefits/.

"Vitex or Chasteberry, the Female-Friendly Fruit for PMS and More." *Dr. Axe Food is Medicine.* https://draxe.com/vitex/.

"History of Lavender?" *What About Lavender.* http://www.what-about-lavender.com/history_of_lavender.html.

"What Is Licorice Root Good For?" *Mercola Take Control of Your Health.* March 21, 2016. http://articles.mercola.com/sites/articles/archive/2016/03/21/licorice-root-uses.aspx.

Wenzel, Melanie. *The Essential Guide to Home Herbal Remedies.* Ontario Canada: Robert Rose, Inc. 2014.

"9 Incredible Benefits of Sesame Oil." *Organic Facts.* https://www.organicfacts.net/health-benefits/oils/sesame-oil.html.

"13 Surprising Peppermint Oil Benefits." *Organic Facts.* https://www.organicfacts.net/health-benefits/essential-oils/health-benefits-of-peppermint-oil.html.

"23 Surprising Benefits of Clove Oil." *Organic Facts.* https://www.organicfacts.net/health-benefits/essential-oils/health-benefits-of-clove-oil.html.

"77 Coconut Oil Uses & Cures." *Dr. Axe Food Is Medicine.* https://draxe.com/coconut-oil-uses/.

CHAPTER SEVEN: DETOXIFY YOUR BODY

"All about water filters." http://all-about-water-filters.com/benefits-and-dangers-of-drinking-distilled-water-regularly/.

"Choosing Canola Oil." *Weil. Ask Dr. Weil M.D.* https://www.drweil. com/diet-nutrition/cooking-cookware/choosing-canola-oil/.

Fontenot, Beth. "Antioxidants Explained: Why These Compounds Are So Important." *The Atlantic.* October 30, 2011. https:// www.theatlantic.com/health/archive/2011/10/antioxidants-explained-why-these-compounds-are-so-important/247311/.

"How Antioxidants Work." *Berkley Wellness.* January 15, 2014. http:// www.berkeleywellness.com/healthy-eating/food/article/ how-antioxidants-work.

"Immune and Lymphatic System." *InnerBody.* http://www.innerbody. com/image/lympov.html.

Krumhardt, Barbara, Ph. D. and I. Edward Alcamo, Ph.D. *E-Z Anatomy and Physiology.* Hauppauge, New York: Barron's Educational Series, 2010.

Langford, Kevin. *The Everything Guide to Anatomy and Physiology: All You Need to Know About How the Human Body Works.* Avon, Massachusetts: Adams Media, 2015.

Merrell, Woodson, MD. *The Detox Prescription.* New York: Rodale, 2013.

Nichols, Hannah. "All You Need to Know about Bone Marrow." *Medical News Today.* December 15, 2017. https://www.medical-newstoday.com/articles/285666.php. Date accessed: January 3, 2018.

Raloff, Janet and Beth Mole. "Vaping May Harm the Lungs: New Toxicity Date Show Why the Inhaled Vapors May Prove Toxic." *Science News for Students.* https://www.sciencenewsforstudents.org/article/vaping-may-harm-lungs.

Spritzler, Franziska. "Distilled Water-What Is It and Should You Drink It?" *Authority Nutrition.* August 22, 2016. https://authoritynutrition.com/distilled-water/.

Stewart, Lisa. "10 Amazing Benefits of Sweating You Didn't Know." *Lifehack.* http://www.lifehack.org/articles/lifestyle/10-amazing-benefits-sweating-you-didnt-know.html.

Ungar, Laura. "Pre-diabetes, Diabetes Rates Fuel National Health Crisis." *USA Today.* Sept. 24, 2014. https://www.usatoday.com/story/news/nation/2014/09/14/prediabetes-rising-diabetes-threatening-usa/15134489/.

"What Are Lymph and Lymph Nodes?" *Breast Cancer.org.* Accessed January 3, 2018. http://www.breastcancer.org/treatment/surgery/lymph_node_removal/lymph_nodes.

Wells, S.D. 'Health Basics: Why are fried foods terrible for your health?" *Natural News.* December 26, 2011.http://www.naturalnews.com/034483_fried_foods_health_damage.html#.

"What affects the quality of olive oil?" *California Olive Ranch.* https://californiaoliveranch.com/olive-oil-101/what-affects-the-quality-of-olive-oil/.

"What Are Phytonutrients?" *Fruit and Veggies: More Matters.* http://www.fruitsandveggiesmorematters.org/what-are-phytochemicals.

Zimmerman, Kim Ann. "Lymphatic System: Facts, Functions & Diseases." *Live Science.* http://www.livescience.com/26983-lymphatic-system.html.

CHAPTER EIGHT: MOVE YOUR BODY

Castleman, Michael, M.A. 'Want to Prevent Colds? Have Sex Weekly." *Psychology Today.* June 1, 2009. https://www.psychologytoday.com/blog/all-about-sex/200906/want-prevent-colds-have-sex-weekly.

Castleman, Michael. "8 Reasons Sex Improves Your Health." AARP. https://www.aarp.org/relationships/love-sex/info-06-2011/sex-improves-men-health.html.

De Bloom, J, Geurts SA, and Kompier MA. "Effects of Short Vacations, Vacation Activities and Experiences on Employee Health and Wellbeing." *Stress Health*. October 28, 2012. NCBI. https://www.ncbi.nlm.nih.gov/pubmed/22213478.

Fisher, Naomi D.L., M.D. "Stress Raising Your Blood Pressure? Take a Deep Breath." *Harvard Health Publications: Harvard Medical School*. February 15, 2016. http://www.health.harvard.edu/blog/stress-raising-your-blood-pressure-take-a-deep-breath-201602159168.

"Is Sex Exercise? And Is It Hard on the Heart?" Harvard Health Publications. *Harvard Medical School*. June 2011. http://www.health.harvard.edu/newsletter_article/is-sex-exercise-and-is-it-hard-on-the-heart.

"Is Sex Good for Your Heart?" *Diabetes Health*. May 21, 2011. https://www.diabeteshealth.com/is-sex-good-for-your-heart-health/.

Levine, Glenn N. and al. "Sexual Activity and Cardiovascular Disease: A Scientific Statement from the American Heart Association." *Circulation*. 2012; 125:1058-1072. http://circ.ahajournals.org/content/125/8/1058.

Neighmond, Patti. "Overworked Americans Aren't Taking the Vacation They've Earned." *NPR All Things Considered*. July 12, 2016. http://www.npr.org/sections/health-shots/2016/07/12/485606970/overworked-americans-arent-taking-the-vacation-theyve-earned.

Nichols, Hannah. "Ten Health Benefits of Sex." *Medical News Today*. April 13, 2017. https://www.medicalnewstoday.com/articles/316954.php.

Whitebourne, Susan Krauss. "The Importance of Vacations to Our Physical and Mental Health." *Psychology Today*. June 22, 2010. https://www.psychologytoday.com/blog/fulfillment-any-age/201006/the-importance-vacations-our-physical-and-mental-health.

"The Workplace and Health." *NPR, Robert Wood Johnson Foundation, and Harvard T.H. Chan School for Public Health.* July, 2016.

"Top 10 Reasons to Have Sex Tonight." *CBS News.* March 24, 2008. http://www.cbsnews.com/news/top-10-reasons-to-have-sex-tonight/.

CHAPTER NINE: AWAKEN YOUR SPIRITUAL SELF

Barber, Nigel Ph.D. "Faith Healing Shouldn't Work, but It Does: How to Explain Faith Healing." *Psychology Today.* March 2. 2011. https://www.psychologytoday.com/blog/the-human-beast/201103/faith-healing-shouldnt-work-it-does.

Brown, Candy Gunther. "Testing Prayer: Can Science Prove the Healing Power of Prayer?" *Huffpost.* May 2, 2012. http://www.huffingtonpost.com/candy-gunther-brown-phd/testing-prayer-science-of-healing_b_1299915.html.

Carey, Benedict. "Long-Awaited Medical Study Questions the Power of Prayer." *The New York Times.* March 31, 2006. http://www.nytimes.com/2006/03/31/health/31pray.html.

Epel, Elissa, PhD, Jennifer DAubenmier, Ph.D., Judith T. Moskowitz, Ph.D., Susan Folkman, PhD., and Elizabeth Blackburn, PhD. "Can Meditation Slow Rate of Cellular Aging? Cognitive Stress, Mindfulness, and Telomeres." *Ann NY Academy of Science.* August 2009; 1172: 34-53. https://www.ncbi.nlm.nih.gov/pmc/articles/PMC3057175/.

Fung, Gregory and Christopher Fung. "What Do Prayer Studies Prove?" *Christianity Today.* May 15, 2009. http://www.christianitytoday.com/ct/2009/may/27.43.html?start=2.

"Kissing Kids' Owies May Benefit Health: Study: Soothing Moms Lower Stress Hormones Tied to Disease." *Children's Health on NBCNews.com* May 18, 2010. http://www.nbcnews.com/id/37215005/ns/health-childrens_health/t/kissing-kids-owies-may-benefit-health/#.V1WxtpMrKRs.

"Loving Touch Critical for Premature Infants." *Science Daily.* January 6, 2014. https://www.sciencedaily.com/releases/2014/01/140106094437.htm.

Luders, Eileen, Cherbuin, Nicolas, and Kurth, Florian. "Forever Young(er): Potential Age-Defying Effects of Long-Term Meditation on Gray Matter Atrophy." *Frontiers in Psychology.* January 21, 2015. http://dx.doi.org/10.3389/fpsyg.2014.01551.

McGreevey, Sue. "Eight Weeks to a Better Brain." *Harvard Gazette.* January 21, 2011. https://news.harvard.edu/gazette/story/2011/01/eight-weeks-to-a-better-brain/.

"Mom's Kiss More Effective Than Homeopathy in Treating Children's Pain." *The Science Post.* Saturday, February 27, 2016. http://thesciencepost.com/mom-kiss-just-as-effective-as-homeopathy-for-treating-childrens-pain/.

Penman, Danny PhD. "Curing Depression with Mindfulness Meditation." *Psychology Today.* October 14, 2011. https://www.psychologytoday.com/blog/mindfulness-in-frantic-world/201110/curing-depression-mindfulness-meditation.

Schulte, Brigid. "Harvard Neuroscientist: Meditation Not Only Reduces Stress, Here's How It Changes Your Brain." The Washington Post. May 26, 2015. https://www.washingtonpost.com/news/inspired-life/wp/2015/05/26/harvard-neuroscientist-meditation-not-only-reduces-stress-it-literally-changes-your-brain/.

"Stress reduction through meditation may aid in slowing the progression of Alzheimer's disease." *Beth Israel Deaconess Medical Center.* Nov. 18, 2013. *EurekAlert!* http://www.eurekalert.org/pub_releases/2013-11/bidm-srt111813.php.

Walton, Alice G. "7 Ways Meditation Can Actually Change The Brain." *Forbes.* Feb. 9, 2015. http://www.forbes.com/sites/alicegwalton/2015/02/09/7-ways-meditation-can-actually-change-the-brain/#4ac5e24b7023.

"What Is a Telomere?" *YourGenome.org (YG)*. https://www.yourgenome.org/facts/what-is-a-telomere.

CHAPTER TEN: CONNECT WITH OTHERS FOR EMOTIONAL HEALH

"America's State of Mind." *A Report by Medco*. http://apps.who.int/medicinedocs/documents/s19032en/s19032en.pdf.

Carter, Zack Ph.D. "Freedom in Forgiveness." *Psychology Today*. June 13, 2017. https://www.psychologytoday.com/blog/clear-communication/201706/freedom-in-forgiveness.

Entis, Laura. "Chronic Loneliness Is a Modern-Day Epidemic." *Fortune*. June 22, 2016. http://fortune.com/2016/06/22/loneliness-is-a-modern-day-epidemic/.

Harris, Rebecca. "The Loneliness Epidemic: We're More Connected Than Ever – But Are We Feeling More Alone?" *Independent*. March 30, 2015. http://www.independent.co.uk/life-style/health-and-families/features/the-loneliness-epidemic-more-connected-than-ever-but-feeling-more-alone-10143206.html.

"Is Technology Making Us Less Sociable?" *The Wall Street Journal*. May 10, 2015. https://www.wsj.com/articles/is-technology-making-people-less-sociable-1431093491.

Khullar, Dhruv. "How Social Isolation Is Killing Us." *The New York Times*. December 22, 2016. https://www.nytimes.com/2016/12/22/upshot/how-social-isolation-is-killing-us.html.

"Loneliness Among Older Adults: A National Study of Adults 45+." *Conducted for the AARP Magazine*. September 2010. https://assets.aarp.org/rgcenter/general/loneliness_2010.pdf.

Mayo Clinic. "Friendships: Enrich Your Life and Improve Your Health." Mayo Clinic Staff. September 28, 2016. https://www.

mayoclinic.org/healthy-lifestyle/adult-health/in-depth/ friendships/art-20044860.

McDaniel, Brandon. "Technoference: How Technology Can Hurt Relationships." *Institute for Family Studies.* January 27, 2015. https://ifstudies.org/blog/ technoference-how-technology-can-hurt-relationships.

"Mental Health by the Numbers." NAMI National Alliance on Mental Illness. https://www.nami.org/Learn-More/Mental-Health-By-the-Numbers. Date accessed: January 6, 2018.

Miller, Sara G. "1 in 6 Americans Takes a Psychiatric Drug." *Scientific American.* December 13, 2016. https://www.scientificameri-can.com/article/1-in-6-americans-takes-a-psychiatric-drug/.

Olien, Jessica. "Loneliness Is Deadly." *Slate.* http://www.slate.com/ articles/health_and_science/medical_examiner/2013/08/ dangers_of_loneliness_social_isolation_is_deadlier_than_ obesity.html.

Smith, Brendan L. "Inappropriate Prescribing." Monitor on Psychology. June 2012, Vol. 43, No. 6. *The American Psychological Association.* http://www.apa.org/monitor/2012/06/prescribing. aspx.

Sreenivasan, Shoba, Ph.D. and Linda E. Weinberger Ph.D. "Forgiving Yourself." *Psychology Today.* April 15, 2017. https://www. psychologytoday.com/blog/emotional-nourishment/201704/ forgiving-yourself.

Taylor, Jim. "Is Technology Creating a Family Divide?" *Psychology Today.* March 13, 2013. https://www.psychologytoday.com/blog/the-power-prime/201303/ is-technology-creating-family-divide

CHAPTER ELEVEN: TRY DIFFERENT HEALING MODALITIES

"About Homeopathy." *North American Society of Homeopaths.* https:// homeopathy.org/about-homeopathy/.

"Acupuncture." *WEIL Andrew Weil, M.D.* https://www.drweil.com/health-wellness/balanced-living/wellness-therapies/acupuncture/.

"Contraindications of Massage." *Pro's Choice Massage Support Services.* https://proschoicemassage.com/contraindications-of-massage/.

"Facts About Reflexology." *International Institute of Reflexology Inc.* http://www.reflexology-usa.net/.

"The Five Element Theory: What Is the Five Element Theory?" *Acupuncture Today.* http://www.acupuncturetoday.com/abc/fiveelementtheory.php.

Fitzgerald, Michael. "Vibrating Cells Disclose Their Ailments." *MIT Technology Review.* https://www.technologyreview.com/s/410793/vibrating-cells-disclose-their-ailments/.

"The Good Life: Basics of Traditional Chinese Medicine." *Health Point Oriental Medicine.* http://www.healthpointclinic.org/PrinciplesofTCM.

"Homeopathic First Aid Remedies for the Home." *The Healing Haven Homeopathic Dispensary.* http://healinghaven.co.nz/homeopathic-first-aid-remedies-for-home/.

"Hypnotherapy." *Psychology Today.* https://www.psychologytoday.com/therapy-types/hypnotherapy.

Mayo Clinic. "Massage: Get in Touch with Its Many Benefits." The Mayo Clinic Staff. http://www.mayoclinic.org/healthy-lifestyle/stress-management/in-depth/massage/art-20045743.

"Naturopathic Medicine FAQs: A Service for Consumers." *The American Association of Naturopathic Physicians.* http://www.naturopathic.org/natfaqs.

Newman, Tim. "Reiki: What Is It and What Are the Benefits?" *Medical News Today.* September 6, 2017. https://www.medicalnewstoday.com/articles/308772.php.

Nordqvist, Christian. "Acupuncture: How Does It Work and Is It Beneficial?" *Medical News Today.* September 11, 2017. https://www.medicalnewstoday.com/articles/156488.php.

"Origins and History of Chiropractic." *American Chiropractic Association.* https://www.acatoday.org/About/History-of-Chiropractic.

"Pet Therapy: What Is Pet Therapy?" *Healthline.* https://www.healthline.com/health/pet-therapy.

"Reflexology: What is Reflexology?" *Weil.* https://www.drweil.com/health-wellness/balanced-living/wellness-therapies/reflexology/.

Rovner, Julie. "Pet Therapy: How Animals and Humans Heal Each Other." *NPR Morning Edition.* March 5, 2012. https://www.npr.org/sections/health-shots/2012/03/09/146583986/pet-therapy-how-animals-and-humans-heal-each-other.

Sacks, Brianna. "Reiki Goes Mainstream: Spiritual Touch Practice Now Commonplace in Hospitals." *Washington Post.* May 16, 2014. https://www.washingtonpost.com/national/religion/reiki-goes-mainstream-spiritual-touch-practice-now-commonplace-in-hospitals/2014/05/16/9e92223a-dd37-11e3-a837-8835df6c12c4_story.html?utm_term=.aebf86d41e58.

Smith, Brendan L. "Hypnosis Today." *American Psychological Association.* January 2011, Vol. 42, No. 1. http://www.apa.org/monitor/2011/01/hypnosis.aspx.

Taylor, Janice. "10 Reasons to Have a Himalayan Salt Lamp in Every Room in Your House." *Natural Living Ideas.* June 15, 2015. http://www.naturallivingideas.com/himalayan-pink-salt-lamp-benefits/.

Tchi, Rodika. "What Is Feng Shui?" *The Spruce.* December 6, 2017. https://www.thespruce.com/what-is-feng-shui-1275060.

"Traditional Chinese Medicine in Depth." *The National Center for Complementary and Integrative Health.* https://nccih.nih.gov/health/whatiscam/chinesemed.htm.

Ullman, Dana MPH. "A Condensed History of Homeopathy." *Homeopathic Family Medicine.* https://homeopathic.com/a-condensed-history-of-homeopathy/.

"What Happens at the Chiropractor?" *Taking Charge of Your Well-Being. University of Minnesota.* https://www.takingcharge.csh.umn.edu/explore-healing-practices/chiropractic/what-happens-chiropractor.

"What is Reiki?" *Reiki FAQ.* http://www.reiki.org/faq/whatisreiki.html.

"What Is Hypnotherapy? Does Hypnotherapy Work?" *Therapy Tribe.* https://www.therapytribe.com/therapy/what-is-hypnotherapy/.

"What is Naturopathic Medicine?" *AANMC.* https://aanmc.org/naturopathic-medicine/.

GLOSSARY

"Are Phytoestrogens Good for You?" *Healthline.* https://www.healthline.com/health/phytoestrogens.

Collins Dictionary. https://www.collinsdictionary.com/us/. Date accessed: January 5, 2018.

Concise Medical Dictionary 7th Edition. Oxford University Press, 2007.

Dorland's Illustrated Medical Dictionary 31st Edition. Philadelphia, PA: Saunders Elsevier, 2007.

Medical Dictionary. Merriam-Webster. Accessed: January 5, 2018. https://www.merriam-webster.com/medical.

"5 Ways to Avoid Hydrogenated Oil." *Healthline.* Accessed January 14, 2018. https://www.healthline.com/health/ways-to-avoid-hydrogenated-oil.

INDEX

acne, 113, 121, 126, 127, 129, 131, 132, 135, 136

acupuncture, 11, 35, 222, 236-240

addiction, 4, 8, 77, 79, 83, 140, 146, 207, 216, 228, 244

adrenal glands, 164, 264

affirmations, 76-78, 82, 213, 214

Al Anon, 80

almond oil, 128

alcoholism, 83, 263

allergies, allergies (food), 59, 75, 86, 252

Alcoholics Anonymous, 79, 146

Alzheimer's disease, 4, 10, 90, 102, 117, 148, 195, 261

American Medical Association (AMA), 24, 26, 44, 107, 273, 274

Analgesic, 112, 119, 130, 132, 261

Anesthesia, 20, 25, 27, 30, 74

Animal Welfare League, 96

anti-aging, 118, 128, 129, 135

antibiotic, xx, 10, 27, 59, 88, 89, 93-96, 118, 120, 125, 126, 132, 135, 140, 145, 154, 258, 263

anti-depressant, 44, 48, 145, 211, 212

antifungal, 129, 130, 133

anti-inflammatory, 114, 116-120, 123, 125, 126, 128-130, 132-134

anti-microbial, 129, 130, 133, 134

antioxidant, 87, 111, 112, 114, 116-118, 120, 126-129, 132, 135, 141, 147, 148, 249, 261

antiviral, 116, 120, 122, 129, 130

anxiety, xxiv, 4, 44, 47, 48, 74, 117, 119, 122, 123, 126, 130, 133, 134, 140, 146, 156, 164, 170, 175, 183, 185, 193, 195, 197, 199, 202, 205, 211, 212, 219, 220, 224, 228, 231, 235, 252

aromatherapy, 126, 223, 243

arthritis, 3, 116-118, 131, 196

Ashwagandha, 119

Ayurveda, iii, xvii, 29, 30, 97, 123, 155, 160, 183, 203, 205, 213, 240, 241, 244 Ayurvedic, 110, 111, 130, 139, 155, 159, 160, 183, 224, 240, 241, Ayurvedic medicine, xxii, 22, 23, 29, 30, 81, 96, 110, 131, 183, 224, 237

behavior, 5, 8, 76, 79, 80, 140, 146, 184, 184, 197, 199, 206, 207, 209, 210, 212, 217, 231, 234, 245, 261, 262

beliefs, xxi, xxiii, XXV, 41, 77, 80, 180, 205, 213, 214, 217, 229, 256,

biosolids, 92, 93

bladder, 80, 154, 161, 174, 202, 262, 263

blood cell, 72, 73, 122, 127, 131, 149-152, 191, 261

blood pressure, 11, 54, 60, 61, 63, 72, 74, 112, 115-117, 124, 149, 152, 170, 173, 174, 190, 191, 197, 219, 222, 225, 226, 228, 236, 247, 265

blood sugar, 3, 11, 112,-114, 123, 133, 190,

bramhi (see gotu kola)

breast cancer, 37, 38, 90, 94

breastfeeding, 113, 114, 117, 124, 156

breathing, 146, 152, 164, 169-173, 228, 230, 230, 231, 241, 253

bronchitis, 117, 133, 134

ABOUT THE AUTHOR

Michelle S. Fondin is the owner of Fondin Wellness and teaches yoga, meditation, and Ayurvedic lifestyle. She's the author of over six non-fiction books and romance fiction. Michelle has made the commitment to write and publish over 40 non-fiction health and wellness books over the next twenty years to help heal the planet. She commits much of her time to her YouTube Channel: MichelleFondin-Author and has plans to open up affordable rehab centers that focus on integrative health. You can connect with Michelle on social media and on her website at the links below. To contribue to Michelle's non-fiction works and video production, go to www.patreon.com/michellesfondin.

Connect via Instagram: michellesfondin
Connect with Michelle via Facebook: https://www.facebook.com/michellesfondin/
Connect via Twitter: https://twitter.com/michellesfondin
Website: www.michellefondinauthor.com

89425464R00189

Made in the USA
Columbia, SC
14 February 2018